boundary 2

Special issue

Charles Bernstein:

The Poetry of Idiomatic Insistences

Edited by

Paul A. Bové

boundary 2

an international journal

of literature and culture

Volume 48, Number 4

November 2021

Duke University Press

boundary 2
an international journal of literature and culture

Founding Editors Robert Kroetsch and William V. Spanos

Editor Paul A. Bové
Victoria Glavin, Assistant to the Editor

Managing Editor Margaret A. Havran

Contents

Editor's Note

Paul A. Bové

> The kind of poetry I want gums up the works.
> —Charles Bernstein, *Pitch of Poetry*

And yet, Charles Bernstein is a node, a switching station, of poetic experiment. Something about gum makes so that he can slow things down, especially the regular machine, and yet make things flow through and across staying on the rails as they touch crossing or parallel, sometimes stopping and often moving on—holding together. For this issue of *boundary 2*, Charles made over to us a gift of lots of words, mostly from beyond the US, from which I tried to make a constellation that shows not only the way people talk about what he does but how he talks back and across, making new stresses and things from the interviews and conversations. When you read the Cento in this collection, you'll see the cyclonic effect. Questions give him a chance to play, measure, and invent, but those questions have often come from, have had their own start in other words he's set in motion or offered. He's given his hearers words in a momentary rest, a base for

boundary 2 48:4 (2021) DOI 10.1215/01903659-9382004

interrogation or a tentative assertion by a friend of the work; it's the thought. A truth tested and measured by a response that will take its own direction.

The switching node of Bernstein's art and manner is on display. The art lies in the freeing up of words, in the getting them ungummed so they move in the writing, or so they are reset to show their movement. The unsettled, unsettling, and pleasing thing about words is that they are never alone. When the poet sets out the entanglement of words and their measures, voiced and counted in varying song styles and inherited forms, then new lines, new meanings, new forms for old emotions, new truths for new emotions—all this becomes possible. All this rests upon language available, shaped already, sometimes loosened, sometimes coagulated, sometimes keeping irregular time—but potential for *poiesis* wherever the chance allows art to make the connections.

Charles has a name for this art: "Echopoetics is the nonlinear resonance of one motif bouncing off another within an aesthetics of constellation. Even more, it's the sensation of allusion in the absence of allusion. In other words, the echo I'm after is a blank: a shadow of an absent source" (Bernstein 2016: 2). And this happens within not only one natural language (one national language) or within one pitch of high or low speech but across and within all the uses of words that come into view or hearing. As a network node for language as itself the echo of an absent source, this poetry and poet don't stop at political or language family borders. This volume shows the movement across so that the echoes resound softly and elusively not only with other poets' arts but in the ears, eyes, and memories of readers who, as in the essays added to this volume, make the faraway echoing come to the fore as the potential for this art to suture even shadows along its way. Yet, this is not an art of redemption. It keeps going in time. It is bricolage in its learning, in its consumption of poetic lines, advertising, comic routines, family speech, subway vernacular, and the high cultures of classical writing and its inheritors. This poetry is "a network of stopgaps," for which we are thankful.

Charles Bernstein has been part of the *boundary 2* project for decades. His work belongs to a tradition of journal projects that began with writing on and by Charles Olson, Robert Creeley, David Antin, Robert Duncan, up to recent inventions curated by Dawn Lundy Martin and many other poets, often brought to the journal through Bernstein's care. As the journal closes round on fifty years of engagement with a major tradition of experimental American poetics in relation to international poetic achievement, as with the recent issue on Cavafy, this work by, on, and for Bernstein is an internal marker as well as a gift to poetry readers.

Reference

Bernstein, Charles. 2016. *Pitch of Poetry*. Chicago: University of Chicago Press. Kindle.

Gertrude and Ludwig's Bogus Adventure

Charles Bernstein

for Gabriele Mintz

As Billy goes higher all the balloons
Get marooned on the other side of the
Lunar landscape. The module's broke—
It seems like for an eternity, but who's
Counting—and Sally's joined the Moonies
So we don't see so much of her anyhow.
Notorious novelty—I'd settle for a good
Cup of Chase & Sand-borne—though when
The strings are broken on the guitar
You can always use it as a coffee table.
Vienna was cold at that time of year.
The sachertorte tasted sweet but the memory
burned in the colon. Get a grip, get a grip, before
The Grippe gets you. Glad to see the picture
Of ink—the pitcher that pours before

boundary 2 48:4 (2021) DOI 10.1215/01903659-9381020

Throwing the Ball, with never a catcher in sight.
Never a catcher but sometimes a catch, or
A clinch or a clutch or a spoon—never a
Catcher but plenty o' flack, 'till we meet
On this side of the tune.

Gertrude and Ludwig's Italian Adventure

Luigi Ballerini

A sketchy midrash on the translation into Italian of Charles Bernstein's "Gertrude and Ludwig's Bogus Adventure" from *My Way: Speeches and Poems* (Chicago: University of Chicago Press, 1999). Here's the original:

for Gabriele Mintz

As Billy goes higher all the balloons
Get marooned on the other side of the
Lunar landscape. The module's broke—
It seems like for an eternity, but who's
Counting—and Sally's joined the Moonies
So we don't see so much of her anyhow.
Notorious novelty—I'd settle for a good
Cup of Chase & Sand-borne—though when
The strings are broken on the guitar
You can always use it as a coffee table.

boundary 2 48:4 (2021) DOI 10.1215/01903659-9382032

Vienna was cold at that time of year.
The sachertorte tasted sweet but the memory
burned in the colon. Get a grip, get a grip, before
The Grippe gets you. Glad to see the picture
Of ink—the pitcher that pours before
Throwing the Ball, with never a catcher in sight.
Never a catcher but sometimes a catch, or
A clinch or a clutch or a spoon—never a
Catcher but plenty o' flack, 'till we meet
On this side of the tune.

And here's how it might look and sound in Italian:

L'avventura pazzesca di Gertrude e Ludwig

Per Gabriele Mintz

Mentre Billy continua a salire, gli areostati
vanno a sbattere sull'altro lato del paesaggio
lunare. La navetta spaziale s'è rotta—e rotta
resterà in eterno. Ma non è sicuramente il caso
di mettersi a contare—Ora Sally s'è messa coi
Moonies e non viene a trovarci molto spesso.
Che c'è di nuovo?—mi ci vorrebbe una tazza
di caffè Chase & Sand-borne—perché quando
le corde di una ghitarra si spezzano si può
sempre farne un tavolino. Faceva un gran freddo
a Vienna in quel periodo dell'anno. La Sacher
Torte era deliziosa ma nel colon ne rimane
un ricordo bruciante. Sta calmo, sta calmo prima
che una scalmana ti scalmani. E che bellezza l'idea
dell'inchiostro che dipinge, del pittore che prima
spinge e poi punge, e mai che da qualche parte
ci sia qualcuno che colga. Mai uno che accolga
invece, che so, un raccolto o un abbraccio,
una stretta o un cucchiaio—mai uno che colga,
ma critiche quante ne vuoi, e fino a quando
non ci si ritrovi dall'altra parte della musica

A word of warning: what you are about to hear[1] can neither be construed as full-fledged commentary nor as a translator's note. It contains a bit of both and works primarily as an orientation device. It is a preliminary step toward a more substantial and mature critical reflection. Given the explicatory nature of these remarks, a very small amount of information is provided about the author and the Language poets, a movement Charles Bernstein helped found.

First: Who is Gabriele Mintz, the person to whom the poem is dedicated? This inscription is not a simple paratextual item. It conjures up a presence and functions as a sort of sextant, a sighting mechanism, used for measuring the angular distances between objects. It does not point in a specific direction but enables readers to position themselves.

Gabriele Mintz is the birth name of Marjorie Perloff, who, as anyone who reads poetry in America—as well as in several other parts of the world—is one of today's most authoritative critics of poetry and innovative writing. She taught for many years at Stanford University and has authored a number of essential books on the poetry of Frank O'Hara, on Schoenberg, on how to read poetic texts, on Futurism, the visual writings of the European and Brazilian avant-garde, et cetera. Of particular interest to us here is her autobiography, *The Vienna Paradox*, a narrative in which Bernstein's "Gertrude and Ludwig's Bogus Adventure" is fully and purposefully quoted.

Born in Vienna and forced to leave Austria in 1938 due the *Anschluss*, the Nazi occupation of her country, Perloff came with her family to America and grew up in New York. The Viennese cultural atmosphere is evoked, somewhat bitterly, by referencing the *Sachertorte*, a cake that could not be more seductively accurate as an indicator of identity, sense of belonging, and connection. *Sachertorte* is to Vienna what *panettone* is to Milano or (after Proust) *madeleine* to Paris.

There is no such thing as free evocation, however. Rather than pleasure, the memory of Sachertorte *is*, actually *was*, marred by pain. Mind you, not the torte in and of itself but the memory of it "burned in the colon." The choice of the past tense is significant and creates a productive contrast with the present tense deployed in a subtext surfacing at this juncture in Bernstein's poem. An aoristic "once and for all" event is thus nailed to the contin-

1. First recorded as a contribution to Nuovo Commento, a sound project weaving together text, criticism, reading, image, and music, curated by Ivan Schiavone, Pierpaolo Cipitelli, Stefano Colangelo e Cecilia Bello Minciacch. See YouTube: mediumpoesia.com.

uum of the incessant or recurring experience, captured, or at least alluded to, by John Ashbery in his provocative “They Dream only of America”:

> They dream only of America
> To be lost among the thirteen million pillars of grass:
> “This honey is delicious
> Though it burns the throat.”
>
> Sognano soltanto l’America
> Perdersi tra tredici milioni di colonne d’erba:
> “Il miele è delizioso,
> Ma lascia un bruciore in gola.”

True it is that in his poem, Ashbery weaves a series of narrative threads, each of them emerging from either the writer’s memory of the reader’s imagination, while Bernstein’s text works as a magnet drawing to its shifting center a whole range of diversified and yet ultimately compatible ingredients. Their gathering, the liturgy of their apparent dislocation, bears witness to the mystery of their pilgrimage from desire to expectation, from devotion to indulgence, from the circumstances of “departure” to those of “return,” an experience powerfully hinted at by the title of the poem.

The names Gertrude and Ludwig belong to two emblematic Vienna-related figures. Gertrude Stein was three years old (she was born in Allegheny, Pennsylvania, in 1874) when her family moved to Vienna (before Paris) with a retinue of instructors and governesses charged with the task of imbuing the children (at such an early age, in Gertrude’s case) with Mitteleuropean culture and manners. Ludwig Wittgenstein needs no introduction to Vienna, as he was born there in 1889 to a wealthy family whose members, in turn, needed no introduction to the intellectual and cultural circles of their city.

Further down, we shall expand on the significance of their presence. Here, let us simply note how their names have replaced two other names belonging to people (fictional) who, instead, are in need of a great deal of introduction (to some of us): characters whose world and values stand in direct contrast with the sophisticated and refined intellectual milieu summoned by the spirits of Stein and Wittgenstein, and who are still elegantly and substantially active in the persona and the writings of Marjorie Perloff herself.

The first two lines of the poem propel us and actually drop us right in the vortex of American popular culture, featuring not quite Ashbery’s “thirteen million pillars of grass" but Hollywood's science fiction comedy *Bill & Ted's Bogus Journey*, released in 1991 as a sequel to *Bill & Ted's Excellent Adventure* (1989) and stretched to a third film in the series, *Bill & Ted Face the Music* (2020).

The plot is extremely complicated. To unravel we need to acquaint ourselves with the first film in the series. In 1988, Bill and Ted, two perfectly dim-witted American students—the kind Edoardo Sanguineti would qualify as specimens of the genus *boobus* Americanus[2]—must pass a history test. They have much to worry about, for something very big is at stake: should they fail, Ted's father will force him to join a military academy in Alaska. That would be the kiss of death for Bill and Ted's band, the Wyld Stallyns, whose music is destined to change the world (for the better) and in fact establish an era of bliss, peace, and many more desirables. Help comes from the Future (year 2688) on board a time machine shaped like a telephone booth. Rufus, the pilot, persuades Bill and Ted to journey back in time and "kidnap" a good number of historical figures who, exhibited in real time, will enable the two nerds to pass their exam. The "spoils" they manage to corral and display upon their return is truly impressive: Napoleon Bonaparte, Sigmund Freud, Ludwig van Beethoven, Joan of Arc, Genghis Khan, Abraham Lincoln . . . The day they feared most turns out to be the day of their triumph. Their music (which, admittedly, needs to be improved upon) will not come to an end and, consequently, will bring about the happiness everyone has been wishing for.

In *Bogus Journey*—which is here of primary interest to us—things become zanier than ever: Bill and Ted are killed but are brought back to life after winning a wager with Death itself. Should we not join the chorus of those who, in this sequel, see a parody of Ingmar Bergman's *The Seventh Seal*? The protagonists face a thousand enemies and overcome a thousand and one predicaments, but nothing stops them from reestablishing the universal happiness and welfare that their music had successfully established and that evil forces had temporarily managed to subvert. The film comes to an end announcing a tour of the Wyld Stallyns on planet Mars.

Despite the lukewarm response of critics, *Bill & Ted's Bogus Journey* found favor in the eyes of many viewers. Indeed, it has become a cult movie, obsessively watched by young people, both lonely and gregarious.

Other specifically American cultural references in the poems are:

2. ". . .with Corporal and Thor / with Nike and Matador; &: boobus (said the student): 'from booboisie' . . . , / from 'bourgeoisie' americanus!" See Sanguineti 1982: 67.

"The Moonies": the followers of Reverend Sun Myung Moon (1920–2012), a self-proclaimed Messiah also known for his business ventures and support for political causes, who for a while harvested much enthusiasm among people hungering for religious certainties.

"Chase & Sand-borne" coffee: a play on words in the spelling of the brand name Chase & Sanborn Coffee—a coffee roasting and tea and coffee importing company established in Boston in 1862, claiming to be the first to sell roasted coffee in sealed tins—allows a somewhat negative, and decidedly ironic, assessment of the quality of the product advertised: a coffee borne (blown) by the wind, mixed with sand (tasting like sand?).

"Pitcher, throwing the ball, catcher": we are, no doubt, watching a baseball game, or thinking of one. A game of insinuation: one lonely batter trying to cut himself a passage through a well-guarded enemy's territories. A slow game, a series of repeated attempts, during which nothing happens, or very little, until something delirious does happen, and the bases are loaded, and it is a home run, a grand slam . . . anything is possible.

Much like Stein's repetitional writing: there is no there until there is there.

In the wake of this instigation, taking a close look at what keeps together, in Bernstein's text, spatial and temporal ingredients that would, at first sight, seem irreconcilable, we may notice, before proceeding, that a fundamental swerve occurs, beginning with "Get a grip, get a grip," etc. What comes before this paraenetic formula is bound together by means of referential associations; what follows is tightly roped in by a phonological fascination.

Both these procedures lead us beyond the boundaries of analogy and into the realm of homology, a most pervasive drive that enables messages to free themselves of all metalinguistic snares (a filly is a mammal, a female quadruped, and a quadruped is . . . + some exclamation marks) and foster the birth of meaning where none had seemed possible: in the unexpected.

The multiple, unsubordinated synergy created by the speech fragments woven in the first section of the poem as well as the clear reliance on the ontophony borne out by the second section—a trait that could be easily be adopted as a standard of much language poetry—bears witness to the "rite of passage" from sense to sense and from sound to sense that language, deployed at its poetic level, cannot afford to ignore, as it unfortunately happens in 99 percent of the versifying activity that passes for poetry, not just today, *hélas*.

In this rite of passage, which poetry has been called upon to celebrate since Homer's time and must continue to celebrate to qualify as poetry, word formation is "respectful" of language and galvanized by its power, not to repeat but to make meaning (even through repetition and contradiction). In it the curiosity of the poet-reader—hence of the translator—plays a major role, attempting to visit the modalities with which the text has built itself through the poet-writer, but not in his/her image and not according to his/her likeness.

Only God, in fact, has managed to make something in his image and according to his likeness, and did it *in the plural* ("Let *us* make humankind in *our* image, etc."), without revealing who the others were who lent him a hand in the making of this bizarre and violent creature who speaks to obtain things and writes poems to transcend them.

Attempting, in translation, to remain faithful to poetics that conceive saying an ever-renewable opportunity to "make" sense—an action aimed at extricating language from its referential and definitional obligation, without giving up on discourse, and imbuing it, actually, with the felicity of its original restlessness, with the promise of a prophecy that needs no confirmation let alone fulfillment—some of the semantic support of the original alliterative sequences had to be altered drastically:

> . . . the pitcher that pours before
> Throwing the Ball, with never a catcher in sight.
> Never a catcher but sometimes a catch

> . . . pittore che prima
> spinge e poi punge, e mai che da qualche parte
> ci sia qualcuno che colga. Mai uno che accolga
> invece, che so, un raccolto

The pitcher has become a painter, the catcher has moved away from the diamond of the baseball game to put on the costume of one who catches things in general (*colga*, *accolga*, *raccolga*) and can thus be seen as the agent of any catch. A modicum of concomitance can actually be experienced in the signifier *catch* (catch of the day included), but how different the roads leading to it!

In this perspective we may now return to the quite daring (humorous, irreverent, but ultimately very judicious) replacement of Bill and Ted's names with those of Gertrude Stein and Ludwig Wittgenstein and probe its relevance.

The philosophical and literary legacy of this "odd" and yet not so odd couple permeates Bernstein's poetry. (Bernstein, at Harvard, wrote a thesis on their disquieting points of contact.) Wittgenstein has also been a lifelong concern of Marjorie Perloff's, who reflected on him and wrote about his work with the competence and vigor that has helped generations of readers wade through, and appreciate in depth, the art of philosophy and the science of poetry.

What matters most, however, in the excellent (and anything but bogus) adventure anyone with eyes to see and ears to hear could and should embark upon and live through is the light generated by the osmotic, atomistic, reciprocal insemination of two logical and rhetorical dispositions: the consequential, systemic progress of Wittgenstein's inquiry and the phonematic, non-teleological, obsessional, and radically magmatic approach to meaning adopted by Gertrude Stein.

If the strings of their guitar are dissonant or if they break, "You can always use it as a coffee table." For as long as it lasts, of course, and certainly "'till we meet / On this side of the tune."

Which is now, I believe . . . the time to reread the poem, *a voce alta*.

References

Sanguineti, Edoardo. 1982. "Erotoparegnia" (1956–59). In *Segnalibro: Poesie, 1951–1981*. Milan: Feltrinelli.

Cento

Charles Bernstein and Various Voices

Interview with Romina Freschi (Argentina)

Buenos Aires, June 2005 (in person)

Plebella, no. 6, December 2005 (Spanish)

When and why did you start to write and/or feel you were a writer?

I think I write because I can't do anything else as well. Early on, I became obsessed with the verbal texture of things—that is to say, how words distort and distend things, how they make patterns as if on their own. There has always been for me an incessant daydreaming about the different aspects of rhyme, rhythm, the origins of words (real or imaginary). So I guess that is the source of my being a writer and a poet.

That's the why?

 DOI 10.1215/01903659-9382046

Yes, that's the why.

And the when?

Ah, the when, well, it's hard to say. Writing begins in reading, no? And I began reading very seriously at the same time I got involved with visual art, when I was in junior high school. I was living in New York, where there was an enormous potential to see painting, Abstract Expressionist painting and the work that came after, Pop Art, and also theater, music. So that's when I first imagined some possibility of making art myself. I met Susan in high school, in February 1968. '68 was a very interesting year, perhaps now we can say even a famous year. I was a senior at the Bronx High School of Science, and Susan went to Music and Art. We would go to art galleries together and museum shows. Susan's parents were artists; my parents, well, my father was a businessman; we were not an arts-oriented family. And then I went to college and, you know, studied and read, and this is when I did my earliest work that directly relates to what I do now. At college I edited a couple of literary magazines, I did theater, too, a sort of experimental theater, and that was more visible than writing. But I guess writing was always in the back of my mind.

Why do you consider poetry important?

Poetry is not important. That's why it matters.

Which poets do you admire? How do you feel they relate to your own writing and life?

I admire many poets whom I do not like and like many poets whom I don't admire. It's a complex question, but then this is always my problem, so many apparently simple things seem complex to me. There are many poets that are, in some aspects of their lives or thought, not very admirable but who are still great poets; the most famous example would be Ezra Pound, but he's hardly alone.

Among my contemporaries, there's a large number of poets whose work I read with great attention and appreciation. And while, of course, I like specific poems and specific poets very much, I am perhaps most interested in the relationship among them, in the matrix of work and in the field of activity that is created through not just production but also exchange. I think of poetry as a conversation, not just expressing an isolated voice but placing voice in the service of voices, voices that are in dialogue with one another. Poets exist within constellations. To understand what the achievement of any one of us is, you have to read through the field, to know not only the social and historical contexts but also the different approaches taken by each poet. It diminishes or trivializes any one poet if you read her or him in isolation.

My work is informed by such radical modernist poets as Gertrude Stein, William Carlos Williams, Louis Zukofsky, Charles Reznikoff, and Laura Riding. And the New American Poetry generation—Jackson Mac Low, Robert Creeley, Larry Eigner, Barbara Guest, Jack Spicer, Hannah Weiner, James Schuyler, Charles Olson, and many others. I could give you a list that would go on and on; the list could also be found by looking at the poets I've written about or who I teach. But, to come back to this: the poets with whom I am engaged form a series of interconnected ensembles. And, for the most part, these poets were (and are) working outside of the mainstream, outside of Official Verse Culture. I continually learn from the way these poets rethink the relationship of representation to language, meaning to expression, voice to voices, not assuming that these things are unified but actually thinking of them as if they were in conflict . . . dialectically.

What is a day in your life like?

It's not like much. It's like very little. Once in a while there is flickering, and then there's a kind of blank, and then it continues on. Actually, my life these days is much too busy, possessed by things that I must do, deadlines, responsibilities. And too much anxiety about not getting things done or things not going (or being done) right. It's not my imagination of how I would be living, and not much like how I lived when I was younger, when I had more time to stretch, more time to drift, more openness.

You regret that?

No, I wouldn't switch. Time is not reversible (Arakawa and Gins notwithstanding). And besides, I like the things I do. It's almost as if it's too much of a good thing. (There is no failure like success.) And poetry is still a place for turning things, anxieties and responsibilities, around, from the purposeful and the productive, into a kind of purposeless nonfunctional space, which I think is the basis of poetry.

What do you do for a living? (How do you obtain money?)

I'm a professor of English, although I try to teach English not as a limit but as the host language, and to include literature not originally written in English too. I teach twentieth-century poetry and poetics. I started teaching only when I was about forty; before that I was a freelance medical writer, though most of my energy went into poetry and poetry-related activities. Teaching came after.

That's not usual here . . .

It's unusual in the US as well. Most professors, anyway those teaching in a graduate program, have PhDs, while I have only my undergraduate degree (in philosophy). But it's possible in the United States because there are so many universities that occasionally one or another will go out on a limb. And anyway, my circumstance is not very typical. I like to think, though, after directing twenty-five or so dissertations, and serving on another fifteen committees, that I have earned an unofficial doctorate. One of the great things about the Poetics Program at Buffalo was that none of us in the core faculty had a PhD in English: Susan Howe, Bob Creeley, and I never having pursued doctorates, Dennis Tedlock got his PhD in anthropology, and Raymond Federman got his in French.

What do you enjoy reading? What do you read that is not "literature"?

I read the newspapers every day, the *New York Times*. It's not a good way to start the day—it always puts me in a bad mood, and not just the news reported; the cultural coverage, especially regarding books, is quite irritating, as befits one of the leading organs of the mediocracy. Apart from poetry, I read mostly philosophy and critical and political writing. I don't read novels very much, though there are some novelists that I read without fail (Lydia Davis, Peter Straub, Paul Auster, Federman); but then I guess novels are literature, aren't they? What can I be thinking? I end up reading a great deal that is immediately related to my work: essays and criticism about poetry, poetics, many magazines, and books of poetry. I've just put together on a website with which I'm involved (the Electronic Poetry Center [EPC]) a long list of recommended reading for this past year. There's an enormous amount of very engaging work being written in poetry and in poetics, so I do tend to read more of that than other things. And I regret I can't keep up, there is so much more I want to read than I have the time for. I always feel with the books around me, and manuscripts, like the proverbial kid in the candy store who wants it all. Well also, not to forget, I read job-related documents of various sorts, applications, reviews, committee stuff, bureaucratic documents that can be very time-consuming because it's necessary to read them in detail and to sometimes write summaries . . .

And what do you read on holidays?

I don't really take holidays. I think Susan would agree with that! At the beach I read exactly the same things that I just mentioned to you. I enjoy reading what I read, so I just wish I had more time. I always feel hounded by the fact that I don't have enough time. So "free time" allows me to catch up with things that I haven't gotten to, but often in quieter and more pleasant surroundings. If I had more time, I would read perhaps more detective fiction, catch up on the Elmore Leonards I missed, reread all the James M. Cain and Jim Thompson and Dashiell Hammett and Raymond Chandler. Or maybe just Poe and Borges would do it.

Do you know any poetry from Argentina?

I became informed about poetry from Argentina through Ernesto Livon-Grosman, who sits here with us, across the table, at this remarkably charming café in Buenos Aires, where we have come every morning, for espresso and croissants, and to read the paper while sitting across from the park. In the early 1990s, Ernesto brought to Buffalo, and also to New York, Jorge Perednik, whose work I did not know until I was introduced to it at that time. And through that process, I read through the magazine *Xul* as best I could, since I can't read Spanish (much to my regret), but also with the help of some translations. Ernesto published for us a very important book of translations, *The Xul Reader*, where there is a strong selection of work from the magazine. That was very exciting for me. I felt a real connection between what the *Xul* review was doing to what I was doing with my friends in and around *L=A=N=G=U=A=G=E*. So that was my primary introduction. But it's a very limited perspective mainly based on what has been translated. But then, on this trip, I am learning a great deal more, through reviews such as yours and *tsé, tsé* and also meeting so many poets here.

Could you please tell us about your experience of L=A=N=G=U=A=G=E as a person, as a poet, within the group of L=A=N=G=U=A=G=E poets, and in relation to other ways to think about poetry? What changes and contradictions took place since the beginning as an "avant-garde" group till the nowadays relative "acceptance" or "hegemony" of L=A=N=G=U=A=G=E? (I guess I'm thinking mostly about two different positions, you as poet in a group, and you within a group in society, as forces or contradictions to face.)

L=A=N=G=U=A=G=E magazine came out of a collective exchange among a number of poets, perhaps twenty-five or thirty, who, in the mid-1970s, were actively writing letters, reading each other's work, talking to one another in person and on the phone, publishing magazines and books, and organizing readings and talks. *L=A=N=G=U=A=G=E* was a small part of that, but it was the part in which some of us reflected critically and publicly on the activities in which we were engaged. There were many poets interested in this ongoing, multisite conversation as a form of collective exchange. We shared a very strong dislike of the Official Verse Culture of that time, which seemed to favor poems so crippled by their formulas for personal epiphany that personal epiphany was shed at the starting line in favor of a highly mannered voicey voice "indicating" (like they used to say in method acting) rather than expressing the poet's feelings, the so-called feelings of the so-called poet. In contrast, we tried to focus our work more on an acknowledgment of the structures of language, forms, styles, and also the relationship of ideology to syntax, you might say, ideology to grammar, ideology to rhetoric, with the recognition that language is never neutral but also that language always has an unconscious or nonrational dimension to it.

So it was a very good time as a young poet to be involved with other people in this kind of exchange because Official Verse Culture was so complacent, so smug, and so very weak in its literary production. Our work took a certain alternative course that had its impact, even when we were just doing it on our own, on our own typewriters; it was never acknowledged in the mainstream, except perhaps to be attacked. And many of the individual poets, as you said, have continued to work in quite significant ways on their individual books and projects. Even now, some of us continue to be in discussion. And, of course, there are generations of younger poets who, from my point of view, continue this exchange but whose work, necessarily, is decisively different. I think the significance for that moment represented perhaps by *L=A=N=G=U=A=G=E* was that it really gave permission to do a wide range of nontraditional work, to tear off the mask of compulsory sincerity, of compulsory lyric, to do work that on the surface seemed not to make sense. I will always emphasize that *L=A=N=G=U=A=G=E*'s beef was not with meaning or expression but with false ideas of sense and false facades of sincerity that devalued the possibilities for new or unexpected forms of meaning, sense-making, and indeed sensation.

At the same time, the issue of acceptance is a complicated and complicating business, and I don't want to ignore that. I have a very good job, and I have a certain level of recognition for what I do. My own good fortune notwithstanding, I think that overall Official Verse Culture is more reactionary now than it was in the 1960s, when we had some breakthrough figures from the ranks of the alternative poets. And while some of the historical poets that some of us put forward, such as the ones that I mentioned in my earlier answer, have been more accepted, partly because of our efforts, Gertrude Stein being a very good example, I think that the reviewing practices in the nationally circulated publications (the Massed Media) and the prize-awarding practices in the United States are almost always (though not entirely!) reactionary (though my colleague Jim English would be quick to remind me that it's only complaints like this that give those prizes their primary cultural play and allow me to make remarks like this one). Anyway, I don't think we have, quite, a hegemony. Official Verse Culture is still alive and kicking, even if bloated like a mule on hormones. The huge infusion of Ruth Lilly's money into the thoroughly corporate Poetry Foundation is a good example: the most money now being spent to promote poetry is done in such a manner as to undermine a good deal of the most engaging poetry being produced in the US. You won't likely see any of that Lilly money going to the Poetry Project in New York, presses like O Books or Factory School or Green Integer, or the EPC for that matter. Indeed, the EPC, which many might see as a very established website, has never been able to get any external funding, or even a dedicated graduate assistant from the university that hosts it, and has been specifically turned down by the big foundations because it features work that is not "accessible" to the public, despite its current stats of one million visits per year. It has a public all right; it's just not the right kind of public. And Sun & Moon / Green Integer has never been able to attract significant or private funding, despite its being a "major" press in every sense of the word. Nonetheless, you see a huge amount of activity in the United States and internationally that moves against the Lillyfication of poetry. But much of this activity doesn't quite come to the surface, to the degree that Green Integer and EPC do; but if you dig just a little bit, you can find it. And partly that's because poetry is not a form of popular culture. Poetry is decisively unpopular, has a small scale. But its infrastructure is exhilaratingly tenacious.

And how do you relate to the fact that shape gets somehow old, inevitably?

I don't have any formula for what a poem should be like. You can't say, a priori, what style a poem should have, what voice a poem should channel, whether it should be narrative or not narrative, lyric or not lyric, striated or smooth. It's not possible to prescribe because what's most interesting about poetry is how it responds to emerging circumstance and its local languages, local places; to the most local part of your mind; to the intersection of so many different, not necessarily definable, factors, which are specific for every poet and for every different point in time, and even for yourself as you move through time. So there is that provisionality, that response to contingent circumstance, that seems to me what's innovative in poetry. Poetic innovation is pragmatic. Innovation is what lets you resolve emerging problems as they pop up, mostly unexpectedly and often unhappily. But better than innovation, call it ingenuity. It's not something rarified or, well, avant-garde. On the contrary, it's the absence of ingenuity that takes poetry out of everyday life. Official Verse Culture, for example, in its refusal of new forms of poetry, clings to a past that has already passed by, making poetry something that resembles corpses in a museum. But when we are speaking of innovation, we are speaking of the basic condition of poetry. It comes down to the ability to stay attuned to, to stay in touch with, your responsiveness to the world you find yourself in.

I'll give you an analogy: when people disparage what they hear as nonsense or meaningless language, they say, Oh that's just like children, it's babble. It sounds as if, somehow, they have left their childhoods behind them. But for me, on the contrary, the people who say that have lost access to the sonic and acoustic potential within language, have lost touch with a part of themselves, and a part of the human world, that stays with us until the time that we die. The poetry of language, let's call it, is not just for children. The loss, or denial, is not of childhood—we all grow up—but of what even little children know. Blame it on your education, your rationality, your socialized mind. Maybe what is so frustrating about "difficult" poetry is that it is an unwelcome reminder of the loss of poetry in our everyday lives; the fact that we have too quickly and with too little thought turned the paradise of language into a game of cards.

In some of your articles you talk about being responsible in the writing as being conscious of the political consequences of the use of language. How do you see that responsibility in poetry? How do you see that responsibility in other discourses? What about the political leaders' discourses after September 11, 2001, in your country?

"September 11," like the Vietnam War when I was in college, makes me acutely aware of how language is used not just to express but also to manipulate emotions and values. In moments of crisis, where there is genuine trauma, as with September 11, but also with the war in Iraq and as in Vietnam, you see an acceleration in the manipulation of the public language by both the state and the mediocracy. At such time one comes face-to-face with how inadequate the language of the mass culture is, the reports and commentary on television and the newspapers. In such time, the necessity for poetry is all the more palpable—to deal with an ever more complex reality and in a more complex way. Yet the very complexity that prevents poetry from having a mass audience, from being popular, is at the heart of its political value, contradictory as that is to social realism or to populist idealism. Poetry is political to the degree that it refuses the language of Massed Culture and the Official Religions and Corporate State, while at the same time actively engaging political discourses. In this way, poetry might potentially interrogate the ideological presumptions of the dominant language. It becomes, by default, a place to reflect on the meaning of basic terms, including democracy, freedom, terrorism, God, truth, evil, and so on. The meaning of these terms cannot be assumed. So when you begin to interrogate these nouns, you open up into a no-noun space of poetry, where people say "I don't understand it" because they don't have the practice of listening to that which they don't already know. Yet, without that kind of listening, politics is doomed. Poetry is not a form of macropolitics, it's not a form of direct political action, poetry doesn't change governments, poetry doesn't stop wars. It's a prerequisite for political thinking, but it's not a sufficient form of action. Poetry is not the end of politics. It's the beginning of politics.

This idea of being responsible and conscious of the shape in writing makes me think of a new step from surrealism and automatic writing. I mean, I think surrealism may be seen today as a way to dig into unconsciousness to bring things up to consciousness. What do you think about surrealism?

Surrealism is an important movement for everybody involved in a radical formal change within poetry. But I don't accept the idea that there's a surreality, a deeper reality, beyond everyday reality. Strange as my work sometimes is, I'm interested in a poetry of the everyday, of the daily, of the ordinary. Still, I think that the estrangement and displacement that you find in surrealist poetry is very important. My poetics is in many ways contrary to surrealism but also very indebted to it. I'm less interested in the dream imagery, in the symbolism, in the illusion of depth, than in the syntactic openness and derangement . . . I feel more connected to Russian Futurism.

Romanticism had the idea of gathering poetry and critique. How do you see that relationship today?

There are many problems with the way in which Romantic ideology governs the idea of sincerity, and by extension literary value, in contemporary poetry: the great poem as universal expression of man's feelings. I object to that on many grounds, including the very gendered terms that are then universalized. At the same time, the Romantic and surrealist poets, if understood in a social and historical context, were doing crucial aesthetic and political work, which I relate to very profoundly. I think of Blake in particular as an exemplary figure, with his verbal-visual-visionary work. Blake remains the poet of the future. He manages to always be ahead of me, anyway. But I frequently return also to Byron and Shelley, Heine and Hölderlin.

And the critical dimension?

Coleridge's poetics is crucial, and the German Romantics as well . . . Really a model for the importance of poetics, for poetry as going beyond the production of poems to appreciate for their beauty. In the 1970s, however, it was necessary to contest not so much the radical thinking of Coleridge or Blake but a Romantic ideology that pitted thinking against feeling, intellect against the emotion; indeed, poetics against poetry.

You've always worked with small and alternatives presses. Would you say more about what you think about the importance of alternative presses?

The poem itself doesn't exist outside of who produces it, what magazine it appears in, how the magazine circulates, who reads it, how they respond to it. All these things are part of what the poem is. A poem isn't just some abstract letters on a page; it exists within its social environment. And not just the given historical world of jobs and states and family, but the ones we make through our writing, our publishing, our exchanges. The value of poetry is also the value of articulating specific, yet contestable, aesthetic values. And this is achieved by poets publishing their own work and the work of poets they believe in, by responding to the work they value, by organizing reading series and websites and small presses in order to take control of every aspect of the means of production and reproduction.

Is there any other question you think should be included in this kind of interview?

Yes, but I prefer not to say. [Laughs]

Frequently Unasked Questions: Interview with Versatorium (Austria)

Der Standard, Album section, January 20, 2011 (German)

This interview was conducted by seminar participants at the Institute for Comparative Literature at the University of Vienna (Peter Waterhouse/Versatorium). The seminar sent me a series of answers, all quotations from my work, in italics, and asked me to write questions following each answer.

Xo.

What is the smallest unit of meaning? Is it a phoneme—the minutest sound you hear as a separate entity? Or is the whole language the smallest unit?

Ideas are dead except in use.

What do you think about the abstract nouns of literary theory, politics, theology, and philosophy: construction and transcendence, being and forgiveness, dialectic and possibility, freedom and ecstasy, materiality and affect, melancholy and citizenship, nation and notion, bewilderment and wilderness, democracy and framing?

At its most effective, the university is not oriented toward marketplace discipline and employment training but rather toward maximizing the capacity for reflection and creativity. When it is most fully achieving its potential, university classes are not goal-oriented or preprofessional but self-defining and exploratory. Attempts to regulate the university according to market values only pervert what is best and least accountable about these cultural spaces. We cannot make education more efficient without making it more deficient.

You started teaching late in life, when you were forty. What do you most value about the American university, and what are your greatest fears about its future?

Exenst aerodole—extremst Autodrom! [Laughs]

Let me follow up on that. What are the limits of critical discourse in the university? Some say anything goes, but you are often critical of constraints on the culture of critical discourse.

More important is a willingness to consider the implausible, to try out alternative ways of thinking, to listen to the way language sounds before try-

ing to figure out what it means, to lose yourself in a flurry of syllables and regain your bearings in dimensions otherwise imagined as out of reach, to hear how poems work to delight, inform, redress, lament, extol, oppose, renew, rhapsodize, imagine, foment . . .

What about making your meaning clearer, about getting across a message, about communicating, about being accessible, about saying just exactly what you feel?

jed jimmsy's cack. ib giben durrs urk klurpf. ig ooburs quwate ag blurg.

Are you a Jewish poet? You have written a libretto, *Shadowtime*, for Brian Ferneyhough, which is about Walter Benjamin. Is this written from a Jewish point of view? You write in your essay in *Radical Poetics and Secular Jewish Practice* that you feel you are, by necessity, continuing the work of the nonreligious European Jewish culture obliterated by the Systematic Extermination Process of the Second World War. But isn't that all past and gone? Can't we put all that behind us?

Marvelous influidities.

Do you like Austrian food?

When a text is dressed in the costume of poetry, that, in and of itself, is a provocation to consider these basic questions of language, meaning, and art. Chronic poetic aporia (CPA).

Is there no way to escape artifice? What about natural language and direct statement? Do you prefer a hall of mirrors to the sublime majesty of a mountain pass at dawn, fog burning off the vistas like angels going home?

Bernstein. Sternbein. I.

What's in a name? Are we there yet? Do you ever mistake a tree for the forest? Bitter tears for joy? *Bitte* for please? *Bernstein* for amber?

Vienna.

Come again?

Let the poem mutate into fruition. Poetry scares me.

What advise do you have for young poets?

Only the imaginary is real. Only the real is real. These lines refuse reality.

What is truth?

Thanks for your of already some weeks ago.

In retrospect, do you think moving to a single European currency was wise? Why is L=A=N=G=U=A=G=E poetry so influential in Burma? Do you value politeness in email correspondence? What is the question again?

Interview with Philip Davenport (England)

October 12, 2012, New York (in person)

The Dark Would: An Anthology of Language Art, vol. 2 (UK: Apple Pie Editions, 2016)

How come you guys lost the battle? [Laughs] It feels embattled, and it feels like we stopped being, in Britain anyway, ambitious. People started to accept "Oh well, I'm in the bunker, and that's where I'll stay . . ."

. . . the poetry battles are different in the UK than in the US, that's for sure, going back to what we were talking about before, Bob Cobbing and the Writers Forum, not to say the whole business with Eric Mottram and the Poetry Society. What I was going to say also, in respect to the *TLS*, when the *TLS* ran a piece about Prynne last year, it was so strange, they just picked this one small book of his, the review was almost written as if . . . here's this odd person who nobody's heard of but who, "obscure and difficult" but, wow, still he is really great. So Prynne is extolled, but he was presented as if he were a cult, hidden from view, which surely he is not. Prynne is one of the most prominent British poets of the time, teaching much of his life at one of the main British universities, and he has a volume of collected poems and scores of articles about his work. But *TLS* chooses to review this one pamphlet. Why treat him in such a miniaturizing, or exoticizing, way? His collected was previously reviewed in *TLS* more than a decade ago, at which time he was billed as the "invisible man of English poetry." I mean if he is invisible, what about all the actually neglected poets in the UK? What are they? Unmentionable or inconceivable, I guess. But there is a conflict between the Official Verse poets and Prynne and Co., Ltd., in Cambridge. But then again there is a conflict between Prynne's Cambridge and Cobbing's London, one that is perhaps more fierce because the poetic values at stake are more overlapping. Which brings us to where you intersect with UK poetry—visual, concrete, VVV, experimental too—a term I don't like—

No, I don't . . .

But that kind of work really has never had much legitimacy and acceptance in the UK or in the US. The advent of the web has changed that. It's made it easier to have alliances and affiliations—transatlantic is what they used to say—across national borders, to set up affiliations which are not so much based in those national cultures. And the web has made available the historical record of visually centered poetry (and verbally centered art) to a much greater degree. But, you know, when Swinburne wrote his book about Blake in 1868, Blake was a completely marginalized figure. The issue for Swinburne and for Blake, the relation of their work to the visual, is crucial in terms of the history we are talking about because the Pre-Raphaelites, like Blake, worked as visual-verbal artists, and indeed their decorative or ornamental approach to visual and verbal art continues to raise, well, if not red flags then pleated ones. As much as the present of poetry needs to be continually claimed, so, equally, does the history of poetry need to be reclaimed. The revenge of history can be an exhilarating force, the return of the repressed. And there remains a powerful desire to repress the material history of the book, which is very much at the heart of contemporary Official Verse Culture and its profound disinterest—if disinterest can be profound—in the history of writing and inscription. I made a joke years ago, in an essay about Johanna Drucker, that there's two things that are ignored about poetry: its look and its sound; that is poetry itself is ignored. [Laughs] So I guess I am just responding to your sense of disappointment and annoyance and anger about poetry histories that you feel were hidden from you. We used to say in the '70s that grammar, that syntax, exerted a kind of control over your thinking, which I think is true, but people would reply, "Oh, you think you can just change the words around and you're going to change the society!" But we didn't think that. We were not naive. Nonetheless, the way in which we use words does affect how we understand and interpret reality. As George Lakoff says, it's a question of framing: what we frame, what we foreground, what we regard as insignificant. I think Erving Goffman's work on frame analysis, along with Lakoff's, is useful to the discussion of the reception of what I, for the moment, like to call pataquerical poetry. Lots of such poetry frames as significant that which doesn't even register as semantic for some readers and critics. And that is surely true of the visual domain of verbal language that is your focus. For some, those who've been properly schooled!, the visual display of verbal language just doesn't count—it's like noise, it's irrelevant; or it's like bad printing, it interferes with deciphering the supposed content. Alphabetic technology is potentially aversive to the embodiment of language (to use a phrase of William Carlos Williams). Accent is the paradigmatic example, since the full range of accents are not typically foregrounded in alphabetic writing, which provides an aphonetic schematic that tends to elide different pronunciation (when you transcribe this, you won't know how I pronounced, or mispronounced, pronunciation). One often noted corollary: standard English—the *koine*, in the UK southern English—is idealized, while other—nonstandard—social, racial, ethnic, regional tongues are stigmatized. Alphabet technology doesn't cause ethnocentrism or class conflict, rather they lay claim to the technology. A substantial part of the history of poetry can be read as those others pushing back. Language is rooted in social interactions: it's never just individuals who speak; the social speaks through the individual. That's the power of verbal language: no matter what you do to it or with it, you're always dealing with a social body. Visualizing language, whether in alphabetic writing or visually oriented poetry, has the ability to make tangible what is otherwise an immersive stream. We get to touch it, hold it, hear it, see it. When I was in China recently, one of the terrific graduate students, in a paper about Rae Armantrout, said that I had always put forward, along with my contemporaries, the idea that the work that we were doing was nonreferential. But, as I tried to explain, I have always argued just the opposite. In 1977, Ken Edwards published an essay of mine in *Reality Studios* that started "Not death of the referent." [Laughs] That was one of my first published essays, refuting an idea that seems to stick to me like zebra's stripes on a panda bear. . . . But the reason that happens is . . . some among those who advocate visual or sound or syntactically sprung poetry proudly wave the banner of meaninglessness and nonreference. But I have always hated that . . . I don't hate the people that say it, I understand what they are getting at . . . but I see it a different way. We are creating new semantic domains, not abandoning the semantic. And the reason that those zebra stripes keep getting put onto my panda ontology, well, it's just that some folks like to think it's only possible to understand verbal language if it sheds its dependence on look or sound. In happy contrast to my friends who celebrate the obliteration of meaning in a Dadaesque way . . . well, I won't embrace this as a positive description, because it seems to me you're giving up on a real struggle over language. Now, I realize a visual mark doesn't have the kind of verbal associations and references that even a single letter has. Visual marking and alphabetic writing are different enterprises, not to say empires. Combining them, of course, is a fundamental project for art, and their separation is a fundamental problem. In *Attack of the Difficult Poems*, I take this back to the archaic—and try to trace the invention of the Greek alphabet twenty-five hundred years ago, emphasizing how much we are still in the thrall of alphabetic technology. Phonetic alphabet script, either Hebrew, which is a little earlier, or Greek, uses letters in an instrumental way to cue sounds. (An *a* stands for a sound that has no intrinsic meaning. Or does it?) The alphabet by itself does not specify the full range of verbal sounds but rather cues them. You have to project the full vocal range onto the script. Acoustically, alphabets are evocative rather than denotative (we each pronounce the same word differently). But the alphabet is not digital code, despite being treated as if it were. And therefore whenever anybody pulls the alphabet apart, or for that matter works outside of the standard grammatical/syntactical patterns, people see red: all they hear is noise, they think there is nothing going on there. And they say . . . that's what you are advocating, the destruction of meaning, isn't it? And it's very hard to get beyond that barrier. Love me for my body, the poem says; but the reader says, your body is distracting me from your mind, your body is just a husk that should fall away so I can understand your meaning. . . . That's the way I understand what we're talking about, in response to your wanting to do a "language art" collection and yet you're telling me you are not informed about poetry . . . that's why I want to take it back to the reception of some of the British poets. That's why I want to connect the fact—the symptom!—that a journal as sophisticated as the *London Review of Books* has such appalling poetry coverage: because they don't actually take poetry as an art form. They can't. There is an enormous resistance to understanding what the art of poetry would be because it presents a challenge to the discourse that they—well, mostly everybody!—operate within, which they take as neutral. But it would not puncture their authority to change their poetry tune, if I can mix my metaphors like a sushi chef in a paddy wagon. Poetry makes nothing happen, right? Like many who abhor the new poetry, such publications are overreacting. It is quite possible to operate at many different rhetorical levels—you can certainly write standard expository prose without that being undermined by poetry. It's almost as if such places take poetry too seriously [laughs] because they are unable to consider it at all, as if it is a kind of virus or black magic they better keep clear of. And maybe it is. As if publishing a pataquerical poem would displace the whole symbolic order. [Laughs] Like deviant sexuality, it has to be repressed. Turns out everything does not come unglued, turns out this dark other side is always operable, whether you acknowledge it or not. Even the person that is most repressed about poetry or its polymorphous perversity still has it in them [laughs] and operates with it all day long, every day. It's always there, and they are living with it. Just relax, accept it . . . (says the poet plagued by anxiety) . . .

It doesn't kill you.

No, on the contrary, it just makes you freer in your choices. I always say, when I teach a seminar that just uses constraint-based and non-expository writing, that a class like this should be required for all students—in addition to the mandatory expository writing class: students need to take abnormal writing to balance their class in normal writing. Non-expository writing will only make your expository writing better: it would potentially enable you better able to conceptualize what you are doing in rhetorical terms. So there's my sophistical sleight of hand . . . because if you don't believe standard-issue expository prose is a rhetorical choice, if you believe that it's rational (or God-given) and it's the best means possible to the most apt expression, then what I'm saying is treacherous, as many people feel. You'd have to accept that there is no "best" expression, only chosen expressions, each of which comes with its own baggage. Rationalized, neo-Euclidian expository writing that represses its look and sound is only one among many possible ways to engage ideas, philosophy, politics. . . . Jump-cut to the present: Why do people occupy Wall Street? Why don't they sound like the Democratic Party and have a platform like the Democratic Party's platform? And yet for some, such departing from the established rule of the road seems akin to anarchy or nihilism . . .

It's really fascinating, because, by accident I met the people who are running the Wall Street occupation protest, because I was sitting beside them in a café, and they were talking about plurality, and that there's a great pressure on them to have a message –

Well, they have a message; they just don't know if it's a poetic message. Perhaps it is ambiguous, but ambiguity is also a message.

I think that there are many groups who would particularly like them to say one thing or another thing.

There is pressure on the Occupy people to have policy goals as defined by the mainstream media and two dominant political parties.

Yeah, but because they're not doing that, I thought it was very interesting that they were sitting talking about existing, sitting and existing with the idea of not having clarity, and it just responds to what you were talking about.

Occupy Wall Street has a very explicit political perspective, couldn't be more explicit, so that when people say that we don't know what they stand for . . . how could it be more apparent? It reminds me still of that nonreferentiality issue: what do you mean, they don't stand for anything? Obviously they have views. It's not put in terms of a congressional legislation, and it's frustrating for people for whom that's the only . . . but, of course, in that, OWS reminds me of the '60s, which was a vexed period, but nonetheless aspects of the New Left moved in a related direction. In England, it was the art schools that were the most magically powerful instigators of that 1968 experience. And so that again goes back aesthetically to radical strands in English art and poetry history. I have William Morris in the back of my mind—it's all connected. And that relates also to the origin of punk, anyway the part that picks up on even people like Burroughs, like Genesis P-Orridge.

Yeah, he very much entwined with Burroughs and the Situationists, I think, via Malcolm McLaren.

A student I worked with at Penn, Greg Steirer, wrote a fascinating dissertation about those connections. One of his chapters made that point that Paris '68 is sometimes remembered as a fight about labor issues or legislative political demands, but mainly it comes out of university reform—*there is no poetry in our classrooms*. It's the students rebelling against the irrelevance and the hierarchy of the classes in France that was a crucial motor to '68. And in England . . . art schools and then punk. Steirer makes an at first counterintuitive argument associating punk with neoliberalism—and he's not against it, he likes this aspect. My less historically accurate sense would have been to see British punk as vaguely connected to the Left, Rock Against Racism and so on; but Steirer sees product branding that celebrates the free market far more central than any ideological critique of capitalism. So for Steirer, the apparently dissident subcultures are the pure product of neoliberal capitalism, which, again, for Steirer is not a "bad" thing. For the successful bands, their brands were worth quite a lot. Poetry culture almost never offers the possibility of lucrative commodification (so our commodification must be done just for the sheer love of it?! or more likely for other kinds of symbolic capital). Well, perhaps hip-hop—given its connection to poetry—is a liminal case. The visual art world has a market dimension unavailable to poetry. But I want to keep returning, Philip, to your sense of injustice in/around poetry and its reception in the UK, which you expressed before we turned on the recorder. You are already seeing, as you meet poets interested in your anthology, that we have a number of overlapping interests. I like to say that the radical poetry web you are beginning to cruise, well . . . let's just say you have fallen through the poetry rabbit hole, just like in *Alice in Wonderland*, and found a subterranean world that's very dense. It's a whole ecosystem, and one not free from hierarchy—everybody can't enter into it in the same way; it's a highly defined and constantly contested space. It is not a subculture as is familiar from music or even the visual arts, which often have a relationship to mass culture or to money that's different. Poetry is to some degree unable to enter into those markets—if it could, it would. I don't think the poets are immune to wanting to have those kinds of success; it's just not open to them in the same way. Poetry is unpopular culture (to use Kenneth Goldsmith's phrase). But the density and the complexity of the infrastructure is something that's extraordinary; and with the internet, these kinds of webs of communication that go back even a hundred years or longer trace a (not so) secret history. Actually, the secret history of poetry that we're talking about really goes back over two hundred years.

When I was talking to Jerry Rothenberg, I'm aware of—

Jerry has done so much to make explicit this history, as, in a different way, has Jerome McGann . . .

I mean, Blake is almost the first, there's a certain trail of outsiderdom, which is—

But it's also the verbal-visual aspect of Blake's work and the fact that it wasn't conventionally published and didn't circulate, which is also true of Dickinson. So that history remains symbolically defining.

For me, there was a sense of, as you said, dropping into a hole—I felt as if I'd gone over a wall and suddenly there was this garden.

Or through the looking glass . . . because Lewis Carroll is part of that history.

Absolutely. But there was a sense then of it suddenly becoming very intense, the experience became very intense, because it was as if this was a rare experience, it couldn't just be accessed.

Poetry isn't really marginal, or it's marginal only to a point. I'm often subjected to this kind of . . . critique, let's say . . . because I have a good university job and I've been published by big presses . . . so some people like to say—how can I advocate what I advocate? But I would like to see more people have the kinds of jobs I have and more of the "kind of poetry I want"—to use MacDiarmid's phrase—get reviewed. And what I'm saying about the *London Review of Books* is not that if somebody I liked was reviewed in there that they would be a sellout; I'm saying the opposite—that it would be fine! I want to see this discussion in their pages! Things would go on even better; the paper's own intellectual projects would be enriched, not harmed, or probably just go on unchanged. I'm absolutely against this "us" against "them" . . . that we should stay away from such places—bunker was the term we used. I'm not sympathetic to the "bunker" as a choice, if it's a choice, and I don't romanticize it, but I recognize the attitude as self-protective for many people and so I accept that (I think of Jack Spicer picketing Duncan because he has sold out by being published by the East Coast elite New Directions) . . . but I think it's an unfortunate situation, and when I criticize the mainstream, it is not to say I don't think it will change or that I won't welcome the change.

Well, bunkers are useful for surviving in, but they also tend to be very limited in their outlook.

I hear it as a World War I metaphor, bringing to mind both the Futurist moment and the trenches. For me, Owen and Sassoon, the whole issue of cacophony, is very important, the gas masks, the explosions—that's a very important part of breaking things apart in the social structure, which then gets reflected and refracted in the poetry. So it's not—"Oh, the poets just decided to fragment things in this way on their own." The world that they were in was doing that, they were responding. Preston Sturges put it perfectly in *Christmas in July*: "If you can't sleep at night, it's not the coffee it's the bunk." It's very explicit in Owen and Sassoon, so that becomes—I'm not the first to say it!—one of the iconic moments for understanding what goes on in modernism . . . not just Gertrude Stein. The problem with the bunker mentality is, bunkers are good when the bombs are dropping, but when the bombing stops and years later you're still in the bunker [laughs] . . . that's a little scary, right? Even a few months later, you can understand, but at a certain point, when some move into houses, and the ones still in the bunker say, "Oh no, you betrayed us, you've sold out, you're not staying in the bunker." But that's a lot of bunk! So you say, "Oh no, you could get another house right next to mine, we'll have a reading series up here." . . . Poetry has a remarkable resilience and also an incredible, even, well, okay, I'll say it, respect within the culture. Despite all that we're saying, it's an art form that has a very resonant and even talismanic power within North American and British culture. No matter how much we talk about the mistreatment of counternormative poetry as something not getting attention, still there's something much beyond that that's even stronger about its cultural station.

Do you have a sense that you are in some way a carrier or a transmitter of that?

"I'm sure we all do the best we can," to echo David Antin (except those that don't!). What's ironic to me is that in an English department, everyone is talking about multidisciplinary while I'm one of the most traditional professors, in the sense that I teach poetry as an art form, which has a claim to being part of the infrastructure of literature departments. Nothing more old-fashioned than that. Even if most people who teach in English departments were to have scant interest in poetry, still, you can't imagine an English department without poetry. Maybe the wrong kind of poetry [laughs] but even so, poetry is built into the foundation of the teaching of the language that everybody speaks. Poetry cannot be completely eradicated. You could say, in K through 12 in America, there's an appalling treatment of poetry, but nonetheless lip service is paid. Then again, a couple of years back I would have said the same thing about classics—before the State University of New York at Albany announced it was eliminating not only its Classics Department but also French and Italian Literature too. So just forget what I am saying; I must be a cockeyed optimist after all ("I'm stuck like a dope / With a thing called hope").

I guess this idea that I was talking about before, it's simply my own personal framing, but that I have a family which has successive generations and that I feel that in what I'm doing right now there's a sense that there are progenitors and there are people who are inheriting stuff, they're being given stuff. That transmission is very interesting to me, and I wondered if you might just finish by talking about that . . . [transmission] from a generation of practitioners to another generation of practitioners.

I have saturated myself in the work of the generations before mine, along with my own and the one after me, and I have, obsessively, taken on the task of archiving and disseminating. At the same time, I'm very critical, or wary, about the nature of how that transmission occurs, and the kind of exclusions that set in. I am not wedded to the group of poets that I came up with in the '70s as the be-all and end-all, and, in contrast, see us as *particu-*

larly particular, brought together by contingent circumstance. Yet, in keeping with the spirit (but not the letter!) of our founding years, I try to stay as open as I can to things that are outside of the histories of transmission that I am deeply, irrevocably embedded in. Teaching the history of such transmission is one way to at least try to break its insulating hold. But it's very hard not to be insular—just time and loyalty work against you. I'm a very loyal person, and so it's very hard for me not to be limited, because the world of poetry is so huge, there are so many different poetry cultures, and there are so many different people working. It's important to keep in mind the limitations of what any of us . . . and certainly I'm very aware of the limitations of my views. But . . . still . . . I have very specific historical interests and lineages of which I am a caretaker. I have a historical and dialectical—indeed a pragmatic—view of lineages and transmission. What I call midrashic antinomianism. That means acknowledging any given path, any given tradition, any given trajectory as contingent, as situational, historical, peculiar—not the "best," not "universal," not formally inevitable. But still the one I have a stake in. That is, to see literary history not as fixed—the one we get too often in schools and in *LRB*, *NYRB*, the *New Yorker*—but as pataquerulous. (By *fixed* I mean both what they do to pets and to sports games.) But circling back to bunkers and Bohemians, I am also wary of the reaction formation, circling the wagons, since pataquerics charts a history of specific and often incommensurable reactions against the norm or standard.

I think that's a very important relationship to broker, isn't it, because if you happen to be in a place, or your contemporaries do, which has involved an element of bunkerism, and then on top of that your own practice is perhaps one that is not easily . . . the transition between that and the rest of the culture around it is at times a vexed one, then there's a double . . . and then there's also the process of aging as well and that idea that you talked about, loyalty—you can only be loyal to so many people: you live a life, there are going to be a number of people and you form alliances with them and you can't keep doing that. So that's a third reason for shutting down, so how do you break that apart?

Loyalty often is seen in terms of both coterie or friendship and the bonding within aesthetic (or political) movements. Both coteries and movements are to some extent built on exclusion. Coterie's problem is favoritism, college chums and all. Aesthetic movements have the problem of going from band to brand, which can be a radical swerve away from opening things up, if, indeed, that was part of the founding mission, as it was with

L=A=N=G=U=A=G=E. In retrospect, anything that gets recognized creates a de facto bunker. The minute something is labeled and characterized, whether as a group (aesthetic program) or individual (voice), if you decide to promote that as a label, then that may lead you into an often overly narrow understanding of both what you yourself are doing and what's going on around you. That's why there was and is so much ambivalence—the lady doth protest too much!—about the "Language" label among many of the practitioners, because resisting branding, while recognizing its inevitability, was one of the aesthetic principals. And that made for difficulties. But it's a paradox: the external acceptance of what you do can increase the bunkerliness of your understanding of what you're doing. Insofar as you're being labeled as doing one thing, then that's your calling card, your signature, your logo, and so that recognition comes with . . . to some degree, you're going along with this . . . And artists often have that problem—they become narrower as a result of their public recognition or characterization (you're the person who does *x* or is part of the *y* group). Or maybe they dig in and become deeper. Maybe the resistance is futile! Like any other identity formation, this occurs externally, because no man (or woman) has an identity formation entirely unto him- or herself. Our identity is formed by the way other people recognize us. Now, you can reject those characterizations, in a kind of neoliberal humanist way, "I Am a Sovereign Self I Am / a Total Original not Part of any Clan"; but at the same time, if you cling too much to identity formation, that can be very narrowing too. This is especially interesting to me in terms of Jewishness, a marvelous arena of complexly contested identity formations. I'm interested in radical poetic practice in a secular Jewish context. In that frame, the Jewish understanding would be to resist certain kinds of identity formation, so we have our slogan from Kafka: "What do I have in common with the Jews? I don't even know what I have in common with myself." But also, I do not reject or undermine my Jewishness; on the contrary, I see it as a primary frame of my identity. Let's just say I am more Jewish than Jew. I would say that of art movements too. The thing about *L=A=N=G=U=A=G=E*, which I edited with Bruce Andrews (1978–82), at least from my point of view, not shared by everyone else involved . . . I was very conscious of questioning and exploring the way in which language operates to categorize and identify and also the way that it can end up being reductive. So our poetic practice—both having essays that were not expository or discursive, and focusing on poems that departed from conventional modes of representation—was an attempt to get outside of . . . the way language operates to close down. Maybe I have always been too phobic about singular identities, starting with the singular voice of the poet; I know a lot of people accept and even welcome and promote such things. I am obsessed with these issues. As I get older, the diachronic (transmission) issue you raise creates ever new problems, as family, aesthetic, or personal loyalties fray and regroup. Anyway: I was born in this briar patch. The basis of my poetics is to question characterization, labeling, and, in that Steinian way, the dominance of nouns. Keeping in mind, though, that frames and categories are the means by which we both perceive and measure the world: I am not against framing any more than I am against meaning or history. But I am interested in pushing back against frames in a dialectical way. As I say, maybe it's futile! You don't dispense with frames any more than you dispense with your body. But what is your body? How does it work? One of my students yesterday at my grad seminar was talking about how in Stein visual images of the body are rarely presented: there's a lot of sex but you don't have depictions of her body ("Lifting Belly" being an exception). Similarly, in the new disabilities poetry anthology *Beauty Is a Verb*, the point is made that Larry Eigner rarely describes his disability. It's an interesting point, but I would never think of it that way. You don't see the representation of the body, but the work is made of language perceived as or in or on a body: it's not letting you look at the body as a voyeur, it's actually letting you share an experience, as if you're getting satellite transmissions from the mind experiencing the world as it is perceived in and through that body.

[break in recording]

. . . It's fascinating, thinking of Cobbing, the visual poems that he would read as sound poems. Other people do this too; there is a tendency to take visual poetry as scores for performance—I mean, Cobbing could be given a carpet as a script, and he would perform the carpet. Johanna Drucker writes about this in her essay on visual poetry in *Close Listening: Poetry and the Performed Word*. You create a visual work that doesn't have obvious phonic dimensions—of course, if you're messing with the alphabet, then it isn't something that would necessarily have a phonic dimension—think of Gomringer's "schweigen" ("silencio"); but still, the analogy is very . . . *evocative*.

It's an unwritten space, isn't it, I think, that you're talking about it, and it's the work that exists in that unwritten space that is almost being accessed that becomes so fascinating.

A wonderful thing about poetry that foregrounds its visual dimension is that it plays with resisting the phonetic. But at the same time, I'm fascinated when such a visual poem becomes the basis for a phono-tour-de-force, as with Steve McCaffery's *Carnival.*

Well, it's a leaping-off point, isn't it, I suppose.

Maybe I'm wrong, but I think the classic 1950s Noigandres concrete poetry or Gomringer . . . there aren't performances of those pieces because of the very nature of their gridlike repetition and iconic signage. So they're called neat concrete; don't they say neat versus messy?

Clean, yeah.

Clean concrete might not be performed, while messy concrete does seem to lend itself to a sound poetry performance. And yet you can hear "silencio."

And yet somebody like Robert Lax I think of as being very related to clean and concrete.

And he performs.

Yeah, yeah. They link minimalism, don't they?

How about somebody like Thomas A. Clark? He's almost a concrete poet in a way. I've never actually heard Thomas A. Clark read. Does he?

I've seen pictures, very pretty pictures.

. . . when you get to that extreme minimalism, or maybe in his case *miniature* is a better term—there is also a sound dimension, silently heard within the context of the book. A murmur.

I'm going to pull us back to the two questions that arise out of what we're talking about. I would like to just come back to how you started, and you were talking about the brutality of ignoring certain people and their achievements. So, in Britain, you were talking about Maggie O'Sullivan . . .

Maggie O'Sullivan is one of the great British poets who should be celebrated, as she turns sixty; but, in fact, she has received little support in a culture that prides itself on its literary and cultural traditions. That was true of Bunting too; Bunting was virtually impoverished at the end of his life. About ten years ago, Maggie applied to the Arts Council in her region . . . I wrote a letter, as did Keith Tuma—who was the editor of the Oxford anthology of British and Irish poetry—and there were other distinguished references from Britain, but despite that the Arts Council said her work was not poetry! And they wouldn't fund her. What a travesty. She applied for a modest amount of funding to do her work. And here is where this ties into your project: my sense is the work was rejected as poetry because of its strong visual element.

I think there's a terrible split in Britain between the overground stuff and then anything that has a notion of experiment about it, and it's really been a problem. I think that that is changing now.

If you look at the way poetry is represented in many forums with wide circulation, you realize it is treated as a kind of ugly stepchild who needs to be invited to the table but is best kept as quiet as possible. People do not read the *London Review of Books* or the *New Yorker* for its poetry coverage, but if they think that if this is what poetry is about these days, they will also think that it really is fifty years behind the other arts. The poetry coverage many of the general readers of these publications see is slanted toward those who are adamantly opposed to formally radical poetry of the past hundred years, work which is either trashed or ignored, with a few signature exceptions, such as John Ashbery, who provides a lot of cover, or let's just say plausible deniability. In contrast, in the art world, comparable formal developments are extolled on museum banners. So there is that famous asymmetry—not in terms of practice, which is comparable, but in terms of reception. The economic value some visual artworks attain is not something possible for a poem. Yet it still needs to be noted that most visual artists see little or no economic returns for their costs or labor and operate—this is truly shocking!—like poets. But the huge amount of money in the art world skews the economic picture, and the expectations, for everyone. Still, the fact that poetry operates in its own symbolic economy, somewhat removed from a lucrative market economy, has its advantages. There is a way that the market culture in the arts has turned active works of visual thought into trophies. And this has also led to a straitjacketing of critical discourse and curatorial choice exemplified by the compulsory orthodontics of *October* magazine (*where even a grin looks grim*). In this canon, neither poetry plastique nor radical poetics can have a place, except if it is certified as uncontaminated by poetry, as with Carl Andre or Lawrence Weiner or Jenny Holzer. That radical poetics remains unsettling for both official literary and art culture is telling. The banality of much of the verbal language in blue-chip art allows it to be assimilated into a market and museum culture that resists linguistic complexity while supposedly celebrating visual difficulty. But you can't have one without the other. Think about Décio Pignatari's "beba coca cola / babe / coca / caco / cloaca" [drink coca cola / drool / glue / cocaine / cesspool], which remains incendiary; and then think of the excruciatingly bland use of language in Ed Ruscha's work of the past decade (yes, I understand it's supposed to be nondescript, as with the verbal material in so much hyper-dry conceptual art, more filler than poetry) . . . I still go for Pignatari's startling use of logo. That's the sort of visual-verbal work I admire, along with, now, the work of Johanna Drucker and Robert Grenier. I feel a deep connection with Grenier and O'Sullivan, poets so connected to wilderness and the pastoral, even though I would appear to be living a life, and doing work, quite aversive to that. Bob, as you know, has wanted to present his work in an art context, with disappointing results.

I think that there are various things mitigating against it, one of them being that perhaps, as well, he is so comfortable in that pastoral context. As a person, I felt that I discovered Bob much more spending time with him in Bolinas and that he does have a level of discomfort when he's in an urban environment, but if you're in the gallery world it is about selling and hustling — I've spent the last few days walking around SoHo, shaking people by the hand, doing little card exchanges, and all of that kind of stuff, and you have to be able to do that and he's just not.

There are certainly examples of people in the visual arts world who are extremely resistant to professional socialization, in the way that Grenier is, who nonetheless are successful for one reason or another. But what I think is interesting about your description of what the art world is like . . . and this is what I mean that you could say that poetry is fifty years ahead of the visual arts . . . because this professionalization and corporatization of the art world is a detriment to the exchange economy that's possible within poetry. So Stein remains a vexed figure in official literary *and* art culture in a way that is not true of Picasso. It's telling that the Museum of Modern Art is comfortable including Cendrars, Apollinaire, and Kruchenykh in their upcoming "inventing" abstraction show (but only on the condition that there be no translations), but Stein is persona non grata. What's that about? I guess because Stein wrote in English so people would be able to read it! And then let's come back to the present. Allen Fisher would be an interesting example: Why is Allen Fisher so obscure and Rachel Whiteread so successful?

What does Rachel Whiteread do that is not what Allen Fisher does?

They're both interesting, they're both about at the same level of difficulty, and they both have entirely individual projects. One is enormously successful and the other has tremendous presence as a poet in the alternative poetry world but yet isn't able to break through. That's an interesting fault line that probably has nothing to do with either of those people. The *London Review of Books* would fall apart if they had an Allen Fisher piece. I guess that's what they must feel!

We'd love to, Allen, but unfortunately we'd fall to pieces!

But it presents no problem for the comparable art magazines to have a piece of an artist of his generation who is comparably difficult and conceptual.

But Rachel Whiteread—famously one of her early pieces was a cast of a house in London and that caused a great furor, and there was a lot of viciousness about that, and that piece was actually destroyed.

I've seen that piece. She may be controversial, but the controversy is reported on, she's in museums, and she has a presence that someone like Allen doesn't have. Also, Allen's work has to be understood more the way you would understand a visual artist's work: the way he uses materials, the way he uses shapes, the different kind of book projects, and so on.

They are actually diptychs, aren't they, a lot of them—they are a painting and a piece.

Right, but you can't understand Allen within a traditional literary context. You have to have some sense of him working within the larger art field. I just give these examples because we're talking about England.

Well that's where I come from, and I have to be careful because that's where I sit, and I come, to an extent, with a chip on my shoulder, as we say, that there's that kind of annoyance, because I only came across Cobbing in my thirties and it was by accident almost, and I felt extremely annoyed, at myself partly, because I hadn't figured that this was going on, but also because I felt, well, how come this wasn't passed on to me? Because this seemed to me extraordinary work.

Official Verse Culture in the US and in the UK never gave Cobbing or Jackson Mac Low their due. *Conservative* isn't even really the right word . . .

In any case, Cobbing and Mac Low were not conventional. In contrast, much of the prized poetry of our time is quite dull, though I know that is not the experience of those who give the prizes, nor of many readers.

Maybe it actually parallels what you're saying about the art world, you know. I do wrestle with this, and the people are nice. I don't like being annoyed or having confrontations or being horrible about somebody, but at the same time, I have a boredom threshold and I feel that it's being taxed severely.

Boredom threshold. I like that way of putting it.

Well, I'm trying to be gentle.

I've come to terms with my annoyance. While I'm annoyed by my annoyance, I realize I have to live with it.

Interview with Maurizio Medo (Peru)

Transtierros, 2014 (Spanish)

I wanted to interview you for so long, Charles, that now, in front of you, I feel I'm listening to 4'33" *by Cage. Do you like Cage?*

I don't like John Cage: *I love John Cage.* That's the way my kids might have put it, back in the day. The thing about *4'33"* is that it lasts forever, and yet the time frame, the specificity, is the key thing. Cage invented so many ingenious ways of patterning sound; he greatly expanded the realm of what can be heard as music (rather than noise). In poetry, it's Jackson Mac Low who was the great pioneer on a parallel track. My take on Cage's and Mac Low's work is that it isn't noise that is being made but music and poetry: I see it as generative, not degenerative. But I wonder where that leaves us if we think, as I do, that anything can become music if framed as art. Noise is the outer limit of human sense, a dead zone, a zone of pure animalady (the human malady of being and resisting being animal). We're one foot in the world of things, of fauna and flora; but that other foot, the foot of our human consciousness, filters that; even the experience of brute sound is transformed to "brute sound." *We are most familiar with the estranged.* So perhaps estrangement gets us up close, puts us next to, what is beyond the real, the symbolic, "silence" and "noise": the darkness in the dark, the hearing part of listening.

Can we relate your poetics with Cage's compositions as they juxtapose densities—resounding, psychic, and linguistic ones—reaching heterogeneous textures, which seem to constitute a leakage path *from the traditional poetic field?*

Sure, and I like the way you put it. I produce manually what Cage and Mac Low produced by algorithm (a set of procedures), which I call algorhythmia to add to Pound's *phanopoeia*, *melopoeia*, and *logopoeia*. The manual method allows for leakage, I think more than a procedural form, because you can build the cracks in and use the leakage like Jackson Pollock drips. Leakage is ornament in my practice. There is a line in "Reading the Tree" in *Rough Trades* that speaks to this:

> . . . I would have a house
> of my own, with a bay of pastel
> miasma, reality leaking
> from its edges, as the context
> conditions. . . .

Leaks are there so the radiance can spill out. I feel uneasy with the abusive consideration of certain kind of poetics as "experimental"—

I can hear tacet tacet tacet again when I ask you—isn't the poetic act axiologically experimental? With what do we experiment, with language or with thought—assumed as another form of referring to reality? [Cage uses "tacet," Latin for "silent," as the titles of the three movements of 4'33"*.]*

Experimental: I too dislike it. It has a scientific association, as if you are looking for *answers* rather fomenting *questions*, rather than, how 'bout?, *syncretizing perceptions*. Cage's and Mac Low's work can be seen as research and in that sense experiment: What happens if we take this vocabulary and run it through this procedure? But even such radical approaches can be sublimed into craft once you get a sense of what you are doing. Then the poet is more like an architect making a blueprint for a verbal construction that the reader/perceiver will move through. To do that, you need to project the site of reading and then go on instinct and experience. I like the Dewey words: *process*, *doing*, *inquiry*, which I associate with another word, *essay*. *Essay* as *try*—as here I don't know what I will say next, let my mind take leaps—but if I fall crashing to the ground, it's not an experiment to see if I will break any textual bones, it's because I like the sensation of clamor. *Essay* comes to us courtesy of *assay*, to take the measure of something, subject it to a trial. I like the idea of a poem showing the results, for example, of disturbance in a verbal system, or malformation. The poem *endures* this trial, and that endears us to it. I don't think a poem has experiences like a person, but readers invest it with these qualities, as if the symbolic were real. (Then again, ain't that what the real is, or have I been misled?) Maybe the problem is the connotations *experiment* has taken on in discussion of art. I don't present to you my experiments but their fruit or, anyway, fruitiness! *Experiment* and *experience* share the same root, *experīrī*, Latin for *to try* (but that gets us to *expert* too, the opposite end). *Based on experience* sounds very solid. But something *experimental* has not yet proved its worth, as you'd take an experimental drug only if the ones which which (sorry, *with which*) there was experience failed to cure the malady. We could say that conventional poetry has proved its worthlessness, but I doubt there is a cure for animalady. The point is that poetry is a making of something, going from *say* (speak) to a *say* (a cloth of silk or wool, a textile). *Say what*? It's only me testing the words. If this had been a real emergency, you would have been instructed to switch to the emergency broadcast frequency.

Have you ever thought that in many of your "impermeable" poems in which you break the hypnosis of certain effects you were also breaking the versus in which genders use to confront? Could these constructions be impermeable for their syncretic value, in which the words are reconstituted?

I made up a term a while back—*com(op)posing*: the idea that in composing in an aversive way (against settled understandings) one creates new syncreticisms. So I do see an analogy to breaking down, or I'd rather say expanding/spinning/echoing binary oppositions such as male/female (gender). Language runs on binaries—you can't eliminate them, at least in my theology. But you don't have to be ruled by them, can turn the situation around and rule them, take their measure, overturn not in the sense of defeating but spinning, like spinning wool. This is how *versus* becomes again the crux of verse: a turning over and over, the process of which is a homing ground. This contrasts with the idea of *native soil*, which is fixed, unplowed, stagnant. Homing ground is an activity, often born out of displacement, exile, discomfort: an *alien nation*.

I get quite annoyed when it's said that a poem is "the most representative" or a "failed one" in an author's work, almost establishing a ranking of the best and worst. When I read your work, I sense a concatenation of fragments that, articulated among them, make it impossible to find this or that "representative" or "failed" but a speech pulled out of the relativity of a language (with all its faults and norms). Do you think that what critics, at least the most reactionary ones, consider as failed, the failed element, can at the same time constitute the axis that makes the existence of a linguistic construction possible?

Yes. The idea is to fail . . . but in the most successful (resonant?, spectacular?, unexpected?) way possible, including confounding ways of interpreting the poem—not just by a dominating critical approach to which you or I may be hostile, not just by readers, but first off by myself. I try to trip myself up in endless numbers of ways. I like also to dwell on the experience of tripping, falling, failing, flailing. I think in any one of my books I am pretty good at including a mix that even a sympathetic reader will find something off, wrong, failed; but of course I like sore thumbs and bad puns, so it has to be more than that. Then there are those who would say the whole approach to poetry that many of us take is failed, wrongheaded, not fit for literary prizes for sure, which ironically just adds to a certain poetry street cred, no? Going back to *experiment:* there is a sense you are trying to find something that works. But I want poems that *don't work.* So, yes, impossible to find "representative" poems except to say characteristically unrepresented. But various constellations, such as the selected I put together as *All the Whiskey in Heaven*, can at least suggest a wide range of possibilities. And this brings back your question about binary oppositions, of which failure/success is key for aesthetics. Because you can only succeed in a new modality by failing in an older one (and vice versa). Over time, I became quite expert in my particular modalities of slipping on verbal bananas. I can do it so well that they cease to have the power of failure. And then failure becomes part of the rhetoric of transvaluation, as when nothing is so beautiful as the ugly. It is *failure* in the eyes of those who I think have failed values. But what about failure on my own terms? Plenty of things come to mind: compromise, accommodation, laziness, complacency, condescension, self-importance, dismissiveness, crankiness. I have become quite fond of these failures too; some have become crutches on which I rely. I'd come back to this: failure in the sense of an acknowledgment of loss, of prolonging sensation and desire for the duration of poem. Animalady is failure. Failure to connect to the object of desire can become the basis of syncretizing a homing ground.

Who is Charles Bernstein inside your poetic structuring, a subject that becomes—victim of the memory of its present—a sign, or only a mask of nobody?

Not nobody, because the somebody I am can easily be marked on the shipping container; those markers of identity are scars that no amount of erasure erases: anybody's work has meaning in relation to those scars. But I live so much inside my work that it has become its own entity, with its own memory and consciousness. I am part of the team of writers that contribute material to the work—well, mostly everyone is gone, so it's only me. But the poem is the boss. You should really be directing your questions to it.

In Latin America, you've probably talked about it with Enrique Winter, when we read American poetry, we are reduced to a determined group of authors, the mainstream ones. Another tendency is to read them by groups—the British modern, the L=A=N=G=U=A=G=E—without taking into account the particularities of each one. I guess, and hope I'm wrong, that this fault—generated by academic alienation—can happen among you too with what we produce. We get along with knowing the tip of the iceberg. In my country, Peru, that is the same as Chile, only a little bit better, I don't think there's a dozen persons who know Hannah Weiner at all. I find her significant and in tune with your work. Which are your Latin American readings? What poets do you like, and what similarities do you find between what's being made in one and another side?

I think the problem with us here is just a general lack of information on contemporary poetry south of the US border, which is made all the more difficult to connect to because of the national fragmentation of Spanish language poetry. To address this issue, Eduardo Espina and I started a magazine several years ago called *S/N: NewWorldPoetics*. We did four issues and hope to start up again: but our initial set is online at the EPC (writing.upenn.edu/epc/presses/SN/). I also am an editor of *Sibila*, a magazine from Sao Paolo, originally a print magazine but now just online (sibila.com.br/). For both magazines, I am primarily involved with the American poetry that appears, in translation of the original; but it gives a context. I have worked a lot with Régis Bonvincino, the editor of *Sibila*, and through him have gotten something of an education in Brazilian poetry. I feel a strong connection to Heriberto Yépez, from Mexico, who headed up a group translating a big selection of my essays for Aldus. Also, my old friend Ernesto Livon-Grosman introduced me to Jorge Santiago Perednik, from Buenos Aires, and I have written about an affinity to his work and a kind of secret *Xul/L=A=N=G=U=A=G=E* connection in terms of the poetics of the Americas; take a look at this film of the both of us since I think it may answer your question: (jacket2.org/commentary/perednik-bernstein). One of the greatest experiences I have had as a poet was visiting Reina María Rodríguez's "tower" in Havana: an amazingly engaging experience, with Reina especially, but also many of the other poets I met there: I felt a direct connection that is all too rare in life. When I was in Buenos Aires visiting Ernesto and Jorge, I met Reynoldo Jiménez, who gave me a copy of his anthology *El Libro De Unos Sonidos: 37 Poetas del Perú* (Buenos Aires: tsé, tsé, 2005), which I read with great fascination.

Interview with Alcir Pécora and Régis Bonvicino (Brazil)

Sibila, 2014 (Portuguese)

Do you read poetry?

You betcha.

What kind of poetry do you read?

I find various gaps in what I've read so get sidetracked, happily, much of the time. Especially poetry from outside the US and before the twentieth century. I try to keep up with the work of old friends but then also to at least briefly attend to current works, especially ones doing something I haven't quite seen before. But keeping up is increasingly hard for me. I buy a lot of new books, subscribe to series, read online (especially when I first am learning of a poet). I've got a couple of hundred recent (and increasing less recent) poetry books on my "to read" shelf.

Do you think that reading poetry would produce any effect?

I am hoping not. Sometimes I am disappointed.

What do you expect from writing poetry?

Less and less. I am moving toward that perfect zero degree.

In your opinion, which is the best effect one can get from practicing poetry?

I've realized (I've known it for a long time) that writing is an obsession for me. I am not trying for an effect just working out the poem at hand. Sometimes I feel my mind is dictating the poems to me, though "I" interfere a lot. Poems often feel like they take over my consciousness and write themselves—I don't mean that in a supernatural sense, it's more infranatural if anything (echopoetics), but just to describe the experience. So I am too absorbed to consider the effect until it's too late.

Do you think your poetry has any public value?

As opposed to private value?

Which is the best support for your poetry?

I've been lucky from near the outset to have good friends and comrades publish my books—Douglas Messerli's Sun & Moon and Green Integer,

James Sherry's ROOF . . . before moving to University of Chicago Press. Alan Thomas had published *My Way: Speeches and Poems*, and after that I suggested to him *With Strings* as a trade book, like my essay book, not as part of a poetry series. He took on *With Strings*. It's been perfect ever since. Earlier on, I liked best publishing in magazines that I felt a direct connection to, as an ongoing contributor whose work was connected to the other contributors, as with Douglas's *La Bas* or James's ROOF, Lee Hickman's *Temblor*, Clayton Eshleman's *Sulfur* and then our work together in *Sibila* as well as the magazine I edit with Eduardo Espina, *S/N*. On the web: John Tranter's *Jacket* and now *Jacket* 2, or the web archives Eclipse (Craig Dworkin), EPC (with Loss Pequeño Glazier), and PennSound (with Al Filreis and Mike Hennessey). I am also very involved with translations and translators and at any given time; those people are the ones I am mostly intimately in exchange: Leevi Lehto (Finland), Peter Waterhouse and Versatorium (Austria), Enrique Winter (Chile), Ernesto Livon-Grosman (U.S./Argentina), Norbert Lange and co. (Germany), Ian Probstein (U.S./Russia), my OEI friends (Sweden), Lianggong Luo, Nie Zhenzhao, & Li Zhimin (China), Zeyar Lynn (Burma), Martin Richet & Abigail Lang (France), Heriberto Yépez (Mexico), Dubravka Djurić (Serbia), and Régis Bonvicino (Brazil).

Which is the best result you expect from the publishing of your poetry?

Expectations are the father of anxiety. It's a long-term business. Fundamentally I hope the work comes out as intended, working hard to proof and make sure the poems look right visually. After that, distribution: knowing the book is available to those who may want to read it.

Who is the best reader of your poetry?

I am engaged with reviews and commentaries and responses—always curious to hear what individuals make of the work. But I don't hold any special store by "best." I can think of some people who could be said to be the "worst" readers of my poetry—and though I can't say I appreciate their commentaries, there are ways in which those hostile responses are proof of what I do.

What would you most like to happen after the publication of your poetry?

Go on to the next works.

Indigo: Interview with Paata Shamugia (Georgia)

Indigo (2016) (Georgian)

Adapted for Warren Motte and Jeffrey DiLeo, *Experimental Literature: A Collection of Statements*, JEF Books (2018)

Poetry is $50 billion behind art. In art world terms, the problem is not that poetry is too elitist but that it is *not elitist enough*. In mass culture terms, the problem is that poetry (of all kinds) doesn't command enough market share, and market share is the sole criterion of what counts as important.

Me, I'm part hoi and part polloi.
I know the problems with that.

Too abstract, don't you think, too much in the head?

I don't know much about affect, but I know what I don't like.

Could you expand on that?

The slow apple catches the worm. In other words, the early bird catches dawn but sleeps through dusk.

But what about poetry as the timeless art?

The only thing that might be timeless in a poem is a blank page. And even a blank page is not timeless.

(The only thing timeless about poetry is the baloney.)

In *Pitch of Poetry* (2016), I introduce the term *echopoetics*. All echo, no origin. But I'd rather say, mired in reversals as I am, all originals and no seconds. We hear or see only the pristine, but the pristine is a composite. On that model, why not say the classics have robbed us of our originality? This moment never occurred before, and I don't mean the moment I wrote that, which is long over. I mean the moment you are reading this. It's not who said it first but who said it last.

"The originals are not original," Emerson writes in "Quotation and Originality." Kant thought you could never see/read the original, in the sense of the *twang*-in-itself. (*It don't mean a thang if it don't got that tang.*)

There are only versions. That is, we are moving both away from and toward the original, we are on our way, as in Emerson's moral perfectionism, but we never arrive, not in this historical life. As Dickinson suggests, echoing Darwin, the world in not conclusion; a series stands beyond.

You are one of the founders of L=A=N=G=U=A=G=E. Should we witness further experiments within this important literary movement?

In *Pitch of Poetry*, I kick the life out of all questions about L=A=N=G=U=A=G=E. I have promised myself that I would not say the same thing when asked questions like this, but I have now run out of different things to say. (The same could be said about questions about the nature of experimental poetry.) Of course, I understand *you* (whoever is reading this) have not necessarily read any of these earlier statements. But I take the question as, Is there anything further to say, to do? Again, I'd go for the reverse (it's getting to be a habit): What else is left but to "further experiment"? It's the only hope left, even if no hope at all. Of course, saying nothing is always an option; but it is very difficult. I am doing the best I can.

When the so-called Nouveau Roman *appeared, people were talking about how this movement terrorized the reader. Can we say the same about L=A=N=G=U=A=G=E? Was literary radicalism your purpose?*

I would like to say there was no purpose—you know, that Kantian idea of arts as without purpose (and there goes that Kant again, sucking the life out of my ideas). And I don't associate literary radicalism with terror. I think our approach was more inspired by the Russian futurists a century ago: opening things up, shifting frames, breaking the insularity of the poet-in-a-self-reflecting-bubble. That didn't mean we made poetry popular, which in America means mass culture. But I'd say there is a lot about mass culture that terrorizes an audience into submission or acquiescence; that is one of the things I like about mass culture.

Who made a significant influence on the formation of your style?

Interesting you say *who* and not *what*.

In your essay "Comedy and the Poetics of Political Form" (from The Politics of Poetic Form *[1990]), you wrote about some conventions and your relations toward them. Would you like to tell us more about some of the conventions? And one more thing: as common scholarly sense goes, the conventional (rhymed) verse was invented as a mnemonic device, in order to easily remember the long stories. Now, in this high-tech era, is that still relevant? That is, can we say that conventional rhymed verse is now completely useless?*

Well, if it's useless, then that must be why I am warming toward it. But, yes, poetry is responsive to material, historical, and technological conditions. As

I say in “The Art of Immemorability” in *Attack of the Difficult Poems* (2011), sound recording, photography, and film freed poetry from the burden of memory storage as much as it freed painting from the burden of representation. The printing press is the earlier key development. I say “freed” and “burden” to bring this statement into line with other media theories, but we are never free and these things were not necessarily burdens. But let's say it makes the choices more centrally aesthetic. Art for art's sake is a mark of technological change. For example, the use of rhyme, *my* use of rhyme, means something different now than it did in earlier periods.

The literature that changes reader's ideas about cultural codes and signs may require more mental tension and emotional involvement. Maybe that's why some important works of poetry are stuck in the circle of literary scholars. How can you break this circle?

Would you accept—*literary scholars and other poets*? There are more poets than literary scholars. Maybe the change is for readers to imagine themselves as poets when they are reading “difficult” poems—we can “deputize” them, as they used to say in the old Westerns (the sheriff would recruit the townspeople to catch the bad guys, deputizing them as assistant sheriffs in the time of need). In any case, I think more people read “difficult” poetry now than in previous periods; maybe they don't read the same poem or poet, but overall. The internet makes distribution easier. The key is that more people are getting access to cultural literacy—not just learning to read and write (in the mechanical sense), not just learning to consume, but to produce and critique. What's fundamental is liberal arts education and free speech.

And how about the function of critics?

Liberal arts education is endangered, often before it takes hold. And not because of its failure but on account of its success. In the US, Donald Trump is least popular among voters who went to college. You could say that it's my class bias against him, but perhaps a college education initiates citizens into a world of critical thought. There is so much skepticism about the value of the humanities. Maybe this is our smoking-gun proof. We can't afford to lose sight of Trump's dismissal of global warming as a “fraud”: the urgent question is how can democracy work when so many people prefer scapegoating (of Mexicans, Blacks, Jews, Muslims) to reason? As for poetry, it is a perfect subject for criticism, and needs informed critical dialogue, even if so many American academics have lost their taste for aestheticized writing. At the same time, the continuing focus on *speech* that offends chills robust disagreement and diverts attention from *policies* that oppress.

Cultural commentators have been constantly announcing the death of poetry. Is this time near or is it just a regular apocalyptic conspiracy?

Poetry died a long time ago; Plato killed it. All the rest is ghost play.

In your poem "Being a Statement on Poetics for the New Poetics Colloquium of the Kootenay School of Writing, Vancouver, British Columbia, August 1985," you say, "I want a poem as real as an Orange Julius." So, you want literature to make the "real things," real love, real "blood," as Antonin Artaud dreamed about as a theater of cruelty. Is that a realistic agenda in our consumer society?

More echoes. That's a satiric reference to a poem by Jack Spicer where he says, I want a poem as real as lemon. Spicer is closer to Artaud. My line refers to a "juice drink" at a chain called "Orange Julius"; it's meant to note the improbability of ever getting outside commodification.

You often write about poetry and politics. Can poetry be somehow apolitical or language itself not be part of ideology and the political structure?

No, it can't! Get used to it!

How much of your writing is based on personal experience? Do you write about yourself even if you write about something else? I mean, is poetry always self-descriptive?

My first impulse is to answer that question ideologically, though if I did, I am not sure what I would say, so much would depend on countering prevailing winds so the boat of poetry can sail in spite of hostile conditions. All language is inflected by individuals, and yet language is fundamentally social. So, hey!, it's a dialectical relationship. I am writing a book of poems now to be called *Against Emotion* [later titled *Near/Miss*]. The title partly mocks those who feel that poetry that is not entirely centered on the conventional expression of the poet's feelings is somehow devoid of emotions. My sense is that so much poetry that follows that prescription is an empty ideological exercise waving a flag of subjectivity and affect but unable to inhabit either. But key in my title is *against*, which does not only mean *opposed to* but "up against," rubbing, close to.

Is there any possible formula to follow in order to be a good poet?

Don't follow formulas, which is itself a formula; but then I am of the school of apophaticism.

Don't take the bait.

Get as much sleep as possible.

In our introduction to the *Best American Experimental Poetry 2016*, Tracie Morris and I resist the series moniker, used also for this collection: "All the standard terms for inventiveness in the arts are vexing, even when well-intentioned. *Experiment* can suggest that the focus is on work-product or test results despite the fact that writing that is open to new possibilities is more likely to be aesthetically accomplished than work that closes off such possibilities."

Tracie and I well understand that, as a practical matter, *experimental* suggests poetry that resists formula and convention, poetry that is more concerned with the aesthetic dimensions of the poem, with artifice, than sharing an anecdote or insight, or giving political or moral lessons. "Some, poor in spirit, record plaintively only what has happened to them; but others how they have happened to the universe," Thoreau writes in *A Week on the Concord and Merrimack River*.

Invention suggests more *know-how* and *pragmatism* than *experimental*. Which is not to say that such poetry doesn't have a message but that the *mediation is the message*, to tilt McLuhan a few degrees windward. *Invention* is not the same as *experiment*, but both suggest a commitment to the untried or unsettled and the necessity of doing something in the face of immediate conditions. But I know I am going against common usage. My resistance to the term *experimental* has become a *bête noire* that long ago turned into an *idée fixe*.

One chilly day in November 1836, in the West Riding of Yorkshire, Emily Brontë wrote "Wild words of an ancient song, / Undefined, without a name."

Color it *indigo*.

Project Transcreation Interview with Runa Bandyopadhyay

Kitaab (W. Bengal, 2019)

Tell us something in a few sentences about the start of your journey in poetry.

The journey never started and so doesn't end. It feels like it is an active presence. A river of words flowing through me, which I tap into, or perhaps which taps into me (which traps me).

Is there a relation between the poetic language and the body language of the word? Is a poetic idea revealed in the physical body of the poem? What do your feelings say about this relationship?

Yes. Yes. I am interested in the body of the poem. This is not a "material" body but as Blake says, "a Spiritual Body." That is to say, the poem is symbolic space, an imaginary space, where the value lies in not "representing" the world but exploring the "real" in and as language.

Poetry is form, or process, or (de-)construction or idol-making—which one of these is closer to your way of writing and why?

I am interested in intensifying metonymy and iconicity. Not fragments but constellations of particulars. Not deconstruction but reconstructions as a process without endpoint. In the Jewish tradition there is a prohibition of "graven images," which is to say images of idols. In my secular mutation of this idea, I would say—in place of images are actions and processes that allow the readers/listeners a space to project their phantasies/desires/anxieties. But I do this not by minimalism or abstraction but by rhythm and association.

Poetry requires space, where the reader participates in the poem while at the same time remains outside it. What is your opinion on this dichotomy?

It's possible to try to break down the divide between viewer/viewed—that is, break down the voyeurism by eliding word and object. Gertrude Stein's *Tender Buttons* is a key work in this respect, part of a "dialogic" space opened up also (in American poetry) by Mina Loy, William Carlos Williams, and H.D., and also such second-wave modernists as Louis Zukofsky and Charles Reznikoff. I explore this issue in *Artifice of Absorption* (writing.upenn.edu/epc/authors/bernstein/books/artifice/), in particular, the possibility for rhythmic oscillation between inside/outside.

Is poetry a search for "reality" and existence, or a search for mystery? Or none of those? Then what is it?

Poetry isn't one thing, even for an individual poet. "Reality" is perhaps always at issue, but whose reality, what aspect of the real? I don't accept the "realities" imposed upon me by family, state, literary history, convention;

but then I can't fully reject them, either. In poems, I explore these "controlling interests," to use the title of an early book.

Is poetry more than resonance of ideas in the mind? If so, if more, what is it? Is poetry to be understood?

Understanding is to *stand under*, whereas I want to be inside. Clarity, coherence, and expression are often shibboleths that stand in the way of the poetic transformation of those values: *clarity* as a means of imposing a rationalized order and standing in the way of a (let's call it) *pluriversity. Coherence* is a form of repressing what David Antin calls a "radical coherence" by imposing plot lines in place of transformative narrative. *Expression* doesn't have to mean rejecting anything other than conventional literary styles as significant. Blake speaks of "Mental Fight," and this fight is aesthetic, to not accept that conventional poetry styles have a monopoly on meaning or emotion. I was going to title my forthcoming collection (which I called *Near/Miss*) *Against Feeling*, in the sense of *up against*, touching.

Untraditional poetry or the poetry beyond the heritage—what, in your view, will be the mark of new poetic language?

The history of poetry is pockmarked by innovation and invention, by the struggle for the new *not as novelty but as necessity.* Over the past two centuries, this *pataquerical* imperative has become Western poetry's activist center (my word for the combination of inquiry and querulousness and Alfred Jarry's pataphysics, the poetics of exception). We never know what the new is until we encounter it in a "now" where it seems as strange, yet intensely familiar, as the dawn.

Is poetry a fully conscious construction? Construction and deconstruction—in your opinion, which one for the poet is the more "conscious" important process?

Rhythmic oscillation: known/unknown, here/gone, speech/noise, familiar/foreign.

What is the relevance of daily incidents, the "indecisiveness" of contingencies in poetry? Does a poem follow its "flow," or does it look for something static?

To give material form to indecisiveness, ambivolence (wanting many conflicting things); to cycle through different moods and tones; to have a language of everyday life that is, as if, never before heard; to weep with laughter . . .

In your view, does the poem or poet have a social responsibility? Is the poet responsible to society or him or her own self? What is the function of poetry in society?

All that I am is also my society. I am neither here nor there. Poetry has no purpose—and that is not its purpose.

What is the relationship among texts—through appropriations or translations or (re)(de)constructions, etc.—in poetry? When a poem triggers a reader and the latter assimilates the original poem into her/his own vision, can s/he rewrite it through expansion or commentary or meta-poems, etc., yet always retain the original inside itself? What is your attitude toward "ownership" of a poem? What is an original poem?

The poem is a like an architectural space that the reader, or listener, traverses. The end of the poem is not a meaning or content conveyed but is rather a *temporary* (provisional) space. The end of the poem is what the reader perceives—and the greatest poems are those that allow for the greatest imaginative projections.

Interview by Habib Tengour in *Pour ainsi dire* (Bernstein poems trans. Tengour) (Algeria: La Collection Poems du Monde, Apic Éditions, 2019) (French)

Seven Questions to Charles Bernstein

An autobiography in a few words.

Every day I am further and farther from what origins I may imagine, until the point-blank when I occupy them.

How to respond to a sudden injunction: "Define poetry."

No. I mean poetry as a "no," as resisting the affirmative in pursuit of the actuality of the incomprehensible (a.k.a. the visceral).

Prose and poetry, does the distinction make sense?

Prose eviscerates sense. Poetry stays stuck in the thick of it, gets lost.

Form (and formal) in times of crisis.

Form is always a crisis—in the kind of poetry I aspire to; a response to crisis and sanctuary from (and for) it.

What future for poetry?

Poetry's future is in becoming attuned to its presents. The dawning of the present is what allows for its futures. This is the most unsettling aspect of the kind of poetry I want, which challenges the most deep-seated assumptions of both form and meaning. Poetry is hated by its officials, including those who exploit their contempt for poetry's incommensurabilities by extolling the banalities of audience appeal or moral virtue. Transience and treble-consciousness are the flesh and fetish of the poem: not a game of symbols but a forging-symbolic.

The part of prosody in the elaboration of the poem.

Rhythm is not sound or gesture nor image or pulse or pitch; neither meter nor rime. Rhythm is marking time by marring it: the becoming material of the imaginary.

The place of translation in poetic writing.

All poetic writing is translation from blank. For this reason, all poetry aspires to the condition of translation.

Interview with Mariano Peyrou (Spain)

El Mundo, 2020 (Spanish)

Some years ago, you wrote, "'That harsher necessity' of going on always in / A new place, under different circumstances: / & yet we *don't seem to have changed." Has your vision of poetry changed since you started writing? In case it has, how?*

I wrote that forty years ago, in one of my first books, *Senses of Responsibility*. A young person projecting into a future. Yet I feel the same way now. Things change, and I have been changed by them. Yet, as a poet I have resisted progressing. I am treading water as furiously as I can, just so I don't drown. But then I *do* drown . . . and come back to life—this is how I imagine what a poem is!—the same . . . only different. I love the expression *beside myself*, which can be with ecstasy or paranoia, but being *next to* oneself, one's own companion on life's journeys. So, maybe my vision of poetry hasn't changed, but I am always grappling with new circumstances and creating poems that meet the new moments. Or another way of saying this: my poetry has always been about change and embodying change: it is *characteristically uncharacteristic*. That is, I have is no single style but multiple, even contradictory styles, even within one book. One becomes many. But even that becomes its own kind of typical.

What does society need from poetry nowadays? What can poetry provide?

Nothing. That may be poetry's greatest asset: that it offers nothing and takes nothing for an answer. That is to say—I realize it's imaginary!—that poetry offers a noninstrumental place where language is not in the service of story, character, message, or a pre-existing meaning, but where language is at the center: its sounds, metaphors, rhythms, puns. The performance of language for the manifold pleasures it affords. And that means I find the meaning in a poem in the process of writing it, just as the reader finds meaning in the process of reading it: a meaning that does not exist independent of the aesthetic experience. As William Carlos Williams once wrote, "No one / will believe this / of vast import to the nation."

Poetry has a subversive potency that was detected long ago—we can think of Plato—and tried to tame. How is that taming process going?

Plato was successful. Poetry is banished from our republics and mostly by poets themselves, who feel the need to express and moralize rather than listen and reflect, deform—go both skinny-dipping and deep diving. I don't want a new world order but constantly changing word orders. "Let's get lost"—I can hear Chet Baker singing Frank Loesser's lyrics. Lost in rhythm, lost in dance. Ezra Pound, in his famous lament for a lost fascist poetics, wrote "I cannot make it cohere." I say, "I cannot make it decohere."

You have a very critical worldview, but also a lot of humor. Is the latter a consequence of the former? Can you talk about the relation between these two things?

I have long planned to call my next poetry collection *The JØker*, but now there's a blockbuster movie with a similar title, so I considered, briefly, changing it to *Due Diligence* [later titled *Topsy-Turvy*]. The concepts seem opposite, but for me they go hand in hand. My poems are riddled with comedy, and that is their due diligence. That's just what Mr. Plato distrusted about poetry: the poet as trickster. Poetry as shadow plays, where the shadows are the souls of the dead come back to haunt us. Shadows as the only real we've got. Plato quotes Socrates as saying "the unexamined life is not worth living." I say, the unironized life is not worth living: not worth the paper it's printed on! Socrates would agree. Plato not. *The JØker* is meant to echo an earlier book title of mine, *The Sophist*. The problem with *the* truth and *the* facts is that the *thes* play into the hands of those who want to claim the *thes*—reality—for themselves with their "the truth" and their "the facts." I am not saying that insidious appropriation of reality negates facts or truth. The attack on science and the press, Trump's Big Lie repeated over and again (#BLT #BigLieTrump), is pernicious and wildly successful at destroying democracy in the pursuit of the consolidation of wealth in the hands of the few. But the kind of poetry I want is not about proclaiming a single truth (any more than science is). My poems revel in metaphor, exaggeration, and paradox: I am a liar, says the poet/liar. I play my lyre.

You use irony in a way that some people may not realize that you are being ironic. What are the pros and cons of that way of being/writing? Or are there no cons, and to be misinterpreted is part of the fun? Or is there no such thing as misinterpretation?

Or is it all cons, in the sense of confidence tricks, scams? We're back to Plato. I want a poetry that is a con but where the reader goes along for the ride, not fooled but fooling around. I am aware of the problem of a zero degree of irony: "My humor is so dark you can't see it," as Lenny Paschen sings in a libretto I wrote. I am the master of the deadpan, which also means the master of nothing, or the master of the pratfall, or the master of unmastering. I am a Groucho Marxist. And because of that, I am plagued by misinterpretation—those who say poets like me are out to undermine meaning, proving the old children's rhyme, "I'm rubber, you're glue, what you say bounces off me, sticks to you." Tolerance for deviant poetry behavior can be very limited. But it takes place in the realm of the symbolic and provides a space to consider issues significant for democracy, to echo Williams again, but without threat of guns or prisons. Poems are made to be misinterpreted; it doesn't hurt them! Poetry can be a space for multiple interpretations and sometimes a "wrong" interpretation can provide valuable insights, if you can enter into a dialogue and recognize the where or why of the misrecognition ("Oh, I see they really loved each other despite the hate."). But there can never been any single, correct interpretation of a poem.

Your poems are very playful. Is it necessary to defend this approach theoretically?

Demagogues like Trump claim that their lies are the truth. The national media helped Trump by early on refusing to call those lies lies (and they still constantly echo, and therefore give renewed life to, those lies, though with a bit more circumspection in the last months, as they reluctantly wise up to this game, well after the damage has been done). At the same time, the mainstream press, including mainstream literary press, will not countenance a poetry that calls sincerity into question. In this way, they are complicit in Trump's triumph, or let's say they have folded (or been fooled) in the face of it, because of their own shibboleths about authenticity and storytelling. I don't defend what I do *theoretically* but aesthetically and comically—in and as performance.

What do you think of the possibility that machines write poems?

When I read most (not all!) the poems promoted by conformist poetry culture, I am struck by the formulaic language. The way many poets chose to articulate their subjectivity, their pain, their joy, their specific life experience, has been near robotized by craft, "best practices," and a hunger for legibility and accessibility. "The human touch" in a poem too often feels machinic. But, like I said years ago, computers will never replace poets because computers won't take that much abuse.

In 2004, Arnold Schwarzenegger, governor of California, said that those who opposed the Republican agenda were "girly men." You wrote then "The Ballad of the Girly Man," where we can read "We girly men are not afraid / of uncertainty or reason or interdependence." Is there any chance to get to rule the world with those values traditionally considered feminine?

Yes. Despite all, we are moving there. We're not there yet, but we are on the way. And even so, every gesture of resistance to masculinist and racist culture is realization of another world, a world we dwell in for that moment, even if we must return to the "real" world or toggle between the two. We are, as Thoreau wrote in *Walden*, "beside ourselves in a sane sense."

Interview with Natalia Fedorova

Translit (Moscow), 2013 (Russian), in-person interview, New York

Who of the Russian writers do you connect yourself with?

My closest friend in Russia was Arkadii Dragomoshchenko, but I also knew, and admired, Alexei Parshchikov and Dmitri Prigov. Sadly, these three generational companions have all died recently. I met Dmitry Golynko at the University of Pennsylvania, where I work, and then I saw him again in Vienna recently. He is terrific. And I very much admire Lev Rubinstein.[1] I also teach a number of stellar Russian poets, from Kruchenykh and Khlebnikov to Mayakovsky to Mandelstam and Akhmatova. Because of the recent translations of Matvei Yankelevich and Eugene Ostashevsky, I have also been reading the OBERIU—I love Kharms; Vvedensky has just been published.

They were absent from school programs and the general public's view for tens of years in Russia, as well.

1. Charles Bernstein, "Albena Lutzkanova-Vassileva's 'The Testimonies of Russian and American Postmodern Poetry' +: New Lev Rubinstein Volume from UDP," *jacket2*, accessed June 6, 2020, http://jacket2.org/commentary/ussr-usa.

boundary 2 48:4 (2021) DOI 10.1215/01903659-9382060

My students at Penn love Kharms. You don't even have to discuss it because they seem to just get it. I was reading Prigov this morning, and now I see that there is a direct relationship between the aspects of Prigov and Kharms, which I hadn't recognized. One of Prigov's "Seven New Stories about Stalin," has Trotsky, Zinov'ev, and Bukharin coming to talk to Stalin, and Stalin takes a revolver and shoots them down.[2] It has this absurdist or OBERIU quality, which, of course, I couldn't have determined before reading OBERIU.

Prigov was also planning in his last performance to be reading from the closet, which is a known Kharms trope.

I didn't know that connection; now it's apparent, so I am readjusting my literary history.

What is your attitude to your works being translated into Russian?

I am especially happy that Parshchikov translated my poem/essay "Artifice of Absorption." Other translations are coming in the *New Literary Observer*, many done by my friend, the great Ian Probstein, who also published translations in *Okno*, *Zhurnal POetov*, and *Innostrannya Literatura*. I was knocked out about Parshchikov (and friends) doing "Artifice of Absorption."[3] Also Arkadii asked me to write an introduction of Charles Olson's "The Kingfishers"—so that was written just for him, along with a piece on September 11 that I included in *Girly Man*. I don't have a very good sense of what is happening in your generation right now. My first contacts with Russian literature were in the '70s when I was reading the Futurists, and seeing the work, the paintings and the visual-verbal. The handmade zaum books, like *Pomade*, with the handwriting and drawings, were transformative both as works and in terms of groups of people working together.

In what way was it transformative?

Within the modernist moment you have too many dystopian examples of individuals or collectives; the Futurists were a positive, if tragic, model. You remember Marinetti famously came to Moscow to read his manifesto in 1909.

2. Dmitry Prigov, "Seven New Stories of Stalin," No. 3, in *Soviet Text*, trans. Simon Schuchat and Ainsley Morse (Brooklyn: Ugly Duckling Presse, 2020), 105.
3. *Artifice of Absorption*, Russian translation by Patrick Henry, Alexei Parshchikov, and Mark Shatunovsky (Moscow: Stella Art Foundation/Poetry Club, 2008). Also published in *Contemporary Poetry* [*Sovremennaia Poeziia*], issue 2 (June 1, 2007) and issue 3 (September 1, 2007).

And nobody was happy to see him there.

No, but still Italian Futurism was a much bigger thing. What I loved in the Russians was the connection between a social movement and art, and that critique of the museums, and the desire to employ the art in everyday life, the engagement with collaborations, and, of course, the wonderful graphic art.

The Soviet state created that curated space.

So, it was part of the social revolutionary moment that ultimately turned against these people and destroyed them. Goncharova and Popova are two of my favorite artists, along with Rodchenko and of course Malevich and Kandinsky. Even the advertisements are fascinating—the ones Mayakovsky wrote. Some are hysterical: a model for "real" ads that also are ironically self-reflective. The vibrant relation of commercial graphics to the fine arts (as traditionally understood) is fantastic. And then "The Word as Such," that is, the poetics, which at first I didn't understand, but after a while I did, as more began to get translated. For a lot of our circle around *L=A=N=G=U=A=G=E*, the Futurists were crucial precursors and inspirations. More so than any of the other modernist movements, per se, and up there with poets like Gertrude Stein, who was so very different, especially in terms of her politics and relation to the collective. Speaking about Mandelstam, before my collaboration with Kevin Platt—he did a collection of Mandelstam and asked me to translate several poems with him—I never really understood his poetry. The problem—the block—for me was primarily the way Mandelstam, Akhmatova and, above all, Brodsky were presented as Cold War figures by the Official Verse Culture of the US and UK. The Cold War tainted their work even as it was put forward by a literary establishment that reviled radical American poetry (and ignored the Futurists, of course). I am still in the middle of my argument with Cold War ideology because I remain very much a product of the 1950s—and I also see my reaction-formation as being a large part of the problem, that I was misframing these Russian poets (in my own mind) as much as anyone else. Milosz was and is used in the organs of Official Verse Culture as the exemplary anti-Communist and anti-collectivist—an emblem of individual, solitary figures fighting the totalitarian state. Of course, for a culture that is not particularly interested in poetry, and hostile to poetry that challenges conventional modes of representation and expression, it is this humanist thematic—resistance to totalitarianism—not the aesthetic, that is of interest. And ironically this neoliberalism is anti-political since it purports to place the poet beyond ideology. You see this Cold War criticism still in full force in mainstream newspapers and magazines, decades after the official end of the Cold War. (I think especially of Charles Simic in the *New York Review of Books*.) So while I have not been able to get to the bottom of the issue, since I can't read the originals, I believe the Cold War framing of the heroic Russian modernists (e.g., anti-Communist or martyrs of the state) has sacrificed the aesthetic radicalism of the work to conform to Cold War ideology, ironically torqued it toward propaganda while proclaiming it to be without ideology beyond neoliberal ideas of human freedom. And also those histories repressed the full range of Russian writing and art, which became increasingly accessible to use in the late 1970s. I don't mean to diminish the suffering or persecution of these poets or many other Russians—but I do object to these poets being enlisted into a program that reduces them to figures of martyrdom (poetry is not Catholicism) or uses them as cudgels to attack politically and formally radical poetics in the US and UK. This also had the effect of, at least for me, not seeing my connections to Mandelstam while being immediately drawn to Khlebnikov. But you can see how Dragomoshchenko and Prigov had an immediate appeal to me when I first encountered the work, more so than Yevtushenko or Voznesensky. So, I have been recalculating since then, learning more of the history and trying to make up for my prejudices and ignorance.

For example, now I see Mandelstam in the context of the New York poet Louis Zukofsky, who is a little bit younger than Mandelstam, but not by much. Zukofsky, sympathetic to Marxism in the '30s, living on the Lower East Side, wanted to move outside of the context of his Jewish and Yiddish background, to be part of, let's just say, international modernism, while keeping attuned to where he comes from and the local particulars that give his work its resonance. So I think about Zukofsky in relation to Mandelstam's "Notre Dame": looking up at the cathedral and thinking how does that relate to me, can I make art that goes beyond who I am, my own given history or tradition? Make art that is non-national and non-ethnic, or *not only*.

Notre Dame (1912)

Where the Roman justice judged a foreign people,
Stands the basilica; first and joyous,
Just like Adam, with nerves stretching,
The vault, a cross of air, flexes its muscles.

But outside a secret plan emerges:
Here labored the strength of arching stone

So the freighted mass won't crush the walls,
And the cocky vault's battering ram is still.

Elemental labyrinth, inscrutable forest,
The gothic soul's rationalized abyss,
Egyptian awe and Christian timidity,
Reed by oak and plumb-line's king of all.

But, citadel of Notre Dame, the closer
I studied your preternatural ribs,
The more I thought: from crude weight
Someday I too will fashion the beautiful.
(trans. Charles Bernstein with Kevin Platt)[4]

Related to this is Frank O'Hara's engagement with Pasternak. For O'Hara, Pasternak was attractive as a liminal figure, who worked in a space between public dissidence and the private. Perhaps that wasn't really quite accurate to Pasternak, but that's the way O'Hara thought of him. So that is one moment where a Russian poet intersects with the New American poetry in the Cold War, quite different than Allen Ginsberg's engagements with Yevtushenko or Voznesensky. At a recent memorial event for Arkadii, the Russian scholars mentioned his relation to Lyn Hejinian and language poetry in terms of an unusual Cold War encounter that suggested Arkadii's alignment with the West. But I think those accounts misread or perhaps better to say are reductive. At the risk of eliding the very Cold War frame I am otherwise insisting on, what was most powerful to me about my relation to Arkadii was our personal relationship based on a shared aesthetic value. I see this in terms of nonnational affinity, not to say we could ever negate our Soviet or US shells but that we shared roughly similar views toward the US and the USSR, if I can put it that way, and that indeed our aesthetic and political affinities (and aversions) might have put us closer to each other than to most of our fellow poets in our own countries. As I say this, I realize how hopelessly utopian it sounds, but it suggests a different kind of kinship and one which perhaps you may be related to yourself. And I feel this echoes with friends like Matvei Yankelevich and Eugene Ostashevsky who have one foot (and one ear) in both worlds. It's one of the hopeful possibilities about non-national poetry just now.

4. Published in *Modernist Archaist: Selected Poems by Osip Mandelstam*, ed. Kevin Platt (Lincoln: University of Nebraska Press, 2008).

Saying all that, I don't want to negate Arkadii's relation to Russian poetry and Russian literature or mine to American poetry, but I'd say we were company for one another; and for Arkadii this was most true of his relation to Lyn and hers to him. At the same time, the everyday life situation for Arkadii was diametrically opposed to what it was for us. So, the social circumstances, possibility of publishing, the possibility (and nature) of being public, the severe financial hardship . . . Obviously, there was a great difference in material existence for Dragomoshchenko and for me in 1991, the year he and Zina came to Buffalo for a semester.

Jacob Edmond has a fine new book on just this subject called A Common Strangeness*: Contemporary Poetry, Cross-Cultural Encounter, Comparative Literature*—do you know that work?[5]

Yes. With chapters about Prigov and Dragomoshchenko.

I like Edmond's concept of "common strangeness." The place of exchange has to do with common strangeness, not common similarity, but also simultaneity within cultural conditions, and also historical conjunctions of traditions and engagements. Some of the new writing-exchange technologies (email, translation engines, social media) make possible different modalities for translation than we've had previously—for example, compared to relying on the exchanges of letters between the US and Russia in Soviet times. And while valuing language, economic, and cultural differences, we also exist together in some "nonspaces"—again the web and social media, the transnational economy. So, translation again would be the fundamental . . .

Tool?

Tool and also medium, because we have to reinvent what translation is and how it allows people to be in exchange with their contemporaries, translating . . . rather than selecting an individual poet translating another individual poet (often older or historical), why not a collective translation of a rich creative context that would include multiple poets, translating the poems but also the poetics. Such an exchange would be more engaging and have a much broader base on both sides. The poetry culture that exists in St. Petersburg or in New York has many people involved. Translation tends to lose the base for the superstructure. It is not that the superstructure of

5. Jacob Edmund, A *Common Strangeness: Contemporary Poetry, Cross-Cultural Encounter, Comparative Literature* (New York: Fordham University Press, 2012).

selected poets is not valuable, but what might be most useful, initially, is translating a wider context to allow an exchange to emerge. Otherwise, it is like skimming the cream off the top and losing all the milk.

If we look back to samizdat practice . . . Do you see any parallels between this self-publishing practice in the US and this self-publishing practice in Russia?

I did a radio show with Matvei discussing these parallels.[6] While I think there are similarities, I'd want to emphasize the differences first. In the US, the small press flourished unhindered, and to a large extent unread and unacknowledged (as now). So, there is the famous inversion of cultural capital, with free and easy circulation losing some cultural status (and audience) versus censorship creating acute value (and mass interest). You don't as a poet get to choose the means of reproduction in your culture, but I think the virtues of cultural and state indifference to our work—its unpopularity!—are worth noting: there is a great freedom in the lack of necessity, where the stakes are aesthetically high but on your own terms, and the risks are not state sanctions but artistic failure or isolation. Not that your life, inner life anyway, doesn't depend on what success you may have, on your own terms. There is an aspect to samizdat that is like that—not so much dissident (or clandestine) as unofficial. In any case, I'd say the unofficial is dissident but perhaps diffident too.

What is the relation of poetry to tragedy? Would you share Badiou's claim in The Century *on the necessity of terror to provoke thought? What would then be the relation between poetry and thought?*

I don't know the Badiou essay, but I'd say poetry exists in spite of terror or maybe to spite it. Poetry may be a site of our mourning and a register of tragedy, but more often than not both those things shut down thought. Here's what I mean by a reductive Cold War reading: Charles Simic, who often writes against what I take to be the most compelling US poetry, in one of his haughty dismissals, makes an invidious comparison: who would you read if you were in prison—Gertrude Stein or Emily Dickinson—in this way trying to put down work in the traditions of Stein, as if Stein and Dickinson were not in the same tradition, as if you could dismiss all nontraditional poetry by this swipe at Stein, as if the criteria of value for poetry was to

6. Matvei Yankelevich, *Close Listening*, *PennSound*, accessed June 6, 2020, https://writing.upenn.edu/pennsound/x/Yankelevich.php.

imagine you were in jail. Simic jails himself, all our imaginations, and indeed the *New York Review of Books*, where his is the prevailing sentiment on poetry. The kind of moral seriousness about poetry which is tantamount to moral bankruptcy. Poetry should be wild, frivolous, and mock death—well, though you should never say should, should you (or so I like to say)?

Let me give you another more mundane example and one that makes my point more troubling, I am sure. The PEN International writers conference this year has the theme "Bravery." I totally applaud supporting free speech and its activist approach to condemning governments that put writers in jail. But the "Bravery" frame reduces the literature presented to examples of political conscience and also to a very internationally readable and rudimentary criteria for literary value. The good, the bad, and the ugly all suffer from political violence and oppression—a large part of the young black male population in the US are locked up at one time or another for political reasons, under system-generated drug charges. The kind of poetry I want is not "brave," and many of my favorite poets would better be described as timid, to use the word Benjamin dwells on in his essay on Hölderlin.

What makes Mandelstam or Kharms great is not that they were subjected to barbaric treatment—if that human story of courage is what you read them for, then I don't think you read very far in their work. Which is not to say that we don't admire such courage in many, poets and piccolo players and podiatrists. That is not a special office of poetry but of citizens. Mandelstam and Kharms were great poets in spite of the persecution, not as a result of it; and there is no question both would have done more and as great work without it! It goes without saying but needs still to be said, perhaps not in Russia, I assume not!, but in the USA where the highest value attributed to poetry, for Official Verse Culture—or so it sometimes seems, I know I exaggerate!—is the heroic dissidence or the survival narrative (poems arrayed around a personal tragedy), which just adds insult to very real injury. As for poetry itself, whatever that is, who cares? Mandelstam writes in one of his late poems that the one thing you cannot take from me is my words (#372 of *Last Poems*: "If our antagonists take me . . . But [still I] will write what I am free to write, / And yoking ten oxen to my voice / Will move my hand in the darkness like a plough / And fall with the full heaviness of the harvest . . ."). And in a way the Cold War reading of Mandelstam in the US is one more go at taking his words from him, when we make him into a product, celebrating him as a symbol and not for his aesthetic innovation and style. But if you don't care about poetry as an art, then moral action is your only criteria for judgment—and you separate the good from the bad with merit badges. But great poetry is written by the good, bad, and ugly—and that is Mandelstam's true company, not the righteous, not the victims, and not the anti-Communists. Lord, save us from Representative Poets.

So, as to samizdat, I appreciate the pragmatism of it—that it got the work out as best as possible under the circumstances.

And now, with the web, and less physically constrained exchange (other kinds of constraints still seem to be in full force), we can see what develops. As I was saying about Arkadii—the potential for affinity increases if we share similar readings and similar engagements, across national lines, against national lines. The connection over Pussy Riot is a remarkable example. There is something that goes beyond Russian dissident export product and becomes a shared struggle. We become our own self-identified constellations.

In the national context, Pussy Riot brought forward the vocabulary questions, starting with anecdotal use of "holy shit" innumerous times by the court officials and continuing with the use of the word "feminist" as a swear word by the witnesses.

And when it happens, as with this stigma against homosexuality, which wouldn't have been the case in the '60s, even in the '70s: the more people say it—the more it changes.

One of the things that I thought about with the magazine *L=A=N=G=U=A=G=E* in the late 1970s . . . it is impossible to try to do . . . because things tend to get grouped and things seem more similar the further you are away . . . but it was difference not sameness that I wanted to be the basis of our formation—not at the level of ethnic or cultural or racial or gender difference, but rather a difference in form. I suppose you could call it a demented kind of aesthetic Trotskyism: the collectivity would be that of particulars that didn't fit in, that didn't follow the norm: anomalies. I don't know how this would translate into a Russian context, but within the US culture, I see the possibility of poetry (and of thought!) in places where you can explore radical forms of eccentricity: disaffiliations and reaffiliations . . . which is not possible in popular cultures, which has other lambs to roast.

Poetry then, and kind of now, too, is still seen as a form of prophecy in very traditional or in Neo-Marxist ways. You were saying that eccentricity reaches a narrower audience, right?

Not sure about prophecy, but, yes, poetry as a genre has an infinitely small audience compared to popular cultures of other kinds. And that's what makes it a place for exploration, articulation, and exchange of the non-normative. Ironically, it is the lack of commercial potential that creates the specific conditions for the work and great (if often unrealized) possibilities. And that does affect our international exchange. So, coming back to Parshchikov, you can see him writing intimate, microcosmic poetry that has enormous resonance but that sets its own rules, so that he can explore some unfinished business in radical modernism. And while that would not have wide or mass appeal in the US or Russia, it does have an appeal to me in terms of its non-national affinity that begins to open up a virtual constellation where such poetry may find a home ground.

This is all background to your multiple questions about the small press. I would say . . . it is hard for me to say—and impossible for me to give any kind of guidance or advice, because of the asymmetry of our circumstances. Similarity in appearance is a trap, because it is the dissimilarity that is most significant and opens the possibility for affinity.

In what ways do you see the web facilitating the emergence of this common ground?

Certainly, the web creates new possibilities for exchange, but technological change offers as many problems as opportunities. In poetry, the English dominance of the web, or beyond that the dominance of four or five languages, is a good example of the mixed blessing: it's a global tide with an undertow that will cause many languages to drown or require artificial resuscitation. For this reason, as a counter, translation becomes ever more crucial in our digital present. Translations can take place quicker and with more mobility than in the past. For example, I envision (or let's just say, I am waiting for) collectives of young poets translating each other as a form of daily exchange.

Such collective efforts may counter the Great Poet model that tends to read individual poets in isolation from the field in which they work, often to the detriment of even those poets who are picked out from the crowd (sometimes for good and sometimes for bad reasons). What I mean is that to understand why a poem or poet is great, it is necessary to have some sense of the overall field and the kinds of exchanges that take place through publications and performances. This field of poetry—you can call it the tradition if you think about it diachronically, but equally significant is the synchronic field—is the ground against which individual poems articulate themselves. So, this activity of poetry is—ontologically!—more significant than any individual great poem or great poet. And sometimes great poets and great poems—as a concept—can obliterate this synchronous field of the contemporary. Perhaps this is more apparent with music than poetry: the recognition of the primary significance of musical experience, people playing the piano themselves, people hearing music in everyday life in that John Cagean way. That's what's sublime about music: not the beautiful object of the work but what the work allows as an experience for the listener. The greatness of Chopin is not the composition "itself"—but the aesthetic experience it engenders. What makes great poets great is that their work intensifies aesthetic engagements in the verbal life beyond the poem, where poems are seen as part of a semiotic economy that draws upon and transforms the everyday verbal life (as you draw money from a bank and spend it). By everyday verbal life I mean something like what you might call in Russia folk knowledge, something we don't have quite the same sense of here . . . the vernacular, indigenous language experience of the culture, which is channeled, refracted, and intensified by the particular poem. (Something along the lines of what Bakhtin proposes for prose but which really is the heart of poetry.)

It is probably more obvious with our sense of collectivity, but less obvious at the same time with the authoritarian habits, too.

There is a magnificent pathos to that contradiction, which haunts Gogol and Dostoevsky, no? And the more recent poets I've mentioned too. It's necessary, for this reason, to understand the lyric not as an individual voice of the solitary person resisting the authoritarian state but as a collective voice, as dialogic. This is what I have been trying to get at—I am not sure I have been able to.

So how do you see translation transformed in the technological society and applied to Translit *practice?*

I'd like to try, just try, to imagine new forms of web-based translation as Socratic. In other words, the translation does not provide a series of answers—accurate summaries of meaning—but a series of responses: translation as conversation, not master/slave original/copy. The open-ended use of sound files, homophonic and machine translations, collaborations would all sit next to more traditional forms of "faithful" translations. These would not be unfaithful, just a different kind of faith, closer to Pascal's wager.

On PennSound we have very little material in Russian, but here's what I think is possible: recording of a poem in Russian with a simple English interface: title and author, date and place, perhaps a literal translation, quick, or a paraphrase or basic description or commentary suggesting style, subject, something about the poet—whatever is possible for first pass. So, an English speaker could listen to the sound file and, without knowing Russian, would have some orientation, as he or she listens to the recording. And vice versa—you could take poems on PennSound and also provide a Russian interface.

You can find all those paratexts that will help contextualize the work.

Yeah, they are all there in one language or the other, but the barrier, probably in both ways, certainly, for a non-Cyrillic alphabet reader is enormous—to look at the Russian archive. So, you can't figure out what it is, so you want to have an English interface—I am using that word instead of "translation." That's a rudimentary way we can have an exchange. There are obviously things that you can do beyond that, but this would be a start. The performance of poetry goes back as far as any knowledge we have that we call poetry. But the ability to exchange such performances across space in a way that is not prohibitively expensive (given the small economic scale of poetry) is recent, with the advent of the web and MP3s. The recordings or ability to record might have existed for a hundred years, but our ability to easily exchange this material is new.

I read Eugene Ostashevsky's translation of Golynko's poems in a print book from Ugly Duckling Presse in New York. Maybe at some point I also read some translations on the web. But that still doesn't include the sound material—and the sound of Golynko reading his poems is crucial for me, hearing him read in Russian, even though I don't "know" Russian. But I do know Russian in some intimate way when I hear that sound file! It is the same way in English. The crucial thing for me about what American poetry is—people with different voices and different sounds and different accents . . . The alphabet is very thin. You don't get those accents and sound textures; you don't get the different rhythmic pattern—you just cannot get that from the alphabet. So, the more we are able to have sound recordings available and accessible through the internet, the deeper will be our exchange. Because listening to a sound file is infinitely richer than looking at a page in Cyrillic, where you don't know how it sounds or anything about it! If the poem is in Cyrillic, given my ignorance, there is very little information I can glean from that. But if I hear that poem being read—it can communicate an enormous amount to me. And that's a huge potential that doesn't involve translation in the traditional sense. I am not saying that the translation of the poem is not useful, of course, but the sound file may spark that translation and is a prerequisite for it. We could do twin pages with recordings from New York and St. Petersburg made the same week, by poets of the same generation. Two poets put up together and have a simultaneous "fast" translation and commentary. The way you have the possibility of autogenerated closed captioning. We could probably get a text roll of autogenerated translation to run alongside the sound file. We'd be on a roll and it would rock!

Interview with Alí Calderón

Círculo de poesía, Mexico, January 2018 (Spanish)

Today, when in poetry the discourses of hybridity are apparently the dominant ones, why do you think it is worthwhile to pursue the fight against absorptive poetry, the poetry of what has already been publicized?

There is a more radical hybridity than the domesticated kind about which you ask. Imagine a poetry that comes from fusing of incompatible and inconsolable languages, making for Frankensteinian collages. Once upon a time, I gave this a name: *dysraphism*. *Dysraphism* is a fantasy of the poetry of the Americas. We come into a new world burdened, butchered, bewitched by the old. With every spark of light, and they are infinite, we are pulled into the dark-matter cauldron of our violent history, where echoes of languages no longer, or little, spoken bubble up. In contrast to *dysraphism*, there is a "highbred" poetry that appropriates (in the sense of *makes appropriate*) aesthetic innovation in service to the holy crusade for cultural assimilation and authentic expression. Such poetry aspires to rise above the chaos, spurning gloriously crazy-quilt mosaics for coded merit badges. What we end up with is a mule masquerading as the superego: a mule that puts on airs. On

 DOI 10.1215/01903659-9382074

the one hand, appropriations, collages, disjunctions, opacities, vernaculars, multilingualisms, invented forms, polyversities—all forms of xenophilia—acknowledge pressing cultural conditions. On the other hand, purity is a fantasy whose object of desire is closely linked to xenophobia. Highbred poetry is like a principal barring you from school because you are not wearing the right uniform (and that could just as well be jeans as a blazer). I am thinking of the disdainful attitude that still greets messy and noisy poetry of invention. The dead speak, but you won't hear them if all you countenance is accessible English.

In a conversation with David Antin, you talked about how, in poetry, the alternative model is "to produce works that are disruptive of perceived ideas of quality, understood in terms of refinement. That alternative may require finding new readers." How should those readers be? What should they expect from a poem?

Expectation is the boogeyman (*El Cuco*) of poetics: best to meet expectations or else. But just as troubling is compulsory bohemianism: that you must display your defiance of expectations, often in a very formulaic way. It's hard to get out of this—it is not a double bind but a serial bind. What was disruptive a generation ago becomes prescriptive now (a.k.a. "hybrid"). But at the same time, what was conventional a generation ago is, well, so yesterday. *Poetry is situational, not universal.* I guess I've spent my life dismayed by how low the expectations are for poetry. Official Verse Culture is founded on lowering expectations. That's why when you find poetry that is a live wire, and there is plenty of it, you recognize it because it has the potential to blow expectations out of the ballpark. It's like a UFO sighting until you realize: it's a domestic product. I don't see the point of reading (or listening to) poetry that doesn't exceed reasonable, or even unreasonable, expectations. And yet I am well aware that the kind of poetry I want falls on deaf ears. Many thoughtful and smart readers, people I respect, adore what I disdain and mock what I love. I don't have an answer for that, except to publicize, which means to speak on behalf of, the kind of poetry I want, while trying, as best I can, to acknowledge how limited that must necessarily be, since my tastes and preferences are avowedly limited rather than catholic. My aim is not to create a stable new audience but rather transient, in the sense of ever newly forming, audiences. Each new book I write holds for me the expectation for a new constellation of readers. That's scary and almost always bitterly disappointing. But making it *now*, what Robin Blaser called *nowledge*, is the only bet worth making in my aesthetic calculus. This *now*, like *no*, is aversive to expectation (the familiar or *heimlich*), in pursuit of the uncanny (*unheimlich*).

The francophone critique of poetry gives today a central place to the enunciation. You have asked in the same conversation "Who is in control? The words or the meaning or 'you' the 'user'?" According to your perspective, who speaks in a poem?

It's not a *who* but a *what*. But that *what* is a constellation of voices but also language without voice. It's a shibboleth of much of today's poetry that it wants to give voice to the voiceless, which is admirable but risks projecting our voice onto the voiceless. Emerson wrote, "things are in the saddle and ride mankind." Lots of what counts as "voice" in our culture is the voice of commodities, of people speaking as if they were commodities. Which is no more than to say we are, most of us, most of the time, alienated from ourselves. I know I am not alone in finding robotic much of what I hear others say. I realize this may sound condescending, but many of the voices I hear frighten me. I don't see the solution, or anyway the only solution, as speaking naturally or sincerely; often that is just another kind of robotic voicing. What would happen if we suspended the illusion of "voices" and looked at language as a made thing? Then perhaps what would be in control is not the words or the speaker, but the reader or listener. Of course, the reader/listener is no freer than you or me. But this approach is a way to work with a poem as an imaginary space for reflection and projection, a moment outside of the everyday, utilitarian, use of words.

In Artifice of Absorption, *you talk about anti-absorptive poetry. Currently, what techniques and/or verbal devises, according to this poetics, are capable of producing those same powerful effects that the strongest drug could achieve?*

It could never be a matter of lists of devices or styles. There are no prescriptions. A poem that is antipathetic to everything I am saying here could do the trick. That is perhaps the hardest thing to grasp. There is no drug stronger than the imaginary. But the imaginary is make-believe.

Gertrude Stein pointed out that oddness gives poetry the character to endure. Where lies the rarity of a poem today?

Permit me to end with a poem I wrote on the day John Ashbery died.

If Sappho Were a UFO

And I were a genie
We'd dance on the surface of Pluto
And dine at Ipanema beach in Rio.
Nothing much else
Glues me to this shredded fabric
Of the marvelous, on sale all these years
With no buyers and just three
Authorized sellers. I'd made it almost to
Mars then went home, too much
Mud in those parts, and I missed
The smell of home ground
Even if it turned out to be imported.

September 3, 2017
for John Ashbery

Introduction to Chinese Anthology of American Poetry (19th–20th c.), ed. Li Zhimin

---

Charles Bernstein

American poetry is always in search of itself. Our newness is not for the sake of novelty but *out of necessity*, "new yet unapproachable," to adapt a phrase from Ralph Waldo Emerson, the nineteenth-century thinker who is a wellspring for American poetics. For American poets, the past is always vexed and the future uncertain; "only the narrow present is alive," as mid-twentieth-century poet Charles Reznikoff put it in a poem about walking in fog.

Each of the poets in this volume are founding figures for our verse because they find themselves in need of reinventing what American poetry is. It is not just that our active poetry tradition is short—just two centuries. For Americans, English is necessarily a second language, even for those for whom it is an only language.

While largely silenced by centuries of violence, indigenous languages lie under all our spoken tongues. But, as a result of this history of suppression, even the poetry of indigenous people is a secondary language,

boundary 2 48:4 (2021) DOI 10.1215/01903659-9382088

sometimes working as a kind of echolocation device for primary inhabitations. African people brought to the New World as slaves, starting in 1619, were also deprived of their native languages and prevented from learning to read or write. Nonetheless, they created the largest body of American poetry from before the twentieth century in the form of "slave songs" and work songs, a collective body of work that has morphed into blues, gospels, jazz, and contemporary popular music, giving it the longest half-life in American poetry. And yet both the poetry and culture of indigenous people and of African Americans remained, until the twentieth century, separate from the poetry of European Americans, even if all our poetry is built upon it and must needs ultimately acknowledge that "fact on the ground."

All the rest is immigration, from the first English settlers in the early seventeenth century to the waves of migrants arriving today. All refugees, seekers of refuge in a new world, whether because life in the old one was intolerable or because America's promise proved irresistible. American poetry is, above all else, a language of immigrants, and the most recent to land on our shores are the ones who most embody this spirit.

English for an American is not the same language as it is in Great Britain. By 1900, about one-quarter of the white US population either did not speak English or learned it as a second language, while in the mid-Atlantic states and New England, only one person in four was a native speaker of English. The heart of twentieth-century American poetry is the echo of other languages, heard in accents and syntax. Our New World English is syncretic: a blend of local dialectics and languages otherwise foreign to one another. Shakespeare is no more our model than the multilectal music of the New York City streets or the rush of the surf in California, the chants of prisoners on a chain gang, or the hum of tractors on a Midwest farm.

It is a poetry created by ear and on the fly.

Li Zhimin is a poet and scholar in both English and Chinese. Our long conversations about poetry have taken place in China and the United States, and, against all rational expectations, we have found ourselves talking as if we were from the same place.

That place could be called poetry. You will find it here.

Charles Bernstein
April 15, 2018
Brooklyn, NY

Introduction to Charles Bernstein's Distinguished Wenqin Yao Lectures at Zhejiang University, Hangzhou, Fall 2019

Marjorie Perloff

Ladies and Gentlemen, dear Colleagues and Students:

It is an honor for me to introduce today the great American poet Charles Bernstein, the author of fifteen books of poetry and many more of criticism, who has just retired from his position as the Donald T. Regan Professor of English and American Literature at the University of Pennsylvania. I want here to give not the usual biographical account—you can read that in your brochure—but to take a minute to tell you what I as a critic think is so special about Charles's poetry.

In the *Philosophical Investigations*, Wittgenstein writes,

> 498. When I say that the orders "Bring me sugar" and "bring me milk" make sense, but not the combination "Milk me sugar," that does not mean that the utterance of this combination of words has no effect. And if its effect is that the other person stares at me and gapes, I don't on that account call it the order to stare and gape, even if that is precisely the effect that I wanted to produce. . . .

boundary 2 48:4 (2021) DOI 10.1215/01903659-9382102

> 500. When a sentence is called senseless, it is not as it were its sense that is senseless. But a combination of words is being excluded from the language, withdrawn from circulation.

Charles Bernstein has been, of all contemporary American poets, the one who has done the most to bring back those important words and phrases that tend to be "excluded" from circulation. His poetic inventions are usually called "Language poetry," so named for the movement he founded when he first published the little mimeographed journal called *L=A=N=G=U=A=G=E*, but the label is a bit misleading and, in any case, Charles is sui generis. Since the late 1970s, he has been a deeply moral voice, questioning human follies and Establishment values in all their forms. His eye and ear are almost preternaturally attuned to false notes in human behavior: boasting, greed, self-importance.

In his first book of poetics, *Content's Dream* (1986), Charles established his notion of poetry as *construction*. The poet does not, he insisted, begin with some feeling or thought and "turn it" into poetry, but he or she begins with *language*. Thus, he wrote in the early essay "Semblance" that words "are not integrated into a field as part of a predetermined planar architecture; the gaps and jumps compose a space within shifting parameters, types and styles of discourse, constantly crisscrossing, interacting, creating new gels." And in one of my favorite essays, "Stray Straws and Straw Men," Charles rejects the Romantic notion that "I look straight into my heart & write the exact words that come from within." Poetry, for Charles, is not "the spontaneous overflow of powerful feelings" (Wordsworth); nor is it merely "natural." On the contrary, "poetry is an art, an art with technique, with media." And again, "there are no thoughts except through language, we are everywhere seeing through it, limited to it but not by it." And its elements are "intended, chosen. That is what makes a thing a poem."

What Charles understood was that in the late twentieth and now twenty-first century, it is no longer enough to just "express" oneself. And indeed, from the first, he regarded poetry as also critique, a time-honored notion that the finest poets of previous ages have always understood. Thus, in a famous prose-poem essay (an exciting combination!) called "Artifice of Absorption" (*A Poetics* [1992]), Charles shifted from verse to prose and back again and used many citations from other poets so as to show poetry is that discourse that cannot merely be *transparent*: "The obvious problem is that the poem said in any other way is not the poem." Rather, the poet uses all the tools at his command to create a new kind of absorption, arresting the reader's attention. This means that sound, syntax, visual prosody—all the devices available must be used as fully as possible. It also means *difficulty*, and the early poems especially are quite "difficult" in their appropriation of dominant jargon and cliché, whether of business, psychiatry manuals, "how-to" books, and so on, and his distortion of normal syntax and word use, so as to show the foolish and destructive behavior of his fellow citizens. Many of these early poems are very funny. I call your attention, for example, to "Standing Target," where Charles presents, among other things, a portrait of his childhood self as a young camper, imitating the letter the counselors sent home to his family:

> Charles has done extremely well in swimming.
> Throughout the season he
> gave close attention to instructions and
> conscientiously practiced quietly on
> his own during part of "free swim" before
> going to fun with the other boys and
> pool assistants. He had only one difficulty—
> one foot persistently
> stuck to the floor of the pool. Last
> week Charlie got that foot off the bottom
> and swam completely across the
> pool.
> (*All the Whiskey*, 62–63)

This absurd account then modulates into a section of broken fragments, showing the real pain behind these "cheerful" outside reports: "fatigue / of   of   / open for /   to   , sees / doubles."

Over the years, Charles branched out by using an astonishing variety of forms from the dramatic monologue to the ballad to the libretto, as in *Shadowtime*, one of my personal favorites. *Shadowtime* is "about" Walter Benjamin, culminating in his terrible fate of not being able to escape from the Nazis in World War II and subsequent despair and suicide. In order to write this libretto for an opera by Brian Ferneyhough that was produced many times in 2005–2006, Charles immersed himself in Benjamin's own writings; his "play" is by no means straightforward or realistic but takes Benjamin's basic theories and casts them in the most various and curious verse forms—often gently satirizing Benjamin's thinking itself and showing its problems and limitations. The variations are dazzling: one, for example, is called "dew and die" and is based on a concrete poem by the Austrian

Ernst Jandl. It is a deeply moving work full of brilliant inventions: here is a little ballad playing on the French word *Mademoiselle*:

> Madame Moiselle and Mr. Moiselle
> Went for a walk with their gazelle.
> The tiger slept on the sewing machine
> And all the children swept themselves clean.
> Rings of desire, floods of wisps
> Who's to say what, what's to say which
> Whether what is is so because
> Or whether what is is not
> Who's to say, what's to say
> Whether was is is not
> Or whether what is is so because
> Is so because it's not

Without any overt moralizing, such little ballads show the terrible confusion and pain of these last days on the Spanish border, where everything falls apart. Here, philosophizing comes to an end. I hope someone here will undertake a translation of *Shadowtime*, which would mean a lot, I believe, to Chinese readers.

In his selected poems, *All the Whiskey in Heaven* (2010), Charles has one of the best poems written about the terrible tragedy of 9/11. It's called "Report from Liberty Street," and it begins, "I took a walk on Liberty Street today. Only it was not the same place as I had known before." It is a moving account, very accurate yet also very poetic about the look and feel of New York City after the attack, using the refrain, about the terrorists, *"They thought they were going to heaven."* The poem is full of aphoristic lines like "'We got what we deserved,' a shrill small voice inside some seems to be saying. But surely not *this* person, nor *this* one, no *this* one, nor *this* one"—a brilliant succinct response to the many callous journalists and even scholars who voiced the view, "It was America's fault so they got what they deserved."

In the same period, he wrote such great philosophical poems as "every lake has a house," with its spoof in inexorable logic and reasoning," and the great title poem, "Not for all the whiskey in heaven," an elegy for Charles's wonderful daughter Emma, whom he lost in 2013 when she was only twenty-three. These Emma ballads are wonderfully moving without being mawkish or sentimental. Only Charles could have brought this off!

Charles's most recent book, with the wonderful title *Near Miss*, won the poet the coveted Bollingen Prize, one of the highest honors in the US. The Bollingen Prize has been won by Ezra Pound, Wallace Stevens, and Marianne Moore, among others. The dazzling range of poems continues: one of my favorites is called "Catachresis my Love." The word *catachresis* means a semantic misuse or error; originally it referred to bad metaphors like "blind mouths." It is full of brilliant aphoristic lines like:

> There are no true colors, just different camouflages.
>
> The desire to add insult to injury is no greater than the compulsion to add injury to injury or insult to insult.
>
> You can only do what you can do and sometimes you can't even do that.

Over and over, reading (or hearing) Charles, we don't know whether to laugh or cry or perhaps both. His poetry is so *engaging* that it will change your consciousness.

Ladies and Gentlemen, please join me in welcoming Charles Bernstein.

The Well-Hung & Well-Stretched Language-Tongues of New York

Pierre Joris

1. Not "the one" but "the many" languages. You can't get rid of what the French call "les faux amis," the false friends. And why bother? For you can kiss them on the mouth (tongue-kiss language? language-kiss tongue?) & turn them into poems: at least that's what Charles Bernstein, the best friend of false friends, puns & other impure or polysensed language forms shouts himself hoarse to endorse. Codicil: "Il s'égosille," for "shouts him-

This text was written in French as a preface to Charles Bernstein's *Pour ainsi dire* (*So to Speak*), a selection of his work translated by Habib Tengour (Algiers, Algeria: Apic Éditions, 2019). Translating it (back)? into English is problematic, as the author does as he claims the addressee does: he puns & plays with words—which is a well-known no-no when it comes to translating. This translation tries to keep this playfulness alive, at the risk of befuddling the audience (but what are audiences for, anyway? Illumination goes through befuddling). Thus the title in French was "Les langues bien pendues and bien tendues de New York." Now a "langue bien pendue" refers to a rich & ready tongue, a great gabber never at a loss for words, though the title means langue not as "tongue" but as the linguistic thing: "language." Literally, the expression gives "well-hung"—& that seems to be the easiest way of punning shockingly back into New Yorkese.

boundary 2 48:4 (2021) DOI 10.1215/01903659-9382117

self hoarse" in the original contains, I felt, ego-cille, something that makes the ego blink, & CB would certainly have played with same, with different sound-sense, for he loves sense-sound sans-sens or with sang song & bloody sound or not. For Bernstein is a New Yorker, and even the most New York poet I know. He is very aware that his city is the world's richest language-alembic—more than two hundred are regularly spoken here and some suggest that number is closer to three thousand: English, Spanish, Yiddish, Russian, Arabic, & Chinese, of course (or also), with looming behind that mesclun (a French salad mix by now also acclimatized in Nueva Iork) the phantoms of Lenape and Mohican coming & going in & out of focus, shaking their heads at some of these other ones also spoken here: Vlashki, Garifuna, Mamuju, Bukhari, Aramaic & Ormuri.

Which puts English back in its place: the young but exuberant kid in the recreation (or maybe creation) area of the world. In his theoretical writings, Bernstein explores this language not so much as an "idiolect" (the individual's distinctive, variegated, but unique use of language) but as "idéolecte"—which would be a given group's or community's distinctive and unique uses of language. A thought that permits to deconstruct that old dialectical formula according to which a language is only a "dialect with machine-guns" & thus purely a question of brute power. And which allowed Bernstein to say one day, speaking of a poet who has immigrated to New York: "American poetry is born in second languages, it is our bounty and the secret of our success, if we have any, as much as Samson's long hair was, once upon a time, the source of his strength. That's why any attempt to homogenize and assimilate undermines the foundations of our poetics."

2. The majority of these poems are built on a cornucopia of found phrases & language fragments (read, heard, overheard, fallen off the back of a passing truck or radio . . .): a collage of fragments of a discourse of extremely heteroclite origins. Origins that are at times visible, at times hidden, & what is at play (in all senses of that word) are the concept and practice (nearly classic by now) of intertextuality, entailing a fast—not to say instantaneous—de- & re-contextualization of language fragments. The effect of this is strangely enough very close to that of painting in that, sensu stricto, one can start to look/to enter the poem at any place in the text, and most of the poems refuse to deploy a narrative continuity that would create a singular direction (in French, a "sens unique," a direction which in American gets translated with the French "cul-de-sac"), developing step-by-step from/into a linear reading.

One effect of this is to create a continuously shifting ground, "true" temblor topographies, seem- & seam-scapes lacking any ontologically secure "ground," in the Heideggerian sense of that term. I have spoken of this elsewhere as "seem- & seam-scapes," thus of view(ing)s, landscapes in which the homophonic "faux amis" (so well loved by CB) "seem" (appearance, semblance, resemblance, etc.) and "seam" (stitching, juncture, visible or hidden; plus excess meanings such as vein, load, corrugation, fold, etc.) meet up. The "seams" in the poems don't necessarily follow the visible poetic markers (such as verse-lines or stanzas) but happen(stance) or (objective?) chance inside a verse or even of a word, making for cracks in the syntax & shifts in the voice(s) at times visible & audible in the discourse, at times invisible & inaudible. A central aim of this constructive approach is to dislocate & dismember the speaking subject in order to refuse the appearance (in both meanings of that word) of an all-knowing "I" claiming to speak from an assumed or implied position of uni-vocal, of unequi-vocal truth.

This does not mean that aesthetics play no role in Bernstein's oeuvre: aesthetics are central, but as something that has to be questioned and critiqued continually, and not as a goal or as a successful polished surface. At the heart of his writing lies the exploration of the relations between aesthetics and politics. As he puts it in *Rough Trades*: "The lines of an / imaginary arc inscribed on the / social flesh by the knife point of history." This political stance is visible in the language itself: one of the effects of using de- & re-contextualized citations is to challenge the conventions not only of traditional poetic language but of public speech as well. In his essay in *The Politics of Poetic Form*, Bernstein puts it thus: "In its counterconventional investigations, poetry engages *public* language at its roots, in that it tests the limits of its conventionality while forging alternate conventions (which, however, need not seek to replace other conventions in quest of becoming the new standard)." And further on: "The poetic authority to challenge dominant societal values, including conventional manners of communication, is a model for the individual political participation of each citizen."

3. The Coney Island Wonder Wheel or maybe just ordinary everyday New York traffic, i.e., what the city taught us, is that, as Bernstein suggests, "the ordinary is never more than an extension of the extraordinary. The extraordinary is never more than an extension of the imaginary. The imaginary is never more than an extension of the possible. The possible is never more than an extension of the impossible. The impossible is never more than an extension of the ordinary."

The opening verses of *Rough Trades* make it clear that if Bernstein “want[s] no paradise,” what he does want is “to be / drenched in the downpour of words . . .” And if words and drops rain on his city, New York, she is also the *atlal* of all the mornings, of this morning: you arrive here surprised by the night that hid away in the city’s light-and-sound show, and as you get off the ferry, the camel, the plane, or the bike, you should be handed free of charge this book by Bernstein as a guide to the city. You’d sit down to read it & you’d be there. Open the book.

Sorrentinostan, Brooklyn, December 2018

Charles Bernstein: Against the Idea of Poetry

Leevi Lehto

This article is a translation of the "Foreword" to *Runouden puolustus*, an anthology of poems and essays by Charles Bernstein in Finnish translation (*poEsia*, 2006). This book has a long prehistory, which at least in part is also a personal one. I first met Charles Bernstein in the fall of 1992, and the oldest translation in the volume (of "Targets of Opportunity") is from that time—it was printed with my interview with the poet in *Helsingin Sanomat* in January 1993.

I can say, without exaggeration, that a connection to Charles Bernstein—and via him to a larger new poetry community, first in North America, then increasingly on a global scale (both geographically, and in terms of orientation [of the poets concerned])—has served as an absolutely crucial reference point to my own later work. I cannot say what directions my work might have been taken without it; what is certain is that the Finnish poetry culture, during the nineties and indeed later on, could not have offered it any reference points at all.

boundary 2 48:4 (2021) DOI 10.1215/01903659-9382131

Enough of personal history. Except that what I just said will also say a lot about the poet Bernstein: it would be impossible to enumerate all the actors at the present world scene of poetry, who share this same line of reference (though each one from his/her own direction) to the same poet. Here, we are of course talking about his role as a poetry activist—a teacher, a critic, an essayist, an organizer, and a "man behind the scenes." These roles alone will easily make him the single most influential person in terms of the development of the serious poetry of our time.

Enough about "communality." Except that, here, these "communal" roles (ones that traditionally may be thought of as being "extra-literal") will at the same time say something essential about the poetry in question, on one hand, and about a communality possible in this world of ours, on the other. If anything, the poetry of Charles Bernstein is wildly individual—not in the sense of a safe and stable "personal voice" but, on the contrary, in its devotion to questioning this kind of voice, and from as many (mostly unexpected) directions as possible. In addition to that, it is—in a more conscious way than any other poet's that I know of—not only happily indifferent to communication but in most times also against communication in a flat sense (and thus also against communality in a flat sense): militantly anticommunal, so to say ("against the idea of political efficacy of poetry," as he put it in an interview in 1995). This is why I don't think that influence, in the case of Charles Bernstein, can be understood as being "extra-literary": it derives from . . . no: it is . . . the same . . . with his poetry.

Except that, it would be difficult to locate a poem by Charles Bernstein that would not also be against poetry—the idea of poetry—itself. And not only against Poetry (understood as an idealized model or essence) but also against various individual poetries—a fruitful way to approach most of Charles Bernstein's poems is to see them as many interventions into various constellations, or power-relations, in the field of poetry, always reacting to something, always against a particular idealization—among them, of course, the idea of interventionism as such: "the work drops away and in its place there are stations, staging sites, or blank points of radical metamorphosis . . . turning ever further away from ideality in the pursuit of an ultimate concretion," as he writes himself in the preface to his collection *With Strings* (2001).

Except that this, of course, is exactly his idea of poetry. I have tried my best to make the selection reflect this continuous state of intellectual awareness that I see as being central in Charles Bernstein's poetry. The poems span his entire active career; there are poems and essays (in a way, my prototype has been Bernstein's 1999 volume of "speeches and poems," *My Way*, University of Chicago Press); poem-essays and essay-poems; short lyrical pieces that often interrogate the fundamentals of epics; longer epic sequences where Bernstein often is at his most lyrical (to me, the long sequence "Emotions of Normal People" is one of the most moving poems of the late twentieth century); sound poems, "conceptual" poems, non-poems, anti-poems, a translation by Bernstein from Finnish to English (which at the same time is a translation from English into Finnish) . . . and, speaking about communality, also poems written by others than Bernstein.

I suggested that Bernstein's poetry is against the idea of a "personal voice" and constantly in work to dismantle the ideology of a "lyrical I"—as it is, except that: what I've said about individuality, about maintaining the critical awareness, openness, et cetera, amounts to the poet letting his (in Charles's case, charming/engaging) personality to impregnate/saturate the work, through and through, and without restrictions. Here, Bernstein's poetry indeed is directly related to two great fellow Americans, Walt Whitman and Allen Ginsberg—though it also effectively trans-illuminates a certain hidden conformism of the latter. Personality and "personal voice" understood as independence vis-à-vis the given communal structures—including the more and more lobotomized structures of traditional publishing—and thus always as a possible starting point for a new, utopian communality (but note that "The Only Utopia Is in a Now").

Communality also as a sensitivity toward one's own background: the question of "being American," in the sense of a transcendental utopianism first outlined by Ralph Waldo Emerson, can be seen as one of the later Bernstein's most prevalent themes (in my reading, the "Bricklayer's Arms" writes about that theme; and the slashing remark in "War Stories"—"War is an excuse for lots of bad antiwar poetry"—seems as if taken directly from a lecture/sermon of Emerson).[1] Finally, voice and sound, as such: even though (or rather: because), an attraction to unexpected or difficult-to-pronounce sound combinations is a constant feature of Bernstein's prosody, I wouldn't hesitate to speak, at the level of the work, of a certain peculiarly Bernsteinian sound. It is not exactly the bright flute sound of a Pound, not the broken willow whistle of the Finnish folk songs, either—perhaps something of these two combined, and then pierced by a besotted adolescent

1. For Emerson in Finnish, see Ks. Emerson, *Luo, ito*, Suom. Antti Immonen. 23°45 niin &. n'ciin-lehden filosofinen julkaisusarja, 2002.

gaiety to such an extent that a certain generalized, but always intellectually controlled, sorrow will most often linger as the final note.[2]

Except that saying "at the level of the work" is begging the question whether, and on what conditions, one can talk about "a work" ("the work") with Bernstein. Even in the original, his poetry is characterized by a certain resistance against the idea of a work's centrifugal movement that will gain momentum now that this poetry is entering its foreign language phase, so to say—something that I see as imminent: during this fall alone, "representative" volumes will come out in Swedish and in Portuguese, in addition to the present Finnish one. "The translation of poetry is never more than an extension of the practice of poetry," Bernstein himself writes. Out of necessity, translating his work will also mean its continuous rewriting—and I mean this in the same radical sense that the poet, in the final essay in the present selection, sees the transition of the old oral poetry to what's happening now. I urge [you] to follow up this process that evidently will produce numerous new "stations, staging sites, or blank points of radical metamorphosis."

2. With this, I am reacting against a certain American reception, where the humor, or satire, of Charles Bernstein's poetry gets foregrounded. Except that his "humor is so dark you can't see it," it is also so visible and all-prevalent, that it ceases to work as a separate "device," becoming an immediate and indispensable basis for (much grander) seriousness.

In the Un-American Tree: The L=A=N=G=U=A=G=E Poetries and Their Aftermath, with a Special Reference to Charles Bernstein, Translated

Leevi Lehto

In his novel *The Unbearable Lightness of Being*, Milan Kundera has an American senator looking at his four children running across a large expanse of grass toward a stadium with an artificial skating rink. "Describing a circle with his arm, a circle that was meant to take in stadium, grass, and children, he added, 'Now that's what I call happiness.'" For Kundera, this attitude represents what he calls "totalitarian kitsch." Something which, to him, "causes two tears to flow in quick succession. The first tear says: How nice to see children running on the grass! The second tear says: How nice to be moved, together with all mankind, by children running on the grass!"

Now, this definition could almost come from an essay by Charles Bernstein on what he calls "Official Verse Culture" of the present-day North

Presented as one of the keynote addresses at the opening session of the International Conference on 20th-Century American Poetry, hosted by Central China Normal University, Wuhan, China, July 21, 2007.

boundary 2 48:4 (2021) DOI 10.1215/01903659-9382145

America, characterized as it is by easy, prefabricated sentiments, the supposedly universal "emotions of normal people," and the rule of "easy acceptability." But note also Kundera's comment, only a page or two later: "The smile at [the Senator's] face was the smile Communist statesmen beamed from the height of their reviewing stand to the identically smiling citizens in the parade below."

I'm using Kundera, a Central European novelist not that close in his artistic ambitions to Language poetries, to suggest that the Language project's merits be viewed outside the quite narrowly American (or Western) context in which it is often represented. My claim here will be that Language as a "movement" may rather be seen as related to, and reacting against, the structures and mentality of the Cold War and the Twentieth-Century Mass Communication Society. As to the Cold War, specifically, I'm not so much interested in its inner ideological antagonisms, as in suggesting that it be seen as (the first) global structure of cultural dominance, and one where the influence of its opposing poles to each other (or indeed a shared set of "values") is more pertinent. It was also a structure that, in East as in West, meant the introduction of simple but powerful state ideologies—much larger than either totalitarian kitsch or Official Verse Culture—and their implementation by means of various kinds of cultural, educational, social, media-related, and other controls. It was the beginning of the development that, in the opinion of many, has led to the shallowing of public life, the emptying out of cultural heritages.

The core group of Language poets can perhaps be seen as representing the first American TV generation, and the "languages" they have been interested in have often been precisely those of the controls I mentioned. More importantly, though, they should, in my view, be seen as the first serious gathering of poets to react to the changing conditions of poetry in this new environment. Where some of their immediate predecessors—the Beats, the New York poets—can be seen as having flirted with the mass consumer culture, most of the Language poets come across as seriously concerned with (even disturbed by) some of the consequences of that "New Society" for poetry and for literature more generally. Against a more conventional view of them as just "hard line" experimentalist, I tend to see in them an almost moving "conservationist" attitude combined with most radical questioning of the fundamentals of "literature." This "paradox" can be where their lasting value comes to be seen.

I know that Charles Bernstein will soon talk more extensively about the "fate of innovation"—so suffice it to say here, as regards this paradox, that I think of the Language movement as having, already, established a new kind of literary tradition: a "tradition of innovation" where some of the central elements are the following: (1) renunciation of the military metaphors so characteristic to many of the old avant-garde movements (Dada, Futurists), (2) abstaining from formulating an "alternative" artistic program or from staging itself as a solution to society's antagonisms and delusions, (3) making use of a kind of a network economy that enables the group (I know it is not correct even to speak about group in connection to Language) to grow organically, (4) a certain peer-to-peer (poet-to-poet) structure that radically changes the dynamics of how the art form evolves: public or critical success, with its attached model of successive "paradigm shifts," comes to be replaced by ongoing interchange between poets; in short, Language has helped to "bring poetry back to the poets," and finally, (5) the imperative of innovation.

In the imperative of innovation, central to my argument is its practical ubiquitousness: the new poetical praxis that language has helped to introduce has a tendency to exclude the idea of "applied poetry"—at least, it has demonstrated that a community of "innovative poets" in the strict sense of the term can continue to grow, even more rapidly than any other part of the poetry community at large. This new situation requires us to reconsider the value of "newness" in evaluating the merits of new poetry—as it is replaced by such notions as "untimeliness," "strangeness," "being-out-of-placeness," etc. We are dealing with a set of new kinds of sensitivities that may sound striking as explained but are felt more than natural by the members of the poetry communities in question. I wouldn't exclude that this has affinities with some changes taking place in the culture at large (networking as a new general principle of group formation, new kinds or subgroups and sects, etc.).

Much of this gets admirably expressed in Charles Bernstein's definition of poetry as "the ultimate small business." This idea could be seen as modeled on Pound's networking activity or on Joyce's organizing his own reception. This is one of the reasons why I think of the contemporary revival of innovative poetry as a descendant of the early poetic and other Modernism proper.

When I leaf through an anthology like *The Other Side of the Century*, by Douglas Messerli, from 1994, today, I'm struck by how strongly "controlled" the writing is. Compared to it, more conventional anthologies from the same period almost seem a series of randomly generated—almost Googled!—versions of a set of few predefined themes. This suggests that, against some still popular misconceptions, the new innovative poetic culture has very little to do with the famous "Death of the Author"—or to put it otherwise, it serves as an example of Roland Barthes's original claim of that death testifying to the birth of writing (only we are not talking about writing that would attempt to express the two successive tears of totalitarian kitsch).

One of the indications of this emphasis of writerly control is how it is reflected in the positions taken by the two most important contemporary tendencies purporting to "carry on" the Language project: Conceptual Writing and Flarf. Both these tendencies are geared to "loosen" or question the control of the author on the poetic work—even in the "nonnaturalistic" and disjunction-oriented way generally found in Language poetry. With Conceptual Writing, the target is precisely the idea of writer as the one "in control"—cf. Kenneth Goldsmith's punch line, "I am a word processor." The author still decides what goes into the work, but the detailed control on individual words and sentences, and their interplay, is renounced—often with the delightful result of the work gaining in "insights." In Flarf, the emphasis is on "writing badly," and in the "disturbing" quality of the content, which often derives from online chatrooms and other internet "rubbish." With a twitch, Flarf thus comes across as poetry that is—once again—interested in "free flow of emotions," and in how the writer personally feels about the "content" (the imperative of "disturbedness" demanding her to loosen her control on that). Conceptualism and Flarf can be seen as examples of how "any true avant-garde provokes a legacy that looks very different from itself" (in Craig Dworkin's admirable formulation)—and I mean that as a compliment to both Language poetry and to its contenders.

The new evaluative criterion of "untimeliness," as outlined above, may today already be applied to the reception of the Language poetry itself. Here I must contradict myself: against what I said about the importance of peer-to-peer, poet-to-poet structures, I would like to suggest reactivating the old Benjaminian idea of "a poem has never been meant for its readers." In this new emerging context, something like this could be seen as happening in Conceptualism (cf. Kenny Goldsmith's claim of "not having a readership") but also as an extension of large parts of Charles Bernstein's practice, where the imperative of innovation is accompanied with the dictate of "difficulty made difficult." Instead of seeing Bernstein's work as "inconsistent" (Richard Kostelanetz) (even in the meaning of consistent rejection of consistency [Hank Lazer]), I propose studying it precisely in its consistent rejection to meet its readers—on a communicative basis. (Something which, to once more (mis)use Kundera, has tended to give it a quality of a certain "unbearable lightness.") To exaggerate a bit, it may be that the work of the most prominent member of the original language group is the most in need of reevaluation.

Before moving on to my conclusions, allow me one more remark, on a theme that in this context can rightly be seen as fundamental: language. In the early discussions between the members of the core group of Language poets, the basically structuralist, Saussurean idea of "language determining the reality" was rather prominent. Taking my lead from a Bernstein poem, "Don't Be So Sure," I would like to claim the following: Saussure and Bernstein agree on a fundamental point, that of language being "in the last instance" socially determined, and they differ in how they interpret this. For Saussure—as for much of the later poststructuralist thinking—the social conditioning (*lien social*) is what determines the famous "arbitrariness of the sign": language is what is socially accepted as such. Compare to this the Bernsteinian formulation: "Poetry's social function is not to express but, rather, to explore the possibilities for expression." Explore, not far from question; question, not far from reject; reject, not far from destroy. In this perspective, the new innovative poetries of today cannot exactly be one with language(s). Their attitude is not that of "a floating signifier," and the imperative of innovation can be seen as expressly opposed to the (still somewhat) fashionable postmodern attitude of "anything goes." On the contrary, nothing (as such) goes. Where for structuralist and poststructuralist theory, the *lien social* determines what is acceptable, we need to concentrate on the other side of the coin: to what does not gain acceptance. Difficulty has to be made difficult.

In fact, I have been talking about the international reception of Language poetries all the time. The scene of innovative new poetry today is fundamentally global—not least thanks to the impact of the internet. Still, I would claim that there are two receptions of Language, overlapping but different: domestic and international. I will close with a set of theses on these.

One. In a certain sense, Language really was and is an American phenomenon. Based on several structural factors that I cannot go deeper into here, the new innovative poetries in the US have come to be very much identified with genuine ("alternative") American values and—on another level—with the tradition of English language and literature.

Two. I would claim that—to a certain extent—the tradition of Language poetry, in a special sense, is not transferable to any other national context. Or put it this way: its influence at that level will come more through works that have not been translated or are not translatable. I may not be the right person to say this, having been responsible for a volume of translations of the work of Charles Bernstein into Finnish, but then again, he can already be said to be part of the Finnish poetry scene—not as imported poetic "content" but as an active actor.

Three. The influence of Language writing outside its "homeland" is bound to happen on a transnational level. The case in point is today's situation in Scandinavian countries, where there is an active transnational movement along the lines of what we have seen in the US and Canada. As in North America, there is a lot of resistance to that new development—resistance that is always expressed on a national basis. On the other hand, the fact that this new development is taking place on a transnational level helps to activate certain fundamental tenets of Language writing: not being directly tied to any native language as such, the new international poetries will come to chart even more unprecedented territories. I have proposed a concept of literature of "Barbaric English"—the English spoken as a second language. This has now developed into an interest in all kinds of barbarized versions of all the languages involved (I just finished a longish poem in Norwegian, a language I don't know enough even to know what I have said in the piece). These developments will evidently pose new challenges for American poets, many of whom, if truth be told, are only too complacent with only disfiguring their own dear English.

Four. More than any other poetry before it, the body of the Language poetry will change when translated. (Something like that definitely happened to a Bernstein poem I translated without even looking at it—and to another, which originally is in gibberish, yet now has definitive content in Finnish and Swedish, as well as more gibberish versions based on those.) In fact, the implanting of the Language tradition into the transnational space will be a process and an undertaking comparable to the radical misprision effected by Pound vis-à-vis traditional Chinese poetry—except that the misplacements here, because of the more "undecided" and heterogeneous nature of "original," will be more substantial. Indeed, it will be more a question of creating altogether new poetry based on beneficial misunderstandings and contextual changes.

Five. A word on China is in place in this context. I started by alluding to the international situation during the early years of Language poetry. Now, as we all know, China will have a growing impact compared to the present one in future. I'm aware that something similar to the process that led to the growth of the Language movement is already taking place in China and in Chinese—the internet acting as a crucial enabler even here.

Of course, one can only regret certain restrictions that the Chinese government, with the help of Western online giants, has effected here. We must hope they will be lifted—as I believe they will. I recently read that with its present internet penetration of 10 percent, China is now the second biggest internet country, only a little behind the US, with its 90 percent penetration. Sooner than we in the West even realize, Chinese will be the dominant language of the internet. This will open enormous new possibilities for Chinese poets to creatively misunderstand also the tradition of Language poetry, perhaps ending up with one more large-scale misprision across the continents.

To describe that eventuality, we could say, along with Charles Bernstein, at the end of his essay "The Revenge of the Poet-Critic, or The Parts Are Greater Than the Sum of the Whole": "I open the door and it shuts after me. That is, the more I venture out into the open the more I find it is behind me and I am moving not toward some uninhabited space but into a maelstrom of criss-crossing inscriptions. The open is a vanishing point—the closer I get to it the greater the distance from which it beckons. And I begin the journey again."

Now that's what I would call happiness.

“Nothing tires a vision more than sundry attacks / in the manner of enclosure”: An Afterword to *Angriff der Schwierigen Gedichte*

Dennis Büscher-Ulbrich

The bilingual collection *Angriff der Schwierigen Gedichte* (luxbooks, 2014) by the prolific US American poet and literary theorist Charles Bernstein, which takes its name from the 2011 *Attack of the Difficult Poems* (University of Chicago Press), throws an important transatlantic bridge for contemporary German-language poetry and its readers. Bernstein is a contemporary author in the best sense of the word, suffering the prevailing zeitgeist as well as the violence of the concept, without giving in to despair. His wide-awake and formally advanced poems are, at the same time, discursive interventions and poetological essays. “One must be absolutely modern,” writes Rimbaud in 1873.[1] But few critics take his insistence on that *necessity* into account—or, worse, they reject the notion of “absolutely modern” as anachronistic right away. This book provides a view of Bernstein as, of necessity, a radical modernist who is, at the same time, unabashedly tradi-

1. Arthur Rimbaud, *Une Saison en Enfer* (1873): “Il faut être absolument moderne.”

boundary 2 48:4 (2021) DOI 10.1215/01903659-9382159

tional: iconoclast and icon, New York's own and "rootless cosmopolitan"—precisely in the sense of what Stalinism abhorred: difference, nonidentity, borderless solidarity, and utopia. Bernstein's poems insist with William Blake, whose *Songs of Innocence and Experience* (recorded by Allen Ginsberg, Elvin Jones, et al. in 1970) he reissued on PennSound in 2006, on "see[ing] the world in a grain of sand."[2] The legacy of the early Romantics, the historical avant-garde, and Jewish-American modernists such as Stein, Williams, and Zukofsky in no way wears Bernstein's poetry down. Rather, it makes it necessarily difficult and, above all, very difficult to ignore.

Although Bernstein's oeuvre cannot be reduced to his work as coeditor and copublisher, together with Bruce Andrews, of the paradigmatically titled *L=A=N=G=U=A=G=E* magazine, it remains the cornerstone and springboard of his writing. The magazine is inseparable from Bernstein's name and has contributed significantly to his international recognition. More importantly, however, *L=A=N=G=U=A=G=E* has served as a forum and resource for critical poetics and theoretically reflected writing practice. As such, it helped catalyze collective avant-garde and experimental activities on both sides of the Atlantic at a time of conservative backlash and aversion to critical theory in "Official Verse Culture" (see, e.g., Bernstein 1986). Together with other so-called Language poets like Bruce Andrews, Ron Silliman, Lyn Hejinian, Bob Perelman, Steve McCaffery, Rae Armantrout, Barrett Watten, Carla Harryman, et cetera, Bernstein indulged in critical theory and counterhegemonic practice. As Paul Quinn put it, "It was as if the Beats had been made in Frankfurt [and Paris-Nanterre] instead of Columbia" (2000). Between 1978 and 1981, Bernstein and Andrews published twelve issues and three extensive supplements that stand as a rich historical archive of critical poetics and experimental writing.

Bernstein's own essays on poetics, German translations of which have appeared on karawa.net, in *randnummer* and *Schreibheft*, are manifesto-like "romantic fragments," informed by French poststructuralism, Wittgenstein's philosophy of language, and Frankfurt school critical theory. Critical interventions into the liberal academy and literary establishment rather than expressions of it, they continued the critique of fetishism, the culture industry, phallogocentrism, and global capital. This holds true, in particular, for "The Dollar Value of Poetry" (1979) and the "Politics of Poetry" double issue of *L=A=N=G=U=A=G=E* (9/10) as well as "Comedy and the

2. William Blake, "Auguries of Innocence" (ca. 1803): "To see the world in a grain of sand."

Poetics of Political Form" (1989), a lecture Bernstein first gave as part of a lecture series at the New School, later published by Roof Books as *Poetry and Public Policy* (1990), and which was republished in *A Poetics* (1992). The latter also contains the essay "Pounding Fascism," which appeared in an expanded version as "Pound and the Poetry of Today" in Bernstein's *My Way: Speeches and Poems* (1999) as well as in *Schreibheft* 80. Here Bernstein discusses Pound's significance for contemporary poetry and poetics, while critically situating it aesthetically and politically. Also of particular note is Bernstein's theoretical reflection on poetics in "Artifice of Absorption" (1987), which takes the form of a highly self-reflexive prose poem. Alongside numerous canonical literary voices and theorists, "Artifice of Absorption" also discusses key concepts of somewhat neglected thinkers, such as Valentin N. Voloshinov and Veronica Forrest-Thomson.

It turns out to be impossible to discuss all of Bernstein's important projects and publications since the late 1960s in an afterword: from his early tape poems, performances, and text collaborations (e.g., in *LEGEND* [1980]) to such weighty poetry collections as *Controlling Interests* (1980), *The Sophist* (1984), *Dark City* (1994), *With Strings* (2001), *Girly Man* (2006), and *Recalculating* (2013), the anthologies *Republics of Reality: 1975–1995* (2000), and *All the Whiskey in Heaven* (2010), to the essays and interventions in *Content's Dream: Essays 1975–1984* (1986) and *Attack of the Difficult Poems* (2011), which is also the title of the present collection. Equally important, however, are Bernstein's inter- and multimedia collaborations, literary anthologies, and extensive archival online projects, such as PennSound and the Electronic Poetry Center (EPC), as well as his astonishing libretto for Ferneyhough's opera *Shadowtime* (2004) on the life and thought of Walter Benjamin. The latter is so unabashedly late modernist and atonal that, in addition to the Viennese school and avant-garde poetry from Dada to Oulipo, one also feels reminded of Adorno's *Philosophy of New Music*. Here Bernstein's concept of a "non-Euclidean (or complex) prosody," developed in the introduction to *Close Listening: Poetry and the Performed Word* (1998), is aesthetically tangible.

Bernstein conceives of modern poetry as a form of immanent ideology critique, as it were, and of critical poetics as a form of counterhegemonic cultural practice in the superstructure. Based on Western Marxist notions of the fate of art under capitalism and post-Marxist discourse theory, Bernstein engages a spectrum of writing that is primarily focused on (the system of) language, signifying practices, and social forms, and, in doing so, "takes for granted neither vocabulary, grammar, process, shape, syntax, program, or subject matter . . . and [instead seeks] to develop more fully the latticework of those involved in aesthetically related activity" (Andrews and Bernstein 1984: x). Bernstein's writing also impressively conveys the strengths of a collective engagement with how writing can articulate, make visible, and generate meanings and values. In light of the repeated accusation by certain critics that "language-centered writing," in its peculiar attempt to criticize the reification of language and its manipulative use in the media public sphere—its central role with regard to political power and class domination—remains trapped in a "nihilistic destruction" or "denial of meaning," Andrews and Bernstein explained as early as 1984:

> The idea that writing should (or could) be stripped of reference is as bothersome and confusing as the assumption that the primary function of words is to refer, one-on-one, to an already constructed world of "things." Rather, reference, like the body itself, is one of the horizons of language, whose value is to be found in the writing (the world) before which we find ourselves at any moment. It is the multiple powers and scope of reference (denotative, connotative, associational), not writers' refusal or fear of it, that threads the essays [in *L=A=N=G=U=A=G=E*] together. (xi)

The latter certainly also characterizes *Angriff der Schwierigen Gedichte*.

The already misguided accusation of a "denial of meaning" can hardly be limited to Language poetry, just as Bernstein himself cannot be reduced to it. Rather, he has become an integral part of what might be called the "long century" of radical modernism in the arts. Bernstein's texts and performances are twice removed from "denying" meaning. Rather, they are constructivist, paratactic, playful, and polyvalent, which is particularly well illustrated by the multiple translations of poems like "Catabolism" and "Dodgem" in the present collection. But they are also weird, atonal, hilarious, and deadly serious at the same time. This is also true of "Asylums" and "Dysraphism," which can be understood as continuations of the American modernist long poem. What these texts further have in common is that they go beyond both aestheticism and postmodern self-referentiality in their attempt to contextualize the reader herself by means of a reflexive writing practice attuned to readerly response. In addition to numerous intertextual montages and other forms of bricolage, which allow Bernstein to juxtapose and yet combine very heterogeneous elements, *Angriff der Schwierigen Gedichte* attacks the reader with a steady stream of neo-Dadaist sound poems, aleatory excursions, beautiful aphorisms, and even lyrical voices of care, gender politics, and explicit social criticism, as in "The Ballad of the Girly Man" (2006).

Bernstein, whose work has attracted the critical attention of such distinguished literary scholars as Marjorie Perloff and Jerome McGann, is himself a scholar and academic who teaches poetry and poetics at the University of Pennsylvania. The scope of Bernstein's scholarship is sweeping yet consistent in its ambition: whether writing about Louis Zukofsky, Laura Riding Jackson, Pac-Man, or Thelonious Monk, Bernstein consistently articulates with wit and precision why and how radical modernism affects what Jacques Rancière has called the "distribution of the sensible [*le partage du sensible*]": "the system of self-evident facts of sense perception that simultaneously discloses the existence of something in common and the delimitations that define the respective parts and positions within it" (Rancière 2004: 12). The "sensible" here denotes two things: first, that which is accessible to the "senses" and thus perceptible; second, that which is "sensible" within a hegemonic regime of signification and meaning and thus *makes* (common) "sense." The term simultaneously points to the material and symbolic conditions for a partitioning of the "sensible" that establishes the common contours of a collectivity and to the sources of a dissensual rupture with this very order (see also Rancière 1999).

Modern poetry cannot make emancipatory politics for us, but it can help unravel the seams of the uniform social quilt that the sewing machine of hegemonic discourse (and social practice) keeps quilting and quilting. In the context of a post-political consensus—what Rancière calls *la police*—Bernstein's inauthentic handling of literary forms and genres, the poetry's constructed indeterminacy, his inventive free play at the border between conventional readability and forms of defamiliarization (*Verfremdung*), which seek to introduce an aesthetic distance, or dissensus, can be understood as a successful attempt to mobilize the emancipatory potential of aesthetic experience without falling back on a mechanistic cause-and-effect formula for political poetry. Bernstein's work, rather, contributes to a shared process of disidentification—that is, with the "*police* distribution of the sensible," which is a condition of possibility for political emancipation. It is in this sense that Bernstein remains a political poet, and his poetry remains necessarily difficult and dissonant. His increasing canonization and institutionalization notwithstanding, Bernstein remains absolutely modern, or, as the title of his talk at the Socialist Scholars Conference at Manhattan

Community College in April 1987 put it: "In the Middle of Modernism / in the Middle of Capitalism / on the Outskirts of New York" (Bernstein 1992: 90).

Hamburg, March 2014

References

Andrews, Bruce, and Charles Bernstein, eds. 1984. "Repossessing the Word." In *The L=A=N=G=U=A=G=E Book*. Carbondale: Southern Illinois University Press.

Bernstein, Charles. 1986. "The Academy in Peril." In *Content's Dream: Essays 1975–1984*, 244–251. Evanston, IL: Northwestern University Press.

———. 1992. *A Poetics*. Cambridge, MA: Harvard University Press.

Quinn, Paul. 2000. "Rattling the Chains of Free Verse: The Surprising Survival of Language Poetry and Poetics." *Jacket* 12 (July 2000). http://jacketmagazine.com/12/quinn-tls.html.

Rancière, Jacques. 1999. *Disagreement: Politics and Philosophy*. Translated by Julie Rose. Minneapolis: University of Minnesota Press.

———. 2004. *The Politics of Aesthetics: The Distribution of the Sensible*. Edited and translated by Gabriel Rockhill. London: Continuum.

Exordium

Enrique Winter

There is another American poetry, which in the absence of a father, Walt Whitman, has two mothers, Emily Dickinson and Gertrude Stein. In their works, instead of the creation of a country or the subjects to inhabit it, we attend to the creation of a new language, expanded through apparent errors and disused uses, composed by ear, extending the formal possibilities of rhyme and meter in Dickinson, and the materiality of words, through philosophical reiterations, in Stein. Both of them address issues that keep distance from the hypertrophied speaker of canonic poetry, which centralizes in himself the totalizing vision of the world, but also from the confessional speaker, who shares exclusively his feelings about the reduced scope of experience. In short, Dickinson and Stein's proposals oppose

Author's translation from the Spanish introduction to Bernstein's selected poems *Blanco inmóvil* (Bogotá: Uniandes, 2018). Preliminary versions appeared in books with the same title (Guayaquil: Fondo de Animal, 2013, and Barcelona: Kriller71, 2014); in *Abuso de sustancias* (Santiago: Alquimia, 2014), and *Grandes éxitos* (Guadalajara: Mantis, 2014).

boundary 2 48:4 (2021) DOI 10.1215/01903659-9382173

those who brought poetry to the place where nobody but the poet himself suffers with the state of the world.

Stein did with literature what cubism did with painting: she gave it a multiple perspective, with all the elements on an equivalent plane, fragments that can become independent instead of necessarily collaborating with a universal, and in which the statements depend more on the receiver's intuition than on their direct link with reality. This search for an active reader, motivated by the need to fill in the lack of moral judgments presented by Stein, together with her consequent questioning of the speaker and, in the long run, of the author, laid the foundations of much of modern and postmodern literature. With humor, she thus shifts attention to language itself, to the language that changes things, which otherwise would only be what they are.

Charles Bernstein's poetry arises from these conditions. He wrote his undergraduate thesis on Stein's *The Making of Americans* through Ludwig Wittgenstein's *Philosophical Investigations*. He discusses two fundamental issues for his own poetry in it: "The real thing of disillusionment," the feeling of always being misunderstood and a stranger, which leads to skepticism; and its philosophical correlate, the dramatic break between "words and things," to use the original title by Michel Foucault, opening here the window for the chiffon of French structuralists and poststructuralists who marked the founders of the *L=A=N=G=U=A=G=E* magazine, Bruce Andrews and Bernstein himself.

This publication, perhaps the most influential in experimental poetry of the last half century—putative heir to *This*, edited by Barrett Watten and Robert Grenier—was the vehicle for proposing an exploration of the intrinsic qualities of language rather than continuing a tradition of verse, which their authors felt had been co-opted by academia and press reviews. They argued that there had been a repressive division between the literary genres and, to a large extent, the arts. The movement generated around the magazine continues to this day, but its interdisciplinary nature was nothing new to the poetic avant-garde of the so-called New York School. Frank O'Hara, apart from being a painter, was a curator at the Museum of Modern Art, while John Ashbery was the editor of *ARTnews*, and Barbara Guest and James Schuyler served as contributors to the century-old *Art in America*, not to mention Robert Creeley's well-known friendship with Willem de Kooning and the abstract expressionists in general, and even Mark Strand's recent monographs on the works of Edward Hopper and William Bailey. The same can be said of music in poets such as John Cage and the Beats, who have made crisscrosses in American poetry the rule rather than the exception, with one difference between poetry and the arts, Bernstein stated at the time: the difficulty of consuming the poetic image in the market.

These and other bonds challenge the delimited apparatuses of social control that operates through institutions and language. Such control is executed, according to Bernstein, thanks to the fact that language is taken for granted and not as something that has evolved over time, a contingent matter, susceptible to change just as societies do. Thirty years later, he writes in "Recalculating," "The problem with teaching poetry is perhaps the reverse of that in other fields: Students come to it thinking it's personal and relevant but I try to get them to see it as formal, structural, historical, collaborative, and ideological. *What a downer!*" One of the ideas of the language poets, in lowercase to also include pre-magazine authors such as Jackson Mac Low, and his West Coast contemporaries Lyn Hejinian and Ron Silliman, is to empower readers to understand how imposed systems work, and thus be able to modify them, whether through language or revolution. Ideally both, but not in the manner of the so-called political writers, who accept the state of language as if it were independent of the power that uses it, under the excuse of greater communicability. The argument is conflicting, of course, and Bernstein himself has recognized for poems such as "War Stories" that war is so real that we cannot even imagine it, so real that we can do nothing but imagine it over and over again, considering them as poems that become crystalline structures of loss. This apparent narrativity of his recent poetry, in relation to the urgency caused by armed conflicts, or from the book *Rough Trades* with the use of short poems, makes advisable to begin reading this anthology from there, to enter afterwards in the radical structural break proposed in the years of the *L=A=N=G=U=A=G=E* magazine. This break also applied to the poem from its poetics, which, through the study of its signs, generates its political meaning. This shift is not without its doubts either, since Bernstein, by explaining the objectives of his work through poetics, somehow resurrects the idea of the author as a valid interpreter, if not the most capable, of what he had supposedly deprived of authorship, given its independence as a construction of language.

By then, and barely thirty-one years old, Charles Bernstein had edited eight individual and two collaborative books. He self-published the first ones, creating in each of them different and internally consistent mechanisms, such as chaos, density of diction, and the clash of multiple voices in the dangers of *Asylums*' institutions, *Veil*'s visual poetry, the fragmentary nature of the verses in *Shade* or the prose in *Poetic Justice*, from which a transcription of the Lift Off correction tape of a typewriter is included here, that is, the waste of the poems, questioning what we really read on the page once separated from the safe ground of words.

It was not until *Controlling Interests* that Bernstein incorporated poems of heterogeneous textures in a single volume, mixing in them the procedures exposed to date through the collage. He embodied the poetic potential of everyday life under the imposition of consumption, with vanishing points toward community consciousness and a certain transcendence in "Matters of Policy," in the same way that he appropriates the discourses of school and clinical reports and the biographies of power, leading to an oppressive normalization, by means of the hesitations of memory and the metaphors of learning in "Standing Target," two of his most important poems, in which he also alters the spacing. With this book he was considered the main exponent among the Language poets and was honored by writers and critics of the avant-garde, a resonance that Bernstein himself puts into question in "Substance Abuse," which belongs to another central book in his work, *Islets/Irritations*. This volume also contains the risky poetics of "The Klupzy Girl"—solidly analyzed by Linda Reinfeld in *Language Poetry: Writing as Rescue*—and "The Measure," with its imagery of blurred lyricism.

Apart from some authors already mentioned, Paul Hoover considers among the disparate influences of Bernstein's group of poets the Russian Futurist Velimir Khlebnikov, creator of the transrational language; *A* by Louis Zukofsky; *The Tennis Court Oath*, perhaps the most radical of John Ashbery's books; and Objectivists in general. All of them share with the projectivist poets of Black Mountain College, like Robert Duncan, a greater attention to the method with which the poem is constructed than to its result, under the premise that the materiality and sonority of words have no necessary relation, if any, with reality. Therefore, like Stein, they displace the main role from the speaker—who practically disappears—to the social processes of constituting the senses of the poem.

Bernstein considers his poems impermeable, opaque because of artifice and digression, in opposition to the absorptive ones, which generate in his opinion a hypnotic state thanks to realism, transparency, and continuity, among other traps. A classic poem is thus like a baby that captivates all our attention without offering us anything in return. On the contrary, one full of nooks and crannies, apart from fulfilling the duty of waking us up from hypnosis, when it lights up it does so with more intensity than the sun. In this he is even related to the Beat poets, who seemed so distant from the conceptual poetry of which Bernstein is the most direct antecedent. This hinge character within the tradition of the American avant-garde is one of the greatest attractions of his work—besides the humor and the use of the jargon of advertising, politics, psychoanalysis, and the press, to name the main ones—since it seduces from the questioning in equal parts of a communicability not exempt from music, which precedes it, and a dogmatic application of the impossibility of saying, where the poem is no longer a vehicle of human expression but the result of a restrictive procedure, which follows it.

The projection of this and other positions has an uncertain prognosis in the conflictive American poetic scene, since precisely one of the most considered trenches today is that of post-language lyricism, which comes to recognize in fullness the historical and political materiality of language and cements its aesthetic emotions from that starting point. While the mechanisms of the French Oulipo, such as writing without certain letters or a single and extended sentence in order to investigate a potential literature, are also revalued, appropriation and erasure constitute, for their part, two of the main techniques of the conceptualist poets, and cyberpoetry appears with random cuts of results from internet searches. While there is a rising resistance to a certain lack of content in these currents—for concentrating too much on the possibilities of the medium, given the enormous ignorance that we still have of the human mind—Bernstein continues to present books with a diversity of sources, such as *Recalculating*, which, apart from the postmodern devices mentioned, includes everything from translations of French (as early as the 1980s, he had published the volumes *The Maternal Drape* by Claude Royet-Journoud and *Red, Green & Black* by Olivier Cadiot) to poems in the manner of canonical authors such as Wallace Stevens; *Pitch of Poetry*, from which he cut into verse the essay "The Pataquerical Imagination" offering it as "Anesthetic"; or the manifestos of *Near/Miss*.

Illustrative of its sources' breadth are the quotations in this volume: for example, the appropriation, word by word, of the characteristics of the total institutions established by the sociologist Erving Goffman in "Asylum"; the pear and peach where Gertrude Stein places reality in "You can't insure it . . . ," "My Life as a Monad," "Dysraphism," and "No Way"; "mind forged" by the poet William Blake in "My Life as a Monad"; "butter that popcorn" by the band Parkdale Funk and the "sitting ducks" by the cartoonist Michael Bedard in "Matters of Policy"; the title "Stove's Out" from the song of the same name by Maurice Jarre, who himself quotes the film and novel *Doctor Zhivago*; the "swoon" and the production of "difference" that poetry does together with “There is no document of civilization / that is not at the same time a / document of barbarism” by the philosophers Jacques Derrida and Walter Benjamin, respectively, in “The Klupzy Girl,” which acts as the distorted mirror of “La belle dame sans merci,” a poem where John Keats loses his identity; “But he has forced us to compel this offer; / it comes from policy not love” by the playwright William Shakespeare in “Dysraphism”; “Who’s on first?” by the humorists Abbott and Costello in “Whose Language”; “Take a Chisel to Write” by the poet Basil Bunting in “Of Time and the Line”; “She wore blue velvet but” by singer Bobby Vinton and David Lynch’s film, plus sayings, a line from the lullaby “To Market, to Market,” and a stanza from Bob Dylan’s “Knockin’ on Heaven’s Door” altered by adjacent terms in “The Lives of the Toll Takers”; the caricature of the prayer “Jesus Loves Me” in “The Boy Soprano”; the title “In a Restless World Like This Is” from the song “When I Fall in Love,” made popular by Nat King Cole and Celine Dion; “The lone and level sands stretch far away” by the poet Percy Bysshe Shelley in “Report from Liberty Street”; “news that stays news” by Ezra Pound in “War Stories”; and “Wandering Jew or Nomad” by the poet Robin Blaser in “Recalculating.”

Linked to them, all dialogue is possible, while many of the phrases that seem to be quotes, either because they are in quotation marks or because they perform as aphorisms, are by Bernstein himself, playing once again with the idea of being scattered in the collective subject. Thus, in order to effectively refer to copyright in “The Lives of Toll Takers,” he plagiarizes without warning a verse from his own “Dysraphism” with a democratizing twist: “steal” instead of the previous “spend,” and another from “The Klupzy Girl” with “spoon” for “swoon”; just as in “Substance Abuse” he replaces with “I feel” the previous “I pretend” from “Ballet Russe.” He does this when he is not bothering his masters, messing up the maxims “Lower limit speech / upper limit music” by Louis Zukofsky and “form is never more than an extension of content” by Robert Creeley, continuing then with a commonplace of male chauvinism. Because apart from being Marxist, the L=A=N=G=U=A=G=E movement is feminist and denounces the “phallocentric syntax” even of avant-garde poets like Charles Olson, whose stance against the speaker’s ego was, however, an ascendant for Bernstein.

After his first poetic phase, he began to publish collections of essays, which could hardly be distinguished from his poetry, both in form and content, if it is suitable to make this difference here. He points out that language is not neutral, nor is only the material for writing, but also the material for thought, which is intrinsically linked to it. He considers that the measure of poetry is music, while poetics is the extension of it by other means, as it is of politics, among various creations of concepts, which in Gilles Deleuze's demand would be nothing other than the pursuit of philosophy. This is not surprising, given the union, perhaps inevitable, between philosophy and poetry, despite Plato's first break reimposed by the alleged end of the "poets' era." According to Martin Heidegger, that era began with Friedrich Hölderlin, and it was characterized for founding nations and exploring the human being, among other essential matters, in which poetry would have replaced philosophy that at the time was a captive of science and politics, due to positivism and Marxism. Alain Badiou insists on the separation and wonders what space is left for the poem without its myth of truth, other than falling back on aesthetics alone. Bernstein's poetry assumes this operative distance but solves it internally, stripping the poem not of its philosophical pretensions but of its seductive features that tend toward the authority without argument that Plato, Heidegger, and Badiou feared. Bernstein asks in "My Life as a Monad": "Is it a possible danger that philosophy will take over the poetry, could it, & if it could would that be a bad thing?"

In 1987, he published the essay "Artifice of Absorption," considered a manifesto of Language poetry. His book of poems *The Sophist*, from the same year, includes some of his main poetic works, such as "Dysraphism," an illness in which the root is sewing, he explains in a note, a root shared with rhapsody, then, a sum of sewn songs. This book is related to the long discursive breath of *Dark City*, which includes poems with incrustations ranging from the annoyances of computing to enlightening maxims, astutely analyzing the current state of poetry. Between the two volumes he published the aforementioned *Rough Trades*, which focuses on the same subject with a different strategy: the containment of some of his most relevant poems, such as "Whose Language" and "The Kiwi Bird in the Kiwi Tree." This volume marks new experiments based on the image, incorporating more humor, through schemes used by comedians that he even names in the subtle biography of "Of Time and the Line." In a way, this is anticipated by the parody of *The Nude Formalism* that, like other of his chapbooks, is illustrated by his wife Susan Bee.

Bernstein bids farewell to the nineties with the union in a single book of essays and emblematic poems such as "A Defence of Poetry," in which the profuse typing errors do not hide the ferocious response to the nonsense that would command proposals like his; the letter "Dear Mr. Fanelli," addressed to a subway station manager, and "This Line." *My Way: Speeches and Poems* is the title of the work.

Increasingly tighter in its presentation, Charles Bernstein's poetry in the last decade does not abandon the multiple reference vectors of each word. He continues to oppose cultural and linguistic norms, but with a greater commitment, according to his own words, to exchange, interaction, communication, and community. Criticism of the dominant culture in *Residual Rubbernecking* operates from an unconscious made explicit by the rhyme in the irreverent *With Strings*, which follows it. The book *World on Fire* includes the sonnet "In a Restless World Like This Is" that can be heard not only in Bernstein's reading but as the basis for an interesting discussion among the poets Al Filreis, Marcella Durand, Eli Goldblatt, and Hank Lazer on the Poetry Foundation website. The three sides of time—past, present, and future—derive toward a perhaps tricky ending like that of Robert Frost in his most quoted poem, since for Bernstein the direction chosen is that of the poem, and he acknowledges that "As far as you go / In one direction, all the further you'll / Have to go on before the way back has / Become totally indivisible." This is why the apparent transparency of his ultimate poetry should not be taken lightly, for as Jason Guriel rightly points out about the poem "Castor Oil," the speaker in quartets, the exaggerated alliterations, and the hackneyed figures should be read as a joke; for this is indicated, moreover, by its laxative title. What happens is that in Bernstein the conventional poetic tone works through a beautiful strangeness, and the warning that he is probably pulling our leg every time he seems legible or uses traditional artifacts such as rhyme does not make our defense any easier.

Only the moving account of the moments following the attack on the Twin Towers, "Report from Liberty Street," interrupts Bernstein's ironic continuum which has since then been characterized by the growing presence of "real" violence, as in the extensive *Girly Man*, which, like its successors *Recalculating* and *Near/Miss*, includes dozens of poems which have appeared in chapbooks and magazines. The latest texts in this anthology operate, to a large extent, as a poetic synthesis of this period, compiling many of its mechanisms in prose and of their unfulfilled desires, not without folds.

Selection

I chose the poems for the first edition of *Blanco inmóvil*, in the first place, from *All the Whiskey in Heaven*, an anthology that Bernstein himself made for Farrar, Straus and Giroux in 2010. I picked thirty-one poems by taste and then by relevance, so that none of the most widely read and discussed poems were missing, which made this sample larger than my original approach.

Being this was the first book of his poetry in Spanish, I wanted it to include his most dissimilar aspects. To this end, I incorporated at least one poem from each of his twenty-eight autonomous publications, whether in book or chapbook format, with *Blanco inmóvil* being the first attempt of this kind in any language. These criteria guided most of the remaining nineteen poems, in which I allowed for requests from friends, and among which there are some that anticipate conceptual poetry, since the act of writing them—the idea—is at the center, as is the case with *Veil*, while others show themes and forms that are unusual for Bernstein, such as the errors of distance tourism in the objectivist "New York 747 Sonnette." Finally, in 2013, after the publication of *All the Whiskey in Heaven*, he presented a new book of poems, *Recalculating*, from which I incorporated five texts that I believe broaden the possible interpretations of his work. For this 2018 edition, I have added a poem from *Girly Man*, which makes for five selections from that work, and another three subsequent to the first publication of *Blanco inmóvil*: one from *Pitch of Poetry* from 2016 and two from *Near/Miss* that appeared in the United States a month after this book.

The most recent anthologies of American experimental poetry do not repeat any of the many poems they selected from Bernstein, which shows the divergences that exist on where to focus his importance. Thus, early on I decided to include the seven poems that Paul Hoover took for his indispensable *Postmodern American Poetry: A Norton Anthology* ("The Klupzy Girl," "Dysraphism," "Whose Language," "Virtual Reality," "A Defence of Poetry," "This Line," and "Castor Oil"), as well as the other eight ("Ballet ruse," "Autonomy Is Jeopardy," "Precisely and Moreover," "Of Time and the Line," "Under the Pink Tent," "Social Pork," "every lake . . . ," and "All the Whiskey in Heaven") chosen by Steven Gould Axelrod, Camille Roman, and Thomas Travisano in *The New Anthology of American Poetry: Vol. III: Postmodernisms 1950–Present*. Edited in 2013 and 2012, respectively, these compilations are subsequent to *All the Whiskey in Heaven*, from which the former extracted every text, and the latter only half. Both anthologies share with the internet sites where readers upload their favorite poems—which I also took as a basis for this selection—the preference for the last phase of Bernstein's poetry, leaving a gap with respect to the years when he edited *L=A=N=G=U=A=G=E* magazine and published one or two annual booklets, now downloadable for free.

The decision to represent these conceptual works is not easy for an anthology, since in books like *Parsing*, only the last two poems have a title and an entity distinguishable from the whole. In it, Bernstein's exploration goes from the limited possibilities of the expression of feelings by a first person, in each sentence equated to a verse in the first half "Sentences," to the destruction of both in the second, "Parsing," which moreover begins in the second person. In this case, I opted for the power of a fragment that, because of the diagramming, enjoys independence in the original. The same happens with *The Occurrence of Tune*, in which one of Susan Bee's photos in the original book cuts a fragment in the poem that seemed suitable for me to translate.

Along with the extensive prologue and selection by Hoover, particularly useful for this selection was that of Loss Pequeño Glazier for *Dictionary of Literary Biography, Volume 169: American Poets Since World War II, Fifth Series*. I thus included the poems that he considers to be points of reference in Bernstein's work and which, despite appearing in *All the Whiskey in Heaven*, have not captured as much attention as the poems mentioned above. He contextualizes the collaborations of *Legend*, from which I took its only individual poem "My Life as a Monad," and *The Nude Formalism*, from which I picked two poems as funny as they are unknown, "Fragments from the Seventeenth Manifesto of Nude Formalism" and "No Way." I continued the revision of anthologies less focused on experimental poetry, but in them I only found the same poems, for example "Of Time and the Line" in *The Giant Book of Poetry* by William H. Roetzheim. The other inexhaustible sources of Bernstein's materials are the video and audio files available on the web. Thus, I discovered a Spanish version of "Dear Mr. Fanelli," by Jorge Perednik, with which I compared mine and to whom I owe the translation of "where we're / headed" that I hope is, more or less, in the same direction.

The order in *Blanco inmóvil* is chronological according to the publishing year, and, in cases where I included more than one poem from each book, I followed the correlation in which the poems appear in it. The exception is *Veil*, written in 1976 and published only in 1987. In the last decade, Bernstein has differentiated the dates of writing from those of publication when the content has been related to contingent events. It is worth mentioning here that *Let's Just Say* and *Some of These Daze* were written in 2001 and *World on Fire* in 2002, while "New York 747 Sonnette" was written in 1993.

Translation

The critic Marjorie Perloff points out that the poem "Dysraphism" playfully exploits "rhetorical figures as pun, anaphora, epiphora, metathesis, epigram, anagram, and neologism to create a seamless web of reconstituted words." It is not an exaggeration to extend this observation to a substantial part of Bernstein's work and, incidentally, to this translation, which attempts to reproduce them. The exercise consisted in transferring a new language into an old one so that it would also become new. Furthermore, and unlike Spanish, in English it is natural for verbs to act as nouns and vice versa without changing a single letter, even as adjectives, a license that Bernstein usually uses. Some word games were lost, therefore, and I trust that the responsibility is at least shared between the limits of Spanish and mine.

Bernstein resorts to polysemic terms from which he ventures ambiguous interpretations by multiplying them with the other terms around. I tried to keep the breadth of probabilities, even adding some when it seemed pertinent. The first time I asked the author if he meant one thing or the other in a verse was for "hankering after frozen (prose) ambiance / (ambivalence)." He answered "both," and on top of that he gave me two more meanings. To these four possibilities he consciously offered, he built on a couple of definitions, as he told me how interested he was in keeping my additions, together with certain alliterations and forced errors from the original. Of course, I didn't ask him again until I had finished a full version of the book. It was clear to me then that I could foresee only a part of all the tricky variables at stake.

Bernstein presents polysemous situations not only on the basis of each written word but also on the basis of those that are not and tend to be read in a row. In some cases, I had to slightly alter the meaning to maintain this intention. It happens, for example, in the strange syntax of "When in tents or families in comparative"—which in "The Klupzy Girl" is part of a series of false meanings or at least connectors, an effect that I want to reproduce in Spanish—in which "in tents" literally means "en carpas," but it is read as "intents" (purposes), which is outside its semantic field. In my translation "Cuando en tiendas o familias en comparada," although the literal tents are read in "tiendas," the shift toward the possible image of commercial tents (shops) seems justified to me in order to preserve the double reading in which what is not there, "entiendas" (you understand), is what is read, out of habit. A political duty of poetry is to notice it, denote it, and, case by case, displace it. Unfortunately, there were cases where this was not possible, as with "common fork," which in English immediately evokes the cliché "common folk" and—since the original poem is called "Social Pork"—"common pork," which would have successfully referred to "common people," but which has nothing to do with the fork that is actually written there.

Anyway, there were a few exceptions where I had to choose one or the other meaning. For example, there is no word in Spanish to convey more than one out of five meanings allowed by the context of "draft" in "Matters of Policy." In "Virtual Reality," I translated "testiness / (testimony)" as "testarudez / (testimonio)," aware that the former means (Bernstein would never use that word for this, he would perhaps say "produces") more precisely "irritability" but due to the slight change of meaning it holds a more relevant effect: the intuitive relationship of "testarudez" (stubbornness) with "testimonio," because of its sound assimilation or, also in Bernstein's terms, its adjacency. The universe of boredom over the absurdity of family holidays is transmitted with both concepts, while the words give an account of a universe of their own, alien to their references, as the author prefers. It is extremely interesting to compare the strategies of this poem with those of Philip Larkin's "To the Sea," in order to encompass the same thematic sensation.

I believe that there were fewer cases in which the idioms and set phrases did not find a literal or figurative channel in Spanish, such as "No / pudiste escapar de donde / las papas queman" for "You / couldn't find your way / out of a blanched potato." The preference in such situations was to preserve the image and the concept, so that the latter did not lose materiality, as in "Nutshells," which I translated as "Resúmenes, cáscaras de nuez" (Summaries, nutshells). Since Bernstein works with the commonplaces of the language of power, and this is exercised worldwide from his own language, country, and even city, it is not surprising that in the translation we find speeches that we have already heard in Spanish from our local politicians, businessmen, and media.

Bernstein also invents words, sometimes writing outside the language's borders. Rarely do the words he uses mean what we normally use them for. He bends them, he makes them do. I replicated the use of neologisms and the widespread possibility in English and in other Germanic languages of joining words, as well as asymmetries such as adjectives in the singular form for plural nouns. Similarly, I maintained the deliberate misprints and omitted the articles and prepositions that the author omitted, but only in the cases where English would have forced its use. In short, what is rare in the original is also rare in the Spanish version.

On the other hand, in the poems in which the author used a classic English foot, I replicated the gesture with the Spanish meter. But Bernstein also plays here on several levels and, once we have discovered the sonnet without strophes or rhyme, he hides it again by modifying verse by verse the feet as one gets used to them. That is to say, he changes the internal accents, generating dissonances that even in a purely rhythmic plane call us to remove the cobwebs of what we believe to be poetry in the devalued territory of classical verse. I intend to produce an equivalent effect in the Spanish version. Thus, for example, in "Stove's Out," translated into eneasyllables and hendecasyllables, I opted for a false beginning like Bernstein's, accentuating the fifth syllable in the first four verses—which gives a coherent rhythm only to them—and adding an accent in the eighth syllable in the next three verses until the ear is already given over to the best-known territory of classical verse, in which I translated the rest of the poem except for the word that "arrests" it. The break occurs, as in English, with the syntagma "En suma" (Altogether). Is this forced? No, it responds to certain "natural" ways of saying what the original evokes.

In other poems of compositional formality, of the style of "In a Restless World Like This Is," Bernstein favors different aspects of language without altering the rhythmic pattern nor the presentation, amplification, and reflection that breaks what has been exposed into an emotional conclusion, typical of each strophe of the sonnet. In them I was faithful in converting the five iambic feet adopted by the Anglo-Saxon tradition into the hendecasyllables accented in the fourth and eighth syllables or in the sixth, with which the Spanish made it its own from the fifteenth century to the present day.

Of course, there are poems translated into free verse, starting with those that do not even have verses and those with loose breathing, which through variations become sustained, in some long poems such as "Matters of Policy." In these cases, the reference followed was their orality in audio files. The above does not imply neglecting the changes in the speed of poems as long as "Standing Target," which I translated first in meter, accumulating material in the manner of a flood toward free verse, and "Substance Abuse," which, although it varies its internal accentuations according to the same breath, I translated fully in meter, which I think favors its personal tone.

In general, where there is rhyme, alliteration, or cacophony in the original, there is also in the translation, with slight adaptations of the content, because when Bernstein uses them, he makes this same adaptation, typical of the relationship of rhyme with the unconscious. Like the other factors mentioned, I considered it as a principle and therefore weighed it against the others case by case. In "shellacked reminisces, sheets of firmness, straight grapefruit & mocks & splits, pity, mercy" in "My Life as a Monad," for example, the alliterations generate a meaning apart from the statement, so that the "sheets" can be felt retroactively in "shellacked," which is an old union between that word and "lacked." In Spanish, we don't have that junction nor that sound, which seems to call us to silence, but another alliteration can be represented, and with it the retroactive effect, by way of sound, with "láminas" (sheets) and "lacadas" (lacquered) and making "reminiscencias" (reminisces) rhyme with "firmeza" (firmness). The apparently arbitrary enumeration that follows—with a rhythm marked by monosyllables that in Spanish require several more sounds—can be tied in another way, in this case, by new alliterations among its literal translating options: "pomelo & parodias & partes, pena, piedad." Similar mechanisms of displacement between poetic figures of each language with the aim of replicating the sound and semantic effects of the original, including its extended metaphors, can be found in many of these versions. In most cases, it was unnecessary to change the figure but only the mother sound, as in the case of the alliteration and rhyme present in "Trina, topa, troca" with respect to the verse "Swish, swash, swap," and in a large part of the poem "Dysraphism," which, according to some critics, consecrates the sound adjacency in Bernstein's project.

Does all this seem too cerebral for poetry? Yes, it does. Then Bernstein makes people laugh and also get excited. Categorically. I was concerned about that happening in Spanish too. I imagine that, aware of these difficulties, perhaps complicit in the delay in the availability of his poetry in our language, the author wrote me to use his poems only as a springboard for my own versions. I did not obey him, like a dog that is taken off its leash and returns home alone. To an increasingly wider home.

Finally, I thank Charles Bernstein for yielding his author's rights to his extraordinary poetry and for responding immediately to each of my requests, and Fernanda Trías and Mary Ellen Stitt for the effort invested in their lucid observations of the first version. Except for "The Measure," "Whose Language," "Virtual Reality," and "War Stories" read by the author at Texas A&M during April 2013, and "The Beauty of Useless Things: A Kantian Tale," "Aneasthetics," "The Lie of Art," and "Wild Turning," which I sent for the anthology *Between the Breath and the Abyss: Poetics on Beauty* in

October 2016, which I include for the first time in *Blanco inmóvil*, this book was built entirely in the second halves of June and July 2013, in a small apartment in Queens, New York. That is, in prose you start with the world / and find the words to match; in poetry you start / with the words and find the world in them.

Bail Out Poetry

Abigail Lang

This piece was originally written in French and meant to introduce Charles Bernstein's poetics to a French audience. It was published as an afterword to *Renflouer la poésie* (Joca Seria, 2019), a selection of poems which I translated over the years, often on the occasion of poetry readings Bernstein gave in France. The task I set myself was to address the twin economic and nautical senses of the title Charles suggested for the collection ("Poetry Bailout") and to nod at the flamboyant cover Susan Bee provided for it (*Jacob's Ladder*, 2019). More generally I also wanted to renew the view that the French audience might hold of his work by focusing on his recent poetry and poetics.

Though Bernstein's three perfectly bound volumes published in French all came out over the past decade,[1] his work has been appearing in maga-

1. Before *Renflouer la poésie*, Olivier Brossard's *collection américaine* at Joca Seria published *Pied Bot* (2012), translated by Martin Richet with an afterword by Jean-Marie Gleize, also featured in this issue, and the Algerian publisher Apic published *Pour ainsi dire* (2019), translated by Habib Tengour, with an introduction by Pierre Joris.

boundary 2 48:4 (2021) DOI 10.1215/01903659-9382187

zines, anthologies, and chapbooks since the early 1980s. The publications that shaped his French reception would have to be the 1981 issue of the magazine *Change*, which first introduced Language poetry to the French audience, and the 1986 *21+1 poètes américains d'aujourd'hui* bilingual anthology edited by Emmanuel Hocquard and Claude Royet-Journoud, which offered a French take on Language poetry.[2] Though not a publication, the 1989 Royaumont conference on the Objectivist poets, at which Bernstein gave a salient talk on Charles Reznikoff, constitutes a third defining moment for his initial French reception (see Lang 2016b). Over the years, Bernstein was regularly invited to France, notably to the Fondation Royaumont, where his work was translated collaboratively (see Bernstein 1995; Lang 2016a). This experience possibly furthered his own already experimental approach to translation, substantiated in his translations of French poets Anne-Marie Albiach and Olivier Cadiot (Bernstein 1994; Cadiot 1990). In turn, Bernstein invited several French poets to SUNY–Buffalo. A Francophile, Bernstein appears less indebted to French theory than many Language poets have been and more invested in French poetry and poetics. As for many US poets before him, going back to Whitman, France appears as the Cockaigne of intellectualism, the land of unabashed aestheticism conferring the *grande permission*—not to embrace art for art's sake but to cultivate the *uses* of aesthetics.

Bail Out Poetry

a scale of values "that is not of this world"
—Simone Weil, *Oppression et Liberté*

Does that mean poetry has gone bankrupt? This is the claim of those who, in France as in the United States, attribute the general public's disaffection with poetry to modernism and its "excesses": all forms fostered by the fundamentally materialistic avant-garde and its techniques (collage, montage, orchestral use of the page, performance, etc.). In the poem that gives the book its title ("Poetry Bailout"), these "cultural leaders" ventriloquize Bernstein, calling for a massive bailout of poetry to restore readers' confidence and castigating the neglect of writing practices and the inordi-

2. *Change* n° 41, *L'Espace Amérique* (March 1981), reissued in *Change numérique* (Dijon: Presses du réel, 2016); *21+1 poètes américains d'aujourd'hui*, ed. Emmanuel Hocquard and Claude Royet-Journoud (Montpellier: Delta, 1986).

nate risks that poets have taken since modernism to compose illiquid, insolvent, and troubled poems—in other words, subprime poems.[3]

A founding figure of Language poetry, a hardened sophist, a recidivist of the swerve and the smeared, a eulogist of the gaffe and limp, Charles Bernstein understands he contributed heavily to poetry's discredit. Today, therefore, he abjures his past wanderings before the Inquisitors General against heretical depravity throughout the entire Poetry Commonwealth. In "Recantorium," a long retraction modeled on Galileo's before the Inquisition, but also reminiscent of the puritan confession and the Moscow trials, Bernstein performs a jubilant penance, disavowing his poetics as he wallows in it, all the while poking fun at the Inquisitors and all those who present poetry as "the Timeless Expression of Universal Human Feeling (UHF)." It is an institutional battle. Under benign exteriors, the proponents of "Official Verse Culture," as Bernstein calls them, are performing a *coup de force*: by invoking common sense and universality, they abstract themselves from the polemical field where poetics clash and values are established. Instead of the ahistorical humanism and essentialism of much mainstream poetry, Bernstein proposes a pragmatic poetics based on context and usage. He opposes its anti-intellectualism with a scholarly though unacademic critique mustering all the resources of contemporary culture. (Bernstein equally quotes Cavell and Seinfeld, Goffman and Batman, Karl and Groucho Marx.) And instead of a poetry of nostalgia and denial, Bernstein composes poems of unbridled verbal imagination, formally inventive and terribly seductive.

In the 1970s, Language poets emphasized the social dimension of poetry. Born during or shortly after World War II, involved in the countercultural movements that opposed the Vietnam War and promoted minority rights, Language poets were acutely aware of the ideological dimension of language and the deviation to which it was being subjected by political power, the military-industrial complex, and the consumer society. They felt the abuse of language was a highly effective way of managing daily life. Poetry, the art of language par excellence, appeared as a privileged domain to study how meaning is constituted, both at the level of grammar and discourse. Their poetry sought to show the socially constructed character of meaning. Such a poetics unsurprisingly broke with the vision of the solitary poet and the cultivation of a lyrical voice of one's own. Language poets favored collaboration and created their own production and distribution circuits, which became forums for collective reflection: magazines, small

3. Both "Poetry Bailout" and "Recantorium" appear in Bernstein 2011.

presses, reading and talk series. In 1978, Charles Bernstein and Bruce Andrews founded *L=A=N=G=U=A=G=E* magazine, which gave its name to the movement. The journal published texts questioning the boundary between poetry and poetics and allowed for a wider diffusion of exchanges that had begun in private correspondences. Since then, Bernstein has sought to broaden the circles of reflection and the channels of dissemination. In 1990, with Robert Creeley (and soon with Susan Howe, as well), he created the Poetics Program at SUNY–Buffalo, which trained many poets. At a time when creative writing departments were downplaying the teaching of literary tradition and critical thinking in favor of the production of personal writing, and when many literature departments were abandoning the study of literary texts in favor of theory and cultural studies, the Poetics Program focused on poetics, encouraging the critical reading of literature and philosophy. Under Bernstein's guidance, the Poetics Program pioneered the use of digital technology in the service of poetry. With Loss Pequeño Glazier, Bernstein created a major poetry website and archive, the Electronic Poetry Center, which offered bibliographies, digitized works, audio resources, and links. In 2004, with Al Filreis, he founded PennSound, the largest online archive of recorded poetry and a model of free access: all files are downloadable to facilitate scholarly, educational, creative, and recreational uses.

PennSound is a good example of what Bernstein calls the "'negative' economy" of poetry: "if you take a sheet of plain white paper, perhaps it's worth a penny, but if you write a poem on it, it's worth nothing. It can no longer be sold. But, then again, that *nothing* is worth quite a lot. You've created negative value," Bernstein explains, quoting an anecdote recounted by James Sherry (Bernstein 2016: 205). For if poetic value is not established on the financial and moral scales that dominate US society, poetry is also not "a utopian space, without hierarchies, without power relationships":

> The symbolic exchange that takes place in the poetry polis is immensely valuable for the people involved. . . . [T]he aesthetic stakes are high—higher than in many more commercial endeavors, where aesthetics are a means to an end—and these values are measured by work produced and the value that it has for the exchange. Given the particular economy of poetry, the exchange often takes place with the cheapest possible means of reproduction, from a photocopy to a reading in a bar to a website or MP3 file. In an economy in which direct profit is not the aim, losses from the cost of reproduction are minimized in an effort of maximize exchange value. (206)

When some bemoan the marginal place of poetry in society, Bernstein chooses to rejoice: since poetry is not subject to the imperatives of mass culture, it has every reason to develop complex and nuanced discourses, to compete on the level of ideas with arguments thus maintaining or (re)inventing a democratic space. This is what Bernstein's poetics of dissensus and paradox is all about.

Poetry draws its social—or antisocial—power from the fact that "it is ceaselessly creating a scale of values 'that is not of this world,'" to quote Bernstein quoting Simone Weil in the epigraph of an early essay, "The Dollar Value of Poetry":

> Social force is bound to be accompanied by lies. That is why all that is highest in human life, every effort of thought, every effort of love, has a corrosive action on established order. Thought can just as readily, and on good grounds, be stigmatized as revolutionary on the one side, as counter-revolutionary on the other. As far as it is ceaselessly creating a scale of values "that is not of this world," it is the enemy of forces which control society. (Weil [1934] 1955: 135; Bernstein 1986: 57)

Because the limits of language draw a limit to experience, it is up to poetry to open breaches in the social order: either by decontextualizing/recontextualizing the watchwords to make them appear as such, or by intensifying the experience of reading. The value of poetry lies in this singular experience, which is worthless in the eyes of the market because it is nontransferable and cannot be generalized. (Incidentally, it is only in this specific sense that poetry can be said to be untranslatable.) This experience, says Bernstein, is always an experience of otherness: a distance to be covered. Where the commodity obligingly shines back our projections onto us, the poem often requires some effort for the encounter to take place. Bernstein's aesthetics go happily against the grain. Against bourgeois good taste, elegant design, neoliberal storytelling, and consensual hybrids, Bernstein cultivates the rebarbative form, the rhythm with a limp, the tortuous phrase, the syncretic, and the polemical/provocative. Against programmed obsolescence, a poetics of debris and hand-me-downs. Against the diktat of excellence, a poetics of bankruptcy.

And against the self-righteousness of certain poetic and academic circles, Bernstein chooses to put his foot in it and question his own complicity, to the point of discomfort. As the satirical delight of the "Recantorium" increases, so does the sense of moral superiority and self-victimization of the abjurer. Bernstein allows himself to be deliberately caught up in his machine running amok: he compromises himself with an unnecessarily hurtful metaphor for the disabled, admits half-wordedly that he is now published by one of the largest mainstream publishing houses (Farrar, Straus and Giroux), and points to the ignominy of his device when writers, scientists, and activists are being persecuted around the world. Beyond the rhetorical mastery and formal intelligence, it is the complexity and tension of the feelings involved that make "Recantorium" such a powerful piece. Bernstein claims,

> I am more interested in sensation than in feeling, if feeling is understood in a narrow sense as the expression of a limited set of predefined emotions: happiness, sadness, grief, et cetera. I don't have a feeling that I, the poet behind the words, want to convey to you the reader. The feelings emerge in the process of the poem, both in writing and in reading it. Turbulence, uncertainly, ambivalence, exhilaration, fear, loss, groundlessness, falling, guilt, error—these are a few of the overlaid feeling tones I explore. (Bernstein 2016: 221)

If Bernstein prefers affects to constituted feelings, it is again to "intensify the experience of the aesthetic" (211). No other Language poet lays such store in aesthetics, to the point of recently placing his poetics under the aegis of Poe, the herald of intensity and anti-utilitarianism in art. "*Poetry's social function* is to imagine how language works within its culture, while pursuing a critique of the culture; this suggests that poetry can be a countermeasure to the reinforcement of cultural values at the heart of both popular entertainment and consumer politics. At the same time, *poetry's aesthetic function* is to refuse even this 'value' in the pursuit of what Louis Zukofsky calls the pleasures of sight, sound, and intellect" (203–4).

To "intensify the experience of the aesthetic," Bernstein embraces discordance: "That's my obsession, to put together apparently incommensurable things that in combination take on an uncanny force" and create "unassimilable textures and experiences." "My work is bricolage. . . . I'm a pataphysician, looking for the swerve," or clinamen—or aversion (230). Favoring aversion over a clean slate, his work is very much based on convention. "As a rhetorician and a sophist, I am committed to those genre distinctions, though one genre is not subservient to the other in my queer practice" (231). In a stunning essay, serious as it is comical, Bernstein recently defined his poetics as a *pataqueric*: queer, pataphysical, and inquisitive in spirit. An aesthetic foundation, discordance is also a compositional principle. Bernstein seeks to create the maximum gap between two successive elements: tonal amplitude, hiatus of register, non sequitur, cacophony. "My approach might appeal to a reader who likes shifting surfaces and intense modulations—*vacillations*—of tone, from the dark to the comic and back again" (233). And indeed, his writing is striking in its extraordinary variety of structures and textures: litanies riveted by an anaphora, zany parables, meditative fragments, political ballads, doggerel, or echoes of famous lines; one may overhear Yeats in "Songs of the Wandering Poet" or Ashbery in the tenth stanza of "Log Rhythms." Bernstein has a knack for koans, a flair for formula and all gnomic pronouncements, but he also possesses the art of unwinding interminable meandering sentences that threaten to founder under their own weight and often make good on that threat, leaving the reader stranded and aghast. For in this poetics, difficulty is above all texture: the poet varies the gradient of opacity, from the most transparent and flat expression to the most obscure and sonorous language. And Bernstein cultivates the comic vein, so underrepresented in poetry, especially in France. His references range from variety shows and stand-up comedy—particularly Henny Youngman, the master of one-liners—to slapstick à la Jerry Lewis, whose exaggerated physical violence and awkwardness he renders by halting rhythms and a fondness for the verb *stumble*.

Discordance also governs the composition of Bernstein's books. They are neither collections organized chronologically or thematically, nor projects designed according to a preestablished procedure or plan: "My work, right from the start in the '70s has been postprocedural or postconceptual," he explains (229). Conceiving his books as Benjaminian constellations or group shows, he selects poems written over a long period of time and presenting highly diverse surfaces and arranges them to maximize contrast between two consecutive poems and increase rebound. Instead of a narrative crescendo or thematic variation, Bernstein seeks the ping-pong effect. Each new poem changes the overall context in which the next poem will be read. This is how he assembled his 2010 selection *All the Whiskey in Heaven*.

The tonal discordance takes on a pathetic resonance in the last two volumes of poetry, *Recalculating* (2013) and *Near/Miss* (2018), published after the loss of his daughter. Faithful to his poetics of usage and context, Bernstein expresses his sorrow both in oblique elegies ("Before you go") and in translations (from Reinaldo Ferreira or Goethe), in which he re-enunciates the words of another.

> Poets are fakers
> Whose faking is so real
> They even fake the pain
> They truly feel

he announces in the poem opening *Recalculating*, a translation of Pessoa's "Autopsicografia" (2013: 3). "This time it's personal": parodying the catchphrase of a blockbuster in which the hero returns with a vengeance, Bernstein's teaser highlights the personal (Bernstein 2018). If his poetry is more personal today, it is in the etymological sense of the term: masks and intermediaries multiply.

Recalculating is the message that appears on a GPS screen when the driver has taken a wrong turn and the computer recalculates the route. Bernstein modernizes the age-old image of life as navigation subject to hazards, and of the mind in the body as a captain at the helm of his ship. From Ovid's *Tristia* to Creeley's "I Know a Man," via Mallarmé's "Un coup de dés," Rimbaud's "Le Bateau ivre" or Hopkins's "The Wreck of the Deutschland," the initiatory crossing and the shipwreck (or car crash in the US), whether feared or experienced, provide opportunities to meditate on a human destiny and to put a poetics into practice. Like Ovid before him, Bernstein gives shape to the chaos that surrounds him and the feelings that grip him. Finding self-mastery in measure, he counts, allusively revisiting traditional meters or counting units ignored by English metrics: "If you lift the hood, from time to time you will see patterns in the words per line or lines per stanza, syllable counting that is ametrical, and many passages with traditional metric but right up against ones that are not" (Bernstein 2016: 220). Counting, and poetics more broadly, are not a priori theories but experiential responses to the world.

> The *art* of poetry is just as much the navigation as the boat. Which is why it's important not to valorize one side or the other, poetry or poetics. I leave theory to those far more confident than we who stumble from point to point, finding ourselves in the blank spaces in between. (205)

References

Bernstein, Charles. 1986. *Content's Dream. Essays 1975–1984*. Los Angeles: Sun & Moon Press.

———. 1994. "Work Vertical and Blank: Working around and through 'Travail Vertical et Blanc' by Anne-Marie Albiach (Spectres familiers, 1989)." *Conjunctions* 23. https://media.sas.upenn.edu/jacket2/pdf/Bernstein/Albiach-tr-Bernstien_verticalblank.pdf

———. 1995. *Un test de poésie*. Collective translation. Royaumont: Format américain.

———. 2010. *All the Whiskey in Heaven*. New York: Farrar, Straus and Giroux.

———. 2011. *Attack of the Difficult Poems*. Chicago: University of Chicago Press.

———. 2013. *Recalculating*. Chicago: University of Chicago Press.

———. 2016. *Pitch of Poetry*. Chicago: University of Chicago Press.

———. 2018. "*Near/Miss* Launches." *Jacket2*. December 1, 2018. http://jacket2.org/commentary/near-miss-launches.

Cadiot, Olivier. 1990. *Red, Green & Black*. Adapted from the French by Charles Bernstein and Olivier Cadiot. Elmwood CT: Potes & Poets Press. http://www.writing.upenn.edu/pepc/books/cadiot/rgb/index.html.

Lang, Abigail. 2016a. "Contemporary Poetry and Transatlantic Poetics at the Royaumont Translation Seminars (1983–2000)." In *Collaborative Translation: From Antiquity to the Internet*, edited by Anthony Cordingley and Céline Frigau Manning. London: Bloomsbury.

———. 2016b. "The Ongoing French Reception of the Objectivists: Transatlantic Circulation and the Vicissitudes of the New." *Transatlantica* 1. Accessed April 27, 2021. https://journals.openedition.org/transatlantica/8107.

Weil, Simone. (1934) 1955. *Oppression et Liberté*. Paris: Gallimard. http://classiques.uqac.ca/classiques/weil_simone/oppression_et_liberte/oppression_et_liberte.pdf.

Afterword to *Pied bot*

Jean-Marie Gleize

Translation with the assistance of Carol Mastrangelo Bové

What we've (so far) never seen
"let me be asked to say how I was able to produce texts so inexplicable, so obviously clear, so obvious."
—Francis Ponge

In French: *Asile*.[1] This is the first book I read by Charles Bernstein, in the series directed by Juliette Valéry, Format Américaine, its twenty-fifth volume (so small), made in May 1998 with the help of the Royaumont Foundation. What I liked were the words: "Tirage illimité" (unlimited edition). A reading, therefore delayed (*Asylum*, had been published fifteen years earlier, in New York, in 1983), of a text about which I could see well why we could wish for an "unlimited" diffusion: first, it adopted a very mobile look, blocks of statements descending on the page, more or less long lines laid on whites

Pied Bot, trans. Martin Richet, Collection Américaine (Nantes, France: Joca Seria, 2012).

1. *Asile*, trans. Paul Keineg (Marseille: Un Bureau sur L'Atlantique, 1998). This book was preceded, in the same series, in 1995, by *Un Test de Poésie* (translation by Collective à Royaumont).

boundary 2 48:4 (2021) DOI 10.1215/01903659-9382201

of uneven length on the right, on the left, text floating irregularly, neither prose nor verse, recalling some known provisions (in our modern repertoire) but with this crucial difference: the ritualized poetic motif, the essentialized landscape, the still life more or less abstract, were not at the rendezvous, which on the contrary erupted into the violence of a brutal reality (prisons, camps, barracks, asylums), a locked universe (doors, high walls, barbed wire), for: disfigurement, humiliation, dispossession, submission, "life history, photographing, weighing, fingerprinting, assigning numbers, searching. . . ." Something black like a "disease," that of a society, ours. Poetry could say (without preaching). Be cut, sharp. Politics as an autopsy.

When I first opened this book, this *Pied bot*, or rather the manuscript of its translation, randomly, the first line that jumped out to me was this (it is in quotation marks in the text): "But that wall could be said." It just so happens that for me, the wall, a wall, is an emblem for the criticism of poetry (by itself). It is against the poetic verse-image of Paul Éluard's "The earth is blue as an orange" that Claude Royet-Journoud gave, for example, a verse like "The back wall is a wall of lime," *literal*, irreducible to interpretation: a poetic of the bias of surfaces, a wall, the white of the wall, poetry and the poet brought back to the foot of the wall. It seems to me that, around the 1980s, Charles Bernstein was determined to take up the question in an equally radical or primary way: What, from the real, could not be said? Are there things that poetry does not say, know, or should and could not say?

Charles Bernstein is one of those poets that one cannot *isolate*. He's intervening. Intervention means the inclusion of a practice in a context where one works with and against others, between one and the other—some hostile, hence the necessarily polemical, offensive/defensive dimension of this kind of practice—, others on the contrary with whom one helps to shift the pieces of the game, to change the face of the territory. With whom we advance word for word. Active and fruitful intervention, in a singular and decisive way, part of a collective effort. Charles Bernstein, in this sense, "intervenes." It was in 1978 that he founded *L=A=N=G=U=A=G=E* with Bruce Andrews. And this magazine (thirteen issues until 1981)[2] was born out of the desire to continue and *share* a theoretical dialogue begun with Ron Silliman and Bruce Andrews. A "small" long-range magazine. A limited-edition magazine, intended to exert a great influence in the field of poetic experimentation in the late 1970s and early 1980s (a selection

2. The complete collection, the thirteen numbers and three supplements, is available at http://eclipsearchive.org/projects/LANGUAGE/language.html.

of critical and poetic contributions led to the publication of a book, *The L=A=N=G=U=A=G=E Book*, in 1984). For us in France, given the dates and general orientation of these texts, it is the magazine *Tel Quel* (for critical poetry and criticism of poetry, as well as the renewed attempt to think about the articulation of poetics to the political) and the collective Change (for proposals relating to the poetry of grammar and the "change" of forms), which will have locally played a similar role.[3] It is thanks to Emmanuel Hocquard (who is responsible for the *ARC*[4] readings at the Museum of Modern Art of the City of Paris from 1977), followed by his collaboration with Claude Royet-Journoud for the first anthology of American poetry in 1986, that we were able to read and hear Charles Bernstein for the first time.[5] If it is above all "American," the context in which Bernstein's poetic practice arises and fits, in continuity-contiguous with the objectivist heritage, and on a construction site opened side by side for poetry "language," extends for us to the Franco-American context: by those who, in 1973, in France, founded the small editorial structure *Orange Export Ltd*, we will have had access to these poets with whom Hocquard recognizes "many convergences of ideas and approaches to writing problems" with the French of the same generation.

Initiating, of course, this poet, grouping, eliciting. Aware that the landscape can be reshaped, that it is possible to turn weakness into strength, and that a wall could be said. The magazine is therefore one of those modest tools that can function as powerful transformer. What follows shows that Charles Bernstein, the critic and poet, will also evolve within the university institution (especially in Buffalo or Philadelphia for the most recent period). Before considering the treatment of language, the "political" or social dimension of the poetic operation lies in this inscription in a context, this ethic of

3. The two journals I have just quoted did not contribute to the disclosure of this American poetry, but the questions they asked about writing, about the primary importance of linguistics for poetics, about the meaning or ideological scope of gestures of rupture within formal and generic conventions—all this constitutes a common theoretical fund that allows the reader to consider these experimental practices as quite "contemporary" of each other.

4. *ARC* abbreviates *Animation, Research, Confrontation Literature*, a magazine published by the museum, edited by Hocquard from 1986–89.

5. *21 + 1: American Poets of Today*, chosen by Emmanuel Hocquard and Claude Royet-Journoud (Montpellier: Delta Editions, 1986). In this volume, Charles Bernstein has an excerpt from *Stigma* (Barrytown, NY: Station Hill Press, 1981), translated by Claude Richard. Bernstein also translated Claude Royet-Journoud's *"Le drap maternel" ou la restitution* as *The Maternal Drape* (Windsor, VT: Awede Press, 1984).

formal responsibility in which the practice of teaching, public interventions, acts of publication, oral or written, personal or collective, are attested to as important in the eyes of Charles Bernstein.

The two texts assembled in this volume belong to the large sequence, "L=A=N=G=U=A=G=E." The first, *Shade*, was published in 1978, the same year the magazine was founded, and happens to be the first book published by Sun and Moon Press, which would later become one of the leading publishers of radical experimentation. The second, *The Occurrence of Tune*, was published in 1981, the year the magazine published its last issue. The text, in the original edition, is accompanied by photographs by Susan Bee, Bernstein's wife. These photographs, like the discursive figuration regime, are "altered." They offer reality, a very immediate and simply decipherable reality, a blurred image, defeated, decomposed, or in the process of decomposition. These two texts are preceded here by a brief (meta)poetic fragment, a kind of "proem" first published precisely in a prefatory position for Charles Bernstein's first critical collection, entitled *Content's Dream: Essays 1975–1984* and published in 1986. This book brought together several theoretical and poetic texts, or poetic-theoretical texts published in various journals, including the magazine *L=A=N=G=U=A=G=E*, since the mid-1970s.

Pied-bot (club foot)—a word, a thing, an image, an idea? (The status or degree of figurative consistency of this "Pied-bot" are here uncertain.) This "Pied-bot" will support the ruminant, errant advance. Thus, as this preface also states, "other means are thus admitted to the circulation of the nowhere seen, everywhere disturbed." These would be the malformations and deformations of the soul, or the body (textual as well), what obliges us and frees us. We will move forward with our eyes closed for the never-before-seen, the misunderstood, the almost perceived, the not yet said.

Here, then, begins or announces a book by *nightfall*. The darkness that comes or falls, which is our environment. And our fate, *a habit*. The question would be (one way to ask it, there are others): what is obscure? Or the poem,—the agglomerate of black dust, or my gaze—it is I, reader, who makes the night fall on each of his words. Victim that I am of my "habits." The text is not waiting for me. Where I expect it, it is not, or is no longer. "Night falls" on nothing: on him I have dropped my habits, to see, to hear, to understand, my reading reflexes. Conflict.

One critique, relating to *Asylum:* "a disturbing poem." Nothing more just. These books, *Shade* and *The Occurrence of Tune*, are disturbing, because they are part of a poetic, or of an apoetic, of transgression, which they perform at the same time as they elaborate it, at the same time as they state it ("show how / it's happening / with each phrase"). Poetry and poetics, diction and theory, fiction and criticism are here inseparable (or even indistinct), as meaning and withdrawal of meaning, verse and prose, "magazine literature" or "ordinary talk" and "pure poetry," conversational and propositional, high voltage and low voltage; the apparent "illegibility" of the poem is due to these overlays, to these confusions, as well as to the systematic implementation of a problematic treatment of the expression-representation system: pronominal instability prohibits any identification of a subject (of enunciation), as well as of description, of narrative proposing no more than only pieces of a motif or situation that cannot be recomposed. Or: "no lyricism, no emotion," no emotional ease or aesthetic complacency, no arrangement of things, no obedience to what they call logic: the space of relationships constructed by the text is unpredictable, juxtaposition thwarts the hierarchical order (syntax), no submission to metric convention, prosody; a dethematized poetry, if one dares to say—where something like a song, a disillusioned singing, a more or less empty, abstract air, could return, arise, as improvisation (*occurrence* . . .), as improvised.

It's no doubt in the poem entitled "St. McC.,"[6] where there is at work in the most extreme way, one could say in the most provocative way, this poetic counterpoetic: a very large number of lines are composed only of one word, and even, for one of them, only digits, a certain number keep only a few elements of the literal skeleton of words, the scholarly lexicon and the standard lexicon flash in the night of sense ("graphemic / hinges"), some word-lines appear in capitals (TURN/DESIRE), but without being able to really detect any mallarméen "latent conductive thread," others mix lowercase and capitals ("wiTh tHaT kiNd oF"), the rule of the lines' autonomy (which accentuates the fact of incompleteness, inarticulation, the collision of vertically juxtaposed units) seems particularly striking ("so find / isn't / TURN"). To put it in the poem's own, self-descriptive terms: a series of "autonomous explosions." The difference between this and an approach to

6. The title of this poem intrigues me. Claude Royet-Journoud, with whom I shared this difficulty, provides me with the answer. It is the name of the poet Steve McCaffery. It was Jackson Mac Low who, in the issue of *The Difficulties* magazine devoted to Charles Bernstein, wrote about *Shade:* "We are then all the more surprised when we find that the next poem, 'St. McC.'—presumably named for our mutual friend Steve McCaffery, the Canadian poet and member of the vocal/verbal/musical performance group 'The Four Horsemen'—consists of disjunct lines of one to four words or word fragments."

a poem (for us, principally, that of Mallarmé) that precisely plays with typography and variable spacing to indicate a tempo (accelerations/slowing down) and that structures internal dependencies around the "common thread" is that here, in Bernstein, there is no detectable hierarchy between the elements. Capitals do not dominate the literal terrain. Total equality between units: from the letter onto the words. So that *all* the particles (the line units exploding, turn after turn), and not just those that immediately sign this direction (hinges/reconfiguration/connections/inter-propositions . . .), possess, in addition to their immediate ability to generate fictional drift, a virtually metapoetic value: from "there is" ("there's") (so obviously transversing the whole work as indicative of a project of objective seizure, without prejudging the "poetic") to the "face to a," or to the "TO FACE" that restores the *adventure* (*enterprise*) (a Rimbaldian word for us)[7] to its committed dimension, of "scratch," inscription "ethical" and polemic in the field of the institution—the poetic academic, but not only.

"here. Forget." The "Poem" (the work that opens the collection *Shade*) begins here. That is to say, by the word "here." Not elsewhere, and especially not in those elsewheres where poetry prevails. On the contrary: *here*, and the poem is made to repatriate us there. There is no elsewhere that heals here. Or, again, and it's a useful variant: elsewhere is here. *Here* is an open space, unknown, indefinite, infinite. Hence the injunction—same line, clean, in order to finish, and to begin, begin to be able to begin: "Forget." It would be too long and tedious to enumerate everything that it is necessary to forget or try to forget, in order to begin to be able to say. And first what we have been taught, inculcated, learned to think, everything that hinders us and habituates us and dresses us, including, and first, a certain way of saying, peculiar to "the" poem. One could simply argue that Charles Bernstein's poetry implies a first gesture of active oblivion. Then "sit down with it," with what's there. With "simply" what's there: this, this, "and so on." I am, understandably, very impressed by *Shade*'s incipit, the first lines of the first poem in *Shade*, and I know that the poem is about the poem, since *Poem* is its title—of what it is *to say in a poem:* it addresses me, summons me here, appeals to my capacity or my desire to forget, proposes to sit "with it" because "It's time." And it is then, only then, that everything could, or even can, engage. For example, say a wall, give the possibility that this "wall could be said." A real adventure (*enterprise*) of *transformation* ("Anyway

7. Rimbaud, in his *Illuminations*: *Dawn*: "My first adventure, in a path already gleaming" (trans. Paul Schmidt).

transform everything"), and of the objective world (words and things, language and reality), and subjectivity ("this thing inside you"), and of perceiving, looking, fantasizing, or dreaming as well, of all that falls within the powers of *desire*. All. "Transform everything." So, the poem says what it does, and does what says.

This sequence of verbs: "flutter & cling," this also: "digress, reverberate / connect, unhook," and this also: "detach, unhinge," for which subjects, which objects? Words ("this . . . set of words / all turns, all grains"), series or volley of words, (of "signs," the poem also says, or of things, because "which are the things") in roundabout movements, which, in their displacement (dance, seemingly aleatoric rotation), such as specks in space ("speck upon speck," word on word, line on line), drag or squirt the meaning, hang it, pick it up, multiply it and disseminate it. "Thought stumbles, blinded," yes, of course, but liberated too. I am not saying that this, the relationship between body and consciousness, space and meaning, the deciphering of signs, clouds, or constellations of particles, poetic commitment, and transformation, is accomplished without violence. It is no doubt "harsh" (Bernstein), "rough" (Rimbaud).

For which subjects? For which subject? Very quickly in the book, the question is settled: "Everyone has feelings. It's always the same." On the face of it, I have nothing of my own, in ownership. The unique is the same. We are all common singularities. I can always (it's endless, bottomless) declare to myself: I've done this, that (I suffered), I'll do this, that (I'll travel), I'm against this and for that (for nature, against drugs), I have opinions on this and that (the stock market, or politics, "is death"), I can confirm, even if it doesn't do much good, that this is not that ("A branch is not a root"). Under these conditions I can say that I am telling the truth and that I will tell it. But when I say "I will tell the whole truth" (as in court), or when I am aware that this truth is nothing (that tautological farce, muddy ideologeme, inconsistent biograph) or indeed that it is something else and that if I say that I will say it (all) it is that also I suppose pertinent to a proposal like (Cézanne, 1905): "I owe you the truth in painting and I'll tell it to you."

Or "in poetry." I owe you the truth in poetry and I will tell you. Literally and in every way. To this *always the same* it is possible to oppose "a proper place," one's own place: "my writing / writing / even talking like this": writing, speaking, thinking, pushing the limits of thought by working on the possibilities of language (writtenspeech [*écritparlé*]), that would be the task, which can always be called "poetry," why not? The question is asked: "It could be my own" . . . My own what? My own voice, my own writing, my *madness*. If I have something of my own, it can only be (from the point of view of the norm) my madness: "this could be sort of the / the source of my crazy hood/ness." A blind spot: *I don't know.* The experience itself is ambiguous: the experience of writing is, no doubt, less the experience of things than the experience of the emptiness between things, a *feeling of space*. It is here that Cézanne could return—who paints less apples than the space between apples, less the rock than a certain abstract structure, emptiness, and distance. But it is Stanley Kubrick who emerges (if we dare say): objects *float* "separately" in the void. They do not induce any particular affect on my part. They are detached; to which my own detachment responds: I witness this floating, it is perhaps my madness, the *source* of my madness, which gives me to write, to experience the truth of writing or the desire to write in truth: in a state that could be defined: a certain positive "indifference" to the real. A "*laissez faire.*" A way to be present to the present. And it is then, thanks to this immediate vagabond immobility, that, beyond the initial and necessary exercise of forgetting, *memory* can return and work, a memory itself capable of refreshing experience. Otherwise to give sense, *some value* for the present, to this otherwise *senseless* present.

wall," as. Again the *wall* comes back. The one that could be said. That has just been said, but the phrase that was heading toward him has moved away, effaced. The wall stays, "as." New effacement, the comparing is off base. Or it doesn't know what to be. The framing here is violent, violently sharp and subtracting, to capture only what is needed, which is necessary for the revelation of what must happen here because it will be said in a didactic parenthesis: "(it may be asked)." A wall, no doubt, incomparable. If the wall is "as," it is nothing but *like* a wall. It is even that, what it is, for this reason. What is standing here. And we understand that here, that is what separates. That? There are *them*, or *those who* . . . There is sharing of space. Just now empty (where things and words, particles of matter or sound and sense circulate) here it is cleaved, there is also *us*, or *all.* And so-called community (each one's own). Because all of this is taking place somewhere. The chair on which the poet likes to say that he is sitting doing *nothing* (when he writes) is not simply an experimental place. But a social place. And the poetic operation takes place in a society where there is something called "poverty," and something also called "*property.*" The poem writes the two words by quoting them, the first is in quotation marks, the second in italics, two words that, in real society, designate positions and maintain a relationship of reciprocal involvement. Alongside poverty, charitable practices ("bread-for-alms") . . . The question posed is a moral one. If it is possible (in connection here of the object of charity) to write "is immoral," it is because values are at stake and the object of many discourses ("duties, statements, virtues"), it is that society, unequal, conflictual, engenders exclusion. The question is in fact moral, social, and *political.* "Certain 'agitations'" cannot be ignored, even if the definition of *protest* ("to protest: is") is suspended, even if "*resists*" is said to be "*in fiction*." The question, therefore, arises, possible or impossible ("happiness?"), dependent or independent, "with others" or not. The word "socialism" crosses the stage. Poetry is concerned, visibly, with the existence of the wall.

Of course there is "emotion" (in this poetry without lyricism and emotion), "felt emotions" (see "For," which is a poem *for*, I mean the opposite of a poem against), "loves" and even love, a subject "in love 'with,'" and even "envy," and, reiterated, "need you," "you," "& me," and "we," and "some physical" (i.e., "present," "desires," "a kind of strength"), an inscription of "lack," the fact of "distance," a climate in which the call is imposed, and the fear of a kind of madness ("come / before I go crazy"). Simplicity grappling with complication (and confusion), intimacy struggling with news (or, probably "the" news, everyday mythology), interiority and effacement, de-personalization, assertive, infirmed, fragile identity at least in its kind of presence—("now, exactly, I," "again, here, I," "you?") you certainly. Enough to compose and recompose (the puzzle is at the same time a motive) a scenario, several, with, as the end of the text says here, "false starts, fresh starts."

The occurrence of . . . With each replay, therefore, a fresh start, a false start, a new beginning. There is no question of giving up. The wall, you also must cross it. Collide with it. Cross. We are familiar (I was going to write specialists) with *the notion of obstacle*. How can we not feel concerned, embarked? But all this (let's say it's a journey) starts badly, and even threatens not to start. Almost initial paralysis. It will take several beginnings for it to slip, and that something "it" can then escape, pass between the lines. For now: "*Something begins to jam me up & I know it won't be possible to pull it out*." In my dialect: "Something forces someone." What "I know" (or rather what I think I know) is first that writing is under duress, and my powerlessness. Would have to do with something that will not be named under any circumstances. And probably not, at least not first, what they call the outside world or what they also call the inner world, interiority: "*no presence, no 'things.'*" That's why, for some, it's *scary*. And how. Since we have understood that there is "*nothing left to say*." We know only too well, on this side of the Atlantic, how much poetry is a matter of *presence*, and of consideration of things. It will have to be treated differently. Take things back differently.

Let it be said. Listen to how it speaks low and fragile, possibly contradictory. Try everything to enlarge the field. Take everything into account, equally: "*radical flattening of interest*." Spread branches, brambles, knots, and "Go for it": determination and *speed* are essential here. Overcome malaise, obstacles. Don't believe too much in the boundary between the outside and the inside, the subjective and the objective. And yet these things, even if "extremely hard to locate," finally appear, and jostle: socks, cats, spaghetti, pies, hat, eggs, etc. They will never be able to invade the field. Neither plays their small role in this story (I mean function as clues or evidence; we know how it works in police series and realistic novels). For, it is understood, life goes on, and the poem is continuously connected to the frequency of life: I-you-it-she-one: I/you: "Don't say that. No. Please."; I/he: "If he wants my help let him ask for it."; "No sooner had she turned the block than it became clear . . ."; One/you: "One hears so much about you but never seeing you. . . ." Something happens, a lot of things happen. And pass. Taken. So the poem insists that it continues in the present. That everything that happens, happens in real time, in the present of writing: "Other things happening now & can't go back." In other words, what is done is done, what has been said has been said, and now it is something *else* that is being said and is happening. What the poem writes of meaning, we can only say of what carried by the current is composed and broken down into narrative, acts, events, feelings, words exchanged : "as if meaning were no more than a dancer."

Thus, I understood the writing as a *spinning*: it turns on itself, and faster and faster; and the faster it picks up the more the landscape drawn on its belly blurs and disappears; it then draws on the surface where it evolves a path that fades as it takes place, "a deconstruction of meanings, coming unglued." I will say of Bernstein's poem that it is this *spinning* dance. The meaning and the landscape, the places and things, the characters and their dialogues are written there in their effacement, are effaced, and peel themselves off by inscribing themselves there. They become, little by little, in my mind as a reader "floating substances."

It is then, of course, that I believe I hear and can respond to the central injunction: "Get back & make your own track in the unseen (so far)."

No, there is no "glyph." So, no key. "Tell you all about it" (proposed here as a writing decision) would involve getting lost in the indefinite of beginnings. What I decide to tell you is not telling, it is a story of stories, there are several leads, what happened, what happens, "what . . . will reemerge," etc. No, no glyph. Yes, a "potlatch."

At the end of the book the poem asks to "imagine a page." In fact, all of them are always imagined, built, redone, written by the reader. Irregular, like the ground, like our face. Unacceptable like this image, in the mirror, or on the screen, or on the window of the photo booth, or in the square of a Polaroid. Unknown, indecipherable. Let's take it back. Let's retouch it. Writing, reading (the one who writes and the one who reads constantly exchange their roles, love each other and kill each other), is this work of rectification of lines, of reprise, of adaptive reformulation, approximate, tense, of uncertain recomposition. And "it becomes," Bernstein writes. I becomes, I "become." For *this* and *I* to become, it must also unbecome (*deviate*): where the "readjustment" is first "punctuation," punctuation, or overdose, "unmake" (*ordinary uses*), undoing ("*borders of logic*").

Thus goes, in this poem, in this book, the desiring, deviant writing, to the *realization* of which I am, we are, very fraternally invited.

Remarks at the Retirement Celebration for Charles Bernstein

Susan Howe

Oh, dear. All I can say is to repeat Bob Perelman: All good things come to a beginning. And I can remember that, Charles, you used to say to me, bitterly—*no good deed remains unpunished*.

But what can I say? I mean, I've known the indefatigable, peripatetic poet, philosopher, essayist, performer, translator, teaching colleague, fellow difficult or eccentric poet Charles Bernstein for all my writing life. Now, admittedly, I was a late-blooming writer, having been a painter first. And he was a very early bloomer. Nevertheless, our paths crossed. I think it was in in the late 1970s.

I remember doing a WBAI interview with Bruce and Charles about *L=A=N=G=U=A=G=E* magazine. Never were there two greater mansplainers, I thought at that moment. I couldn't believe it. My little sentences, a little sliver, and then—whoo!—words, words, words, words.

Remarks made at Charles Bernstein's retirement celebration at the Kelly Writers House, University of Pennsylvania, April 4, 2019.

boundary 2 48:4 (2021) DOI 10.1215/01903659-9382215

But we've remained friends ever since. And he doesn't mansplain. It's a different thing. Anyway, I want to say that, ever since, all these years later, in my sense of what matters in my life, in my poetry and in my living—Susan Bee, Charles, Emma, and Felix were and are family to me and to both my children.

But, also, I have to say that Charles is one of the fastest email answerers. Do you know how? That's part of his generosity. He so generous. I always know I'll get something immediately back from him that's caring.

So, as you all know, the spirit of Robert Creeley hangs over our lives in a major way. We fell, both degreeless, basically, into this Poetics Program at SUNY–Buffalo that profoundly changed our lives and, I hope, students' lives. It was, I think, a great moment, a great ten years, we'll say. And so, anyway, we really did just kind of fall into it. Virgin birth, as was said.

I wonder why the name "Charles" is so omnipresent in my psyche and work. I grew up near the Charles River. One of my favorite authors as a child, and as an old woman, is Charles Dickens. Charles Olson was a major influence on my early poetry and my two prose books. They would be inconceivable without Charles Olson. Then I became obsessed with the fate of King Charles I of England, his trial and execution. Who knows? But it resulted in *A Bibliography of the King's Book, or Eikon Basilica*. Shortly after, the icon Charles Bernstein and I found ourselves at SUNY–Buffalo as full professors. Charles even had a chair in this PhD program. Later, during the Buffalo years, up popped Charles Sanders Peirce, for some inexplicable reason, resulting in another odd book, *Pierce-Arrow*. So, I thought, what better at this event for our Charles than to read from a passage from Charles Dickens's *The Personal History of David Copperfield* that I used in the *Eikon Basilica*.

So, this relates to—I don't know if you have all read *David Copperfield, but you should have*!—Mr. Dick. His full name is Richard Babley, the eccentric character who is obsessed with work on his own memorial, from which he is constantly distracted by thoughts of King Charles's head. And this sort of relates to the position we found ourselves in.

> I was going away, when he directed my attention to the kite [said David Copperfield].
>
> "What do you think of that for a kite?" he said.
>
> I answered that it was a beautiful one. I should think it must have been as much as seven feet high.

"I made it. We'll go and fly it, you and I," said Mr. Dick. "Do you see this?"

He showed me that it was covered with manuscript, very closely and laboriously written; but so plainly, that as I looked along the lines, I thought I saw some allusion to King Charles the First's head again, in one or two places.

"There's plenty of string," said Mr. Dick, "and when it flies high, it takes the facts a long way. That's my manner of diffusing 'em. I don't know where they may come down. It's according to circumstances, and the wind, and so forth; but I take my chance of that."

Anyway, thank you, beloved Charles. I don't know what you guys are going to do without him.

Your Brain on Poetry: The Making of the Poetics Program

Charles Bernstein

One: Called to Buffalo

In the fall of 1989, I was asked to teach a graduate seminar at the State University of New York at Buffalo. I had been to Buffalo a couple of times before, first, in the mid-1980s, at the invitation of Robert Creeley. I remember Bob's call, left on my answering machine at Susan Bee's and my apartment on 82nd and Amsterdam in New York. Bob apologized for not offering very much money, even though what he was offering was as much as I had ever gotten for a reading. As if I could have been a big-time fiction writer commanding thousands for an appearance. Everything about Bob's call was welcoming, charming, unassuming. His short voice mail felt like a Creeley poem: succinct and succulent.

I had first read Creeley's work in the early 1970s, after hearing Robin Blaser talk about him when Susan and I were living near Vancouver, just

Originally published in *K.O.S.H.K.O.N.O.N.G.* #14 (Paris), ed. Jean Daive, trans. Martin Richet.

boundary 2 48:4 (2021) DOI 10.1215/01903659-9382229

after we both graduated from college. At first I had a hard time with some of the poems in *For Love*, with its sometimes self-consciously anachronistic lyric address, but I fell hard for *Words*, *Pieces*, *In London*, and after a while *For Love* too. *A Quick Graph* was a model for writing essays and a fundamental resource for *L=A=N=G=U=A=G=E*, the Poetics Program, and my own quick graphs.

In 1978, I sent Bob a copy of *Shade*, and he wrote me back a postcard noting "the steady resources of the ear," which I have always loved and kept as a kind of motto. Creeley's influence is most marked, of all my books, in *Shade*, with its short lines and cracking voices. In Creeley's *Selected Letters*, there is a typo in the entry for that postcard. Creeley is quoted as writing "the steady resource of the *era*." In any case, between Creeley and me, it was and remains an era of the ear—and an error of the ear too. For when the ear strays, when ear mishears, that's poetry . . .

That first reading I gave in Buffalo, in the mid-1980s, was at the Darwin-Martin House, designed by Frank Lloyd Wright. It is one of the most beautiful buildings in Buffalo. While I was performing a rather long and convoluted poem, a glass-framed painting dropped and broke, making a loud crashing noise. The audience gasped. I went on reading, happy that the glass and I were on the same frequency.

A couple of years later, Bob and Linda Reinfeld, then a graduate student at Buffalo, asked me to talk about L=A=N=G=U=A=G=E for Bob's seminar while Bob was on a trip. I remember I spoke in Samuel Clemens Hall, Room 438, the room that would later become my office and the center of the Poetics Program. Linda went on to publish a revised version of her dissertation in 1992 as *Language Poetry: Writing as Rescue*. The book focused on Michael Palmer, Susan Howe, and me. At Buffalo, Linda worked with Henry Sussman, Neil Schmitz, and Creeley.

In 1988, I was asked by Schmitz to give the summary address at a conference he had organized called "Radical Poetries/Critical Address." Schmitz was one of the shining lights of Buffalo, as generous as he was savvy. He had written a wonderful book on Twain and Stein called *Huck and Alice: Humorous Writing in America*. Sussman, a literary theorist associated with deconstruction, and a scholar of Joyce, Benjamin, Kafka, and Hegel, gave a paper at the conference titled "Prolegomena to any Present and Future Language Poetry." I performed "Poetry and Critical Address (Process)" at the conference, making the case for the kind of poetics that would be at the heart of the Poetics Program. (The essay is included in *A Poetics*.)

In the fall of 1989, I was appointed Butler Chair Visiting Professor at Buffalo, meaning I taught one graduate seminar and one undergraduate class. All new to me. At the time, I was working as a freelance medical writer and editing *Merck Minutes*, a bimonthly publication for independent pharmacists (typical articles were on pharmacists who were still compounding their medications and nonverbal communication between pharmacists and customers). I had graduated college in 1972 but had hardly been on a college campus after that, even to do a reading.

In 1986, Wystan Curnow had invited me to the University of Auckland, in New Zealand, for a three-week visit of lectures and readings. That was a grand time, and I enjoyed every aspect of the visit but especially my conversations with Wystan, Roger Horrocks, Tony Green, and Alan Loney (who had been a particular friend of Bob's when he came to New Zealand in 1976, the trip where he met his wife, Penelope). Susan and Emma, less than a year old, came along for the trip.

Starting in January 1987, I taught a quarter (ten-week session) of undergraduate creative writing at the University of California, San Diego, at the invitation of Michel Davidson. Susan, Emma, and I lived in a small apartment in Mission Beach, a block from the ocean. Rae Armantrout, Jerry and Diane Rothenberg, and David and Ellie Antin were our company. Stephen Rodefer was midway in his three years as curator of the Archive for New Poetry. We also got a chance to get up to Los Angeles to see Douglas Messerli and Howard Fox and Marjorie and Joe Perloff. Not to mention down to Rosarito Beach in Mexico. I can still taste the mesquite-smoked quail with sides of margaritas.

I designed a course for UCSD called "Experimental Writing," which is quite similar to one I still teach. I was ideologically, temperamentally, and aesthetically opposed to traditional creative writing classes—not that I'd ever taken one! But my imagination of creative writing workshops was that they tried to help students find their voice and to clarify and simplify the emotionally expressive focus of their poems, using comments of the instructor and fellow students to improve the poem. I always say, if someone tells you to change something in a poem, then you should consider tacking in that direction: they have possibly spotted something you are doing that doesn't conform. For the incipient poet, improvement is something to be avoided at all costs, lest you become insipient. Anyway, my emotions have never been clear and simple, and what voices I channel are haunted and hardly my own. "Experimental Writing" offered a series of constraints to work off of, using found language and procedures: not necessarily an end to itself but a way to get a feel for the possibilities of verbal language and poetic construction. Those weeks in San Diego were the first time I thought that getting a teaching job might be a good idea and not just for practical reasons. I realized it was something I liked and could do pretty well. Plus, the medical writing was getting more and more tiresome. The work took very little emotional energy but was tedious. Fanny Howe was also a visiting professor of fiction writing at UCSD the same quarter as me and we talked about the appeal of our UCSD students. Fanny had done a lot more teaching than me. She soon ended up getting a tenured job at UCSD, which she kept for a few years.

In the summer of 1988, I taught a summer survey course in twentieth-century American poetry at Queens College. The class met five days a week, three hours a day, for three weeks. I picked about fifty poets for the syllabus. I loved teaching the poems, loved hearing what the students, who had hardly read any poetry before, had to say about them. Charles Molesworth, Marianne Moore's biographer, had given me that modestly paid gig, responding to a letter I wrote him. He was taking a chance, based on my essays and editing, since I had never taught a literature course before.

With the recommendation of Paul Auster, I got a job teaching one undergraduate creative writing class at Princeton, for the spring of 1989. Paul and I used to take the train from New York together; he was teaching a translation course at the same time. But while Paul would go back to New York, I headed straight for the library. That was the first time in fifteen years that I had access to a university library. So every week I carted home an armload of books.

The fall 1989 Butler Chair stint at UB was the first time I had taught a seminar for PhD students. Juliana Spahr and Elizabeth Willis were among a group of about twenty students. The graduate seminar seemed a perfect fit for me: the students kept me in top form, because if I faltered, even a bit, or lapsed into formula or evasion, I knew they would take notice. I have benefited greatly from the ferocity and generosity of the graduate students in my seminars. That first Buffalo graduate class hooked me on the seminar as form, as place for intensive, directed conversation. I asked a lot of the students in terms of reading and leaps of thinking, but it was a point of art not to waste their time. I always came into the seminar ready but not prepared, to use a phrase of Dominique Fourcade's. I brought in no notes, no prepared remarks. The essence of the seminar is improvisation and response.

I flew from LaGuardia Airport to Buffalo on Tuesdays and stayed two nights at the nearby Holiday Inn near UB's north campus in Amherst. When

I could stand that motel no longer, I switched to the nearly identical Red Roof Inn across the street. The UB campus was about ten miles from the city, so mostly I stayed in Amherst.

It's not only that I had never taught a graduate seminar before the fall of '89; I had never even attended one, with the exception of Blaser's MA Dickinson seminar, but that was a half dozen of us reading the poems, with mostly Robin and me talking.

I taught the undergraduate class Wednesdays from 2 to 4:50; it was based on what I put together for Queens and remains close to the American poetry classes I still teach, except at the time I used Richard Ellmann's *Norton Anthology of Modern Poetry*, second edition. After that I relied on anthologies I created myself. The class was titled "The Modernist Experiment in Context: 1910–1940," and I billed it this way:

> This course is an introduction to the unprecedented range of different types of poetry that emerged in the early decades of this century in the US and England. I will cover the best known "canonical" poets of the period, such as Yeats, Eliot, Frost, Pound, Williams, and Stevens; the more formally radical and experimental poets, such as Stein, HD, the Dadaists, and the Objectivists; Afro-American poetry (Langston Hughes, Claude McKay, Sterling Brown, Bessie Smith); the more conventional or popular poets (Carl Sandburg, Amy Lowell, Robert Service, Ogden Nash); as well as the political poetry of the '30s, "high" academic poetry, and other, harder to classify, directions. Sound recordings of many of the poets will be played, and there will be presentations about related visual and other arts of the period. Several visiting poets and writers will speak to the class. You will be asked to keep a notebook detailing your responses to the readings, lectures, and class discussions. A midterm and final writing project, which can be based on your notebook or be a separate paper on an assigned or approved topic, will be required.

I taught my graduate (PhD) class the next day, from 12:30 to 3:20, a pattern I would keep for the rest of my time in Buffalo. I titled it "Investigating Poetry: Topics in 20th-Century Poetry & Poetics":

> A series of interrelated topics will be the focus of wide-ranging explorations of modernist poetic practices and theories, including close readings of a broad sampling of poets, as well as philosophers and critics. Topics include: philosophy of language & the language of phi-

losophy; poetry as ideology; representation/reference/reification/refutation; language & identity; dialect/idiolect/dialogue/dialectic (global English); form's genders/gender's forms; the art of appropriation—or, what is found (in) poetry?; the politics of poetic form (programmatic structures to "anti"-structural processes); collage & its discontents; the visual representation of language (visual & concrete poetry); sound poetry; poetry and comedy; and teaching 20th-century poetry. Among the writers to be considered: Louis Althusser, Bruce Andrews, David Antin, Arakawa & Madeline Gins, John Ashbery, Walter Benjamin, Bruce Boone, Nicole Brossard, Gwendolyn Brooks, Sterling Brown, Lenny Bruce, Basil Bunting, Stanley Cavell, Hélène Cixous, James Clifford, Lucille Clifton, Clark Coolidge, Robert Creeley, Tina Darragh, Alan Davies, Ray DiPalma, Robert Duncan, Johanna Drucker, Marcel Duchamp, Paul Laurence Dunbar, Larry Eigner, Susan Howe, Langston Hughes, Veronica Forrest-Thomson, Lyn Hejinian, Luce Irigeray, June Jordon, Groucho Marx, Velimir Khlebnikov, Jackson Mac Low, Hugh MacDiarmid, Nathaniel Mackey, Bernadette Mayer, Jerome McGann, Alice Notley, Frank O'Hara, Maggie O'Sullivan, Tom Raworth, Charles Reznikoff, Laura (Riding) Jackson, Leslie Scalapino, James Schuyler, Ron Silliman, Michael Smith, Jack Spicer, Gertrude Stein, Rosmarie Waldrop, Simone Weil, Hannah Weiner, W. C. Williams, and Ludwig Wittgenstein. (List subject to change without notice!)

Around this time, Bob Creeley got promoted from the David Gray Chair of Poetry and Letters to the Samuel P. Capen Chair. UB's president, William Greiner, wanted to keep Bob from leaving the university to go to Worcester Polytechnic. Worcester Polytechnic was not a school as grand as UB, but if Bob accepted Worcester's offer, he could have returned to the Boston area, where he had grown up. As much as Bob had become an integral part of the city of Buffalo, and was one of the city's leading cultural lights, he hankered to return to New England. But Greiner made Bob an offer hard to refuse: he would remain a full professor with research and program funding, but he would have no fixed teaching responsibilities. Bob would stay in Buffalo but teach only as and if he wanted to.

Throughout the time I was at Buffalo, Bob traveled incessantly, restlessly. He was in great demand, and he enjoyed being on the road, or anyway, not staying put in Buffalo. His new job meant he was UB's ambassador. So the more he traveled, the more he was spreading the word about the university. But he was also driven. With a wife a generation younger than he was (Penelope and I are the same age), and with two young children, I figured Bob wanted to earn as much money as he could while he could, to provide for the family not just in the present but in the future. A full-time teaching schedule would have made all that traveling difficult.

When Bob was promoted to the new Capen Chair, the English Department was given a full professor "line" to hire a new Gray Chair. So my visiting semester at UB turned into an audition for the Gray Chair. For my job presentation, "Tripletalk," I performed three short essays. The only thing I remember about the job interview is that I proposed we do lectures in bars and poetry readings in lecture halls. With the Poetics Program, we achieved something like that.

As for the search, my impression is that Bob was at first thinking of old friends like Michael McClure or possibly a literary scholar like Donald Wesling. The first intimation I got that I might get the job was in a note from Tom Raworth, who told me he saw a big gray chair in my future. My support, grounded by Bob's strong backing, was from the Americanists, notably Neil Schmitz, as well as the literary theorists, notably Henry Sussman (then chair of Comparative Literature), as well as the graduate students who were in my seminar. But there was also fierce opposition. The poet Irving Feldman complained at the faculty meeting about the incompetence of my homely/homophonic translations of Apollinaire (in *Content's Dream*). Bob's close friend, Bruce Jackson, who had just finished a film about him, was so annoyed by Bob's support of me that he didn't talk to Bob for a couple of years. Bruce later told me he was mistaken, that he thought I was one of Bob's cronies (I hope I became a Creeley crony later, but at this time I was just getting to know him).

I was just forty when I got the job—the first job I had with retirement benefits and healthcare and enough income to support a family. In August of 1990, Emma (four), Susan, and I moved to Buffalo, though we kept our rent-stabilized apartment on 82nd Street.

To be continued . . .

The Epiphany of Language: The Connotation of Zen-Taoism in Charles Bernstein's Echopoetics

Yi Feng

Charles Bernstein, a prominent representative of American Language poetry, is renowned for the use of nonlogical language fragments, multilevel rhetorical superposition, parodies of classics, and the juxtaposition of postmodern elements and classical allusions in his poetry. His poems demonstrate obvious characteristics of postmodernism and poststructuralism. Bernstein's poetry intensely reflects the main characteristics of Language poetry, with a profound abstraction and a variety of forms. Bernstein studied philosophy in college, and it is essential that we understand his philosophical foundation to understand his poems well. Admittedly, Bernstein's poetics has been deeply influenced by Western philosophical thinking, especially Adorno's negative dialectics and Benjamin's philosophy

This essay is a phased result of "The Study on Charles Bernstein's Echopoetics," Ministry of Education of People's Republic of China, 2021 (Project Code: 21YJA752002), and is the adapted translation of a Chinese essay, published by *Foreign Literature Studies*, Vol. 41, no. 3, 2019.

boundary 2 48:4 (2021) DOI 10.1215/01903659-9382243

of language.[1] There are many essays that deal with this topic, so this essay is not intended to discuss this topic. Bernstein's poetry contains another profound philosophy—that is, the traditional Chinese philosophy of Taoism.

Taoist aesthetics and Zen aesthetics have clear boundaries in the history of Chinese aesthetics, but American avant-garde artists often do not make a clear distinction; this is not only due to the limitation of their misunderstanding in the context of knowledge but also because of their own major need to break through the difficulties of traditional and mainstream culture (Zhu Xuefeng 2017: 36). It is undeniable that the two schools of Zen and Taoism merged and influenced each other in the history of Chinese culture. "In the twelfth to thirteenth centuries, Zen spread to Japan. In the early twentieth century, Zen masters, such as D. T. Suzuki, introduced Zen to the United States" (Chen Sheng 2010: 162). In addition, the starting point of Eastern philosophy and Western philosophy are very distinct. For instance, Zen-Taoism emphasizes nothingness and regards unspeakable nothingness as the premise of aesthetics (Qiu Zihua and Yu Rui 2006: 101), but the starting point of traditional Western philosophy is "being," whereas "nothingness" is considered meaningless and unknowable. Heidegger and Hegel are familiar with Taoist philosophy. Hegel once called "Xuwu/虚无," namely nothingness, and "Kong/空," namely emptiness, the highest realm of Chinese philosophy (Chung-yuan 1970: 4), but in *Lectures on the History of Philosophy*, Hegel emphasized the importance of "being" and considered that "nothingness" denies the existence of the world (Mao Xuanguo 2006: 127).

In 1968, the eighteen-year-old Bernstein read Lao Tzu's *Tao Te Ching* and *I Ching*. The 1960s and the early 1970s are a dramatic and rebellious era in American history. During this period, the anti–Vietnam War movement, the women's liberation movement, and the civil rights movement were anti-mainstream and anti-traditional. John Tytell commented on the heated study of Eastern thought at the time: Americans' interest in studying the "various schools of Eastern thinking became both a means of liberating them from the thinking pattern of the West, and a way of getting them out of their predicament" (Zhang Ziqing 2009: 16). Studying the ancient philosophy of Taoism in the East and seeking inspiration from Eastern thought became an important part of the anti-traditional and anti-mainstream movement and the civil rights movements of young poets at that time. Bernstein's original intention in studying Taoist works must have originated from this. In

1. For the philosophical influence of Adorno and Benjamin on Bernstein's echopoetics, please see my essay "On Echopoetics by Language Poet Charles Bernstein," qks.jhun.edu.cn/jhxs/CN/volumn/current_abs.shtml.

addition, the well-known Zen master and poet Norman Fischer[2] was Bernstein's friend, and Hannah Weiner,[3] who was Bernstein's good friend and influenced his poetry, also had a strong interest in Zen-Taoism.

I argue that some of Bernstein's poems must be placed from the perspective of Zen-Taoism to show the extraordinary power and the magnificence of the poetry. At present, scholars at home and abroad are mostly concerned with the deconstruction of language, writing techniques, and strategies in Bernstein's Language poems, and they discuss the connection between Bernstein's poetry and Western philosophy. But there is little research on the connection between his poetry and Zen-Taoist philosophy. Zhao Yiheng points out that Jackson Mac Low, who influenced Language poetry, was himself influenced by Chinese Taoist philosophy and Zen thought, and some American Language poets also visited China to look for common ground among Chinese postmodern poets. But whether there is an echo between Language poetry and ancient Chinese poetics is still a matter of debate in academia (Zhao Yiheng 2013: 57). Studying the resonance of the poetry of Bernstein, the representative of Language poets, with Taoism has academic value and significance. Bernstein has visited China many times. He once pointed out that since the nineteenth century, Chinese classical philosophy has had a profound influence on American poetry (quoted from Nie Zhenzhao 2007: 14). In 2016, Bernstein proposed "echopoetics" in *Pitch of Poetry*, whose key motif and relation with Zen-Taoism will be discussed in the following part of this essay. On the surface, it seems far-fetched to link Bernstein's echopoetics to Zen-Taoist aesthetics. However, in an interview, Bernstein once admitted that "nothingness," or "emptiness," is a major theme of his poetics.[4] I argue that Bernstein's poetry strongly echoes the rebellious point of view of Taoist philosophy and greatly matches Taoist political aesthetics. His poetry echoes the poetics of Taoism and the beauty of "speechlessness" of Zen's "the text doesn't stand / No establishment of the words" (不立文字). Through defamiliarization, Bernstein's poetry echoes the subversive expression of Zen philoso-

2. Norman Fischer (1946–), American Zen master, poet, writer, and founder of Cao Dongzong, published more than twenty-five poetry collections and nonfiction in Buddhist magazines and poetry journals, as well as many poems, essays, and articles.

3. Hannah Weiner (1928–97), an early American language poet, published more than ten poetry collections, including *We Speak Silent* (1997) and *Silent Teachers/Remembered Sequel* (1993). See Bernstein's condolence: jacketmagazine.com/12/wein-bern.html.

4. Please refer to the interview video of Bernstein with UNESCO, Iowa Humanities Organization and National Humanities Foundation, "Writers on the Fly: Charles Bernstein," www.youtube.com/watch?v=DOqXIq7t4Ig.

phy, thereby highlighting the nature of language and forming an important part of echopoetics. This reflects the difference from traditional Western aesthetic thought. The power of Eastern philosophical Taoism hidden in echopoetics is largely ignored, and there are many misunderstandings of Bernstein's poetry. This essay attempts to explain how Bernstein applies Zen-Taoist thinking, to demonstrate the writing purpose of avant-garde Language poetry, and to reveal the poet's profound reflection and strategies toward the chaos and nihility of postmodern society.

1. Mutual Transformation between Nothingness and Truth: The Return of "Nothingness"

Bernstein states that "echopoetics is the nonlinear resonance of one motif bouncing off another within an aesthetics of constellation. . . . In other words, the echo I'm after is a blank: a shadow of an absent source" (Bernstein 2016: x). The expression of echopoetics highlights the central word *blank*. In fact, "blank" is an important motif in echopoetics, and "blank" corresponds to "nothingness" in Taoist philosophy. In Bernstein's poem "High Tide at Race Point," written for Norman Fischer, the poet uses "without/with no" to create multiple fragments of language, showing "the mutual transformation between truth and nothingness" (虚实相生) and reflecting the return of "nothingness." The poem begins as follows:

A commercial with no pitch.
A beach without sand.
A lover without a love.
A surface without an exterior.
A touch without a hand.
A protest without a cause.
A well without a bottom.
A sting without a bite.
A scream without a mouth.
A fist without a fight.
A day without an hour.
A park with no benches.
A poem without a text.
A singer with no voice.
A computer without memory.
A cabana without a beach.
A bump with no road.

A sorrow without a loss.
A goal without a purpose.
A noise without sound.
A story without a plot.
A sail without a boat.
A plane without wings.
A pen without ink.
A murder without a victim.
A sin without a sinner.
An agreement without terms.
A spice with no taste.
A gesture without motion.
A spectator without a view.
A slope without a curve.
A craving without a desire.
A volume without dimension.
A Nazi without a Jew.
A comic without a joke.
A promise without a hope. . . .
(Bernstein 2018: 19–20)

This poem juxtaposes many short fragmentations of "without." The title of the poem is a hidden pun, and the theme of the poem is implicit. What is clear is that, firstly, "Race Point" is a place of significance: located in Provincetown, Massachusetts, in the United States, it was the first stop for European immigrant pioneers who sailed on the Mayflower to come to the American continent. Hence, Race Point is a starting point for seekers of freedom and liberty. Secondly, the word *race* also means a group of people with the same ethnicity. If the racial issues that are prominent in American society are linked, and Race Point is a place that signifies freedom, the poem seems to imply a climax or high tide of racial issues or racial problems. The interpretation of "nothingness" in the poem, represented by the lines of "without," has an important relationship with the understanding of the theme implied in poetry.

Zen Master D. T. Suzuki is widely considered to be from the generation of outstanding Zen masters (Abe 1986: xv) who brought Zen philosophy to all aspects of Western society. In Suzuki's collection of works, he emphasized the wisdom of "emptiness" in Zen: "emptiness is not sheer emptiness or passivity or innocence. It is and at the same time it is not. It is being; it is becoming" (Suzuki 2016: 206). This is an enhancement of Lao Tzu's *Tao Te*

Ching: "For though all creatures under heaven are the products of Being, / Being itself is the product of Not-Being" (1997: 87). The poem depicts a collage of a surrealistic beach, showing the spirit of people and the living conditions around. First, the poem shows the passivity of "emptiness" or "nothingness." "A beach without sand" is beaten by "a surface without an exterior," and "a lover without a love" on the beach endures "a sting without a bite"; people are very depressed, but "a scream without a mouth" seems to indicate that the heart's anxiety and restlessness cannot be dispelled. It is conceivable that people feel horrified, suffocated, and helpless in this atmosphere, and the words "a singer with no voice" and "a story without a plot" show the emptiness and boredom of the human. The juxtaposition of these fragmentations, with the negative "without" as the link, forms a language game, and the "blank" is generated from it, which is absurd and abstract. Then, the two lines "a murder without a victim" and "a sin without a sinner" imply that all these seems to be related to crimes. Combining with the theme of "race" in the pun of the title, the reader can realize the poet's desire to express the absurdity of human existence and the mental state after World War II; it is difficult to heal the spiritual trauma under the haze of racism. The poem says nothing about the flames of war or genocide, but it accurately and profoundly expresses the dilemma of survival under the racial conflicts in seemingly absurd language games. The poetic playfulness is deep and vague, ambivalent and abstract, reaching its concreteness and vividness in the reader's imagination. At the same time, all these are revealed through one side of nothingness.

In *Tao Te Ching*, "the only motion is returning" (Lao Tzu 1997: 87) embodies the multiple meanings of Tao, where one is the opposite of the other and completes the other: the one is characteristic of knowledge; and the second is the "return"—the returning to the reciprocating circle of the natural way (Zhu Liangzhi 2011: 13). This poem reverses the passivity of the nothingness in the latter part, showing the power of the "returning" of Tao. As I noted, "blank," the important motif in echopoetics, corresponds to "emptiness" or "nothingness" in Taoist philosophy. Read the lines at the end of the poem:

> Blank without emptiness.
> Border without division.
> A puppet without strings.
> Compliance without criteria.
> A disappointment without an expectation.

Color without hue.
An idea without content.
Grief with no end.
(Bernstein 2018: 20)

Among them, "Blank without emptiness" is crucial. The double negative of this sentence makes the blank "turn back" against itself. Since the poem is dedicated to Zen Master Norman Fischer, we should understand it by combining the phrase "Blank without emptiness" with the "emptiness" in Zen. This poem largely reflects what Suzuki said: "emptiness is not sheer emptiness. . . . It is being; it is becoming." Then the poem begins to show a different picture from that at the beginning. The word *without* in "Border without division" intends to eliminate apartheid; *without* in "a puppet without strings" frees the puppet, making oppressed people free and independent; *without* in "Color without hue" seems to eradicate racial discrimination based on skin color. The word *end* in the ending line "grief with no end" in Chinese translation consists of a pair of contradictory characters (尽头), with one character literally meaning "end" followed by a character meaning "beginning"; but the word made of these two characters means "end." The Chinese word "尽头" (end) reflects "straight words seem crooked" (Lao Tzu 1997: 165) and "the reciprocating circle of the natural way," but the English word *end* doesn't have this connotation. However, the poet uses the word *without* to show the reciprocating reversal of truth and nothingness, and "nothingness" has a returning power. On the one hand, the last line shows the great sorrow brought about by apartheid and racial discrimination; on the other hand, as the saying goes, "at the high tide is when the tide falls"—it also embodies the poet's attempt to transcend the grievous situation. Scholar Mi Jialu discusses Zen poet Gary Snyder's "Mountains and Rivers without End" in his book, which says that "without end" is "a path without originality" and "the absence of omnipresent logos" (2017: 261). Bernstein also used "no end" to dissolve the logos of the language, and by using *no*, he tried to return to the original, which cannot be achieved anymore. In the perspective of Taoism, "no end" indicates a "return"—the returning to the reciprocating circle of the natural way, where there is no racial discrimination or segregation. Combining the puns in the title of the poem, readers can see that the whole poem was cleverly turned back, forming a pattern of "returning to the circle" and the poetic realm of "straight words seem crooked." If the poem is given a Zen-Taoist reading, the whole poem becomes the tide of nothingness in Taoism, constantly rising to try to reach the climax, the truth.

In addition, reflecting the turning power of the "nothingness" in the Zen-Taoism, the poem also clearly embodies the way of thinking of Zen. Ge Zhaoguang believes that Zen's way of thinking is an internally closed way of thinking characterized by the reciprocal derivation of intuition and inward inspection. Its core is the "inner heart's liberation," and its way of inspecting objective things is intuitive observation, and its imaginary association is irrational in a leaping manner but not logical (Ge Zhaoguang 1985: 148). Obviously, this poem seeks the "inner heart's liberation," and the nonlogical verse leaps and tries to transcend sorrow, so as to achieve the effect that the sorrow is purified in the circle of "nothingness."

2. The Poetics of "Speechlessness"

Taoist philosophy emphasizes the impermanence of all things, highlights the chaos and the indescribability of Tao/the Way, and claims the limitations of language earlier than the West. Ge Zhaoguang thinks that the "Tao" in Lao Tzu's and Chuang Tzu's[5] philosophy is "unable to be seen" and "unable to get through intentional acquiring," so the idea that "getting meanings and then forgetting words" is introduced; this is precisely because concepts, logic, and language cannot express the profound meanings of Tao/the Way, and Zen has accepted more of Lao's and Chuang's ideas, such as "The Way that can be told of is not an Unvarying Way" (3) and "words are not enough," emphasizing that "words cannot stand," which echoes Lao's and Chuang's metaphysics in thinking and language (Ge Zhaoguang 1985: 157–58, 187). Both Zen and Taoism have seen the limitation and the defection of language. Since the Wei-Jin and Southern and Northern dynasties (AD 220–AD 589), Taoist thinking has profoundly influenced the artistic thinking of Chinese scholar-officials and gradually formed the poetics of "speechlessness" in traditional Chinese aesthetics (Ge Zhaoguang 1985: 154–62). The aesthetic conception of ancient China advocated the meanings in "speechlessness" and "there is wonder in the painting of no painting" (Mao Xuanguo 2006: 128). Some of Bernstein's poems directly focus on the "blank" theme, and some poems have a lot of blank spaces inten-

5. Chuang Tzu (369 BCE–286 BCE) was a thinker, philosopher, and writer during the War Period in China. He is considered a founder of Taoism philosophy, together with Lao Tzu. His representative work is *The Chuang Tzu*, which includes his most well-known essays, "Enjoyment in Untroubled Ease," "The Adjustment of Controversies," and "Nourishing the Lord of Life."

tionally left between the lines, just like the blank space intentionally left in traditional Chinese ink paintings. The blankness makes Bernstein's poems grow the wings of blankness, graceful and light; some poems intentionally leave no text, forming a kind of anti-writing or metapoetry of "nothingness." These poems, with the theme of "nothingness," shock readers and form a confrontation with "official poetics culture,"[6] reflecting the political aesthetics of Bernstein's poetry and the innovative ideas of avant-garde poetry. One or two examples are given below for analysis.

The poem "Seldom Splendor" is a poem with a lot of blank spaces. The poem goes:

a fine cold mist descends

on Carroll Park

the swing swings empty

benches bare

(Bernstein 2018: 166)

Obviously, this poem has the charm of emptiness, and it is a poem that echoes the charm of ancient Chinese poetry. The depiction of virtual scenes, such as the depiction of sound, light and shadow, smell and other intangible things, is extremely important in ancient Chinese aesthetic and artistic works (Fan Minghua 2009: 132). This poem depicts the splendor of everyday scenes. There is no direct expression of a misty fog in this poem, but the blank spaces between the lines of the poem seems to show the concealment of a rising mist, showing the effect of the fog, from nothing to a trace. On the other hand, alliterations in both the title and the last two lines of the poem re-create a sense of ethereal atmosphere with the emptiness of the whole poem. In close reading, "descend," "empty," and "bare" seem to

6. Bernstein's criticism and dissatisfaction with the official verse culture in the United States mainly stems from the fact that it maintains the old and stiff poetics, which imprisons the writing of avant-garde poetry and the particularity of history and culture. As Bernstein points out, "Official verse culture lives by change, much as vampires live by fresh blood. Official verse culture in 2010 has adapted to many things that it repudiated twenty-five or more years ago: it is, after all, at its heart, eclectic, incorporating the good, the bad, and the ugly" and "official verse culture plays referee to a game where it validates only those following its rules, despite the fact there is more than one game being played and that each of these games has multiple sets of rules" (Bernstein 2016: 245, 246). See the interview with the *Chicago Weekly* in "Echopoetics," chap. 3 of *Pitch of Poetry*.

show the loneliness in the empty park without any people, but through the title, "Seldom Splendor," and the first line, "a fine cold mist descends," the poem also turns back and reverses that emptiness. It shows the other side of the noisy park during the daytime, revealing the splendid beauty of the empty swings and bare benches, which is often overlooked. Although no one appears in the poem, people have already merged with the scene, since the poem seems to imply that the bare benches are available for people to sit on, and the empty swings are swinging, to show that there used to be people playing on them and also that they are available. The poet and the scene become one, while the poem calls the reader to join in the splendor too. The poem transcends the daily specific scenes, reaches the internalization of the scene, and brings the reader into an infinite space and time of emptiness.

Another poem, "This Poem Intentionally Left Blank," takes the paradox of the blank as the main body of poetry and expresses the poet's reflection on the innovation of poetry. The whole poem is as follows: "This poem is intentionally left blank" (Bernstein 2010: 245). The whole poem is only one line, but it occupies one page. It seems to be an untitled poem, or a poem with no content. All the words and letters are capitalized and italicized, showing the beauty of Chuang's idea that saying no words also says something (言无言,未尝不言). In book layout, editors often indicate "This page is intentionally left blank" on the title page so readers know that the blank page isn't an error. Bernstein seems to use this to express poetics, which is anti-traditional in poetics. After reconsidering it, the concept of it and the implications are profound. The blank space of the title page is important, for it can free up open space before the beginning of the main text and easily lead out the main text. It is worth noting that editors often write on blank pages, indicating that this page is intentionally left blank, but this undoubtedly fills in the blank, forming a paradox. This paradox directly refers to the reversal of the real and the nothing and embodies the transformation of time and space between the nothing and the real. Timothy Morton believes that all poems "include the spaces in which they are written and read—blank space around and between words and silence between sounds," and this poem of Bernstein's is about this: it opens a space to give people an "aperture," "the feeling of beginning" (Morton 2010: 11). Bernstein's poem uses the aesthetics of "speechlessness" vividly to achieve the aperture. Wai-lim Yip states that Chinese poetics emphasizes the value of the aesthetics of the blank, which holds that the meaning of "saying no words" is to attach importance to the emptiness of language, that is, the unwritten void (Wai-lim Yip 2007: 57). Bernstein wants to show a blank, give poetry more free space, and allow poetry innovation and experimental writing to be triggered and released just like the main text to be drawn from the title page. The poem apparently may seem to be funny and careless with its simplicity and anti-traditional poetics, but it does not happen overnight, and it condenses Bernstein's painstaking search for experimental poetry innovation. Another poem, "Poem Loading . . . ," has only one line, "please wait," which has a similar theme to "This Poem Intentionally Left Blank" (Bernstein 2013: 12).

In addition, Bernstein's poem "Concentration (An Elegy)" is a repetition of repressed language, highlighting the silent Other in official history (Bernstein 2018: 102). The writing of the silent Other is obviously often regarded as a topic of Western deconstruction. From the perspective of Taoist thinking, the writing of the Other in Bernstein's poetry has a close connection with Taoist spirit because Taoism advocates "dismantl[ing] the Tao (of kingdom, and of heaven) and the various constructions of language under the feudal system, so that other memories of the repressed, estranged, and isolated natural bodies can be recovered, leading to the recovery of overall humanity and overall life" (Wai-lim Yip 2002: 1–2). Wai-lim Yip thinks that "the Taoist spirit is both aesthetic and political" and that "Taoism virtually provides another kind of practice of language in which the frame of language tyranny is dismantled" (1–2). "Concentration (An Elegy)" is written against a decree of the Polish government, which strictly prohibits the use of the words "Polish concentration camps" to refer to Auschwitz and other notorious German concentration camps during World War II. As we know, millions of Jews were killed at places such as Auschwitz during World War II, so they are sometimes called "Polish concentration camps," even though they were run by the Nazis. This poem is a revolt against official attempts to forget history. Luo Lianggong argues that Bernstein's poetics is the product of the fusion of political and aesthetic consciousness (2013: 94). The forbidden and unspeakable language is that of the oppressed and the silent, which is superimposed in the poetry. Like dripping tears of words, the elegy is clearly written for the Jewish compatriots who died in the Holocaust, and it confronts the authoritative official decree. The spirit of this poem closely fits the spiritual direction of Taoist philosophy, dismantling the law of the authority, and reflects the political aesthetics of echopoetics.

3. The Epiphany of Language in Echopoetics

Zen-Taoist aesthetics uses the "strike the stereotypes with defamiliarization" (以异击常) technique, which is resonant with the "defamiliarization" writing technique in Bernstein's poetry. Hu Min believes that to use "defamiliarization" in language is a common aesthetic pursuit among Chinese literati in the past dynasties of ancient China, and Chinese Zen poetry has a unique system of defamiliarization (2008: 64). Defamiliarization, as a writing technique of Western literature, began in the Russian formalist movement that emerged in the 1910s. It aims to prolong the aesthetic experience by adopting the defamiliarization method and gaining a new understanding of everyday phenomena and stereotypical things. The Russian formalist Victor Shklovsky named this literary and artistic expression much later than Zen-Taoists' practice of it. The Tang dynasty painter Wang Wei's painting "Yuan An Sleeping in a Snowy Night" is a classic example of defamiliarization in art. The plantain tree in the snow is a serious misalignment of time and space, far from the commonly seen and nature, but this defamiliarized depiction reveals the spiritual realm of Yuan An (Zhang Jiemo 1998: 60–61). In addition, the Taoist ideas that emerged during the Wei-Jin and Southern and Northern dynasties used the subversive language strategy of "strike stereotypes with defamiliarization" to release new ideas, first trying to confuse people but then later making them realize the truth in it. The "different/idiosyncratic words and deeds" (异言异行) conducted by Chuang Tzu have played a greater role in Zen (Wai-lim Yip 2007: 120–22). As Wai-lim Yip points out, "The most important spiritual direction of Taoism is that we must always question our internalized regular principles" so that we can live and escape from the restriction of imprisonment (2002: 2). In addition, one of the important strategies for Zen is to subvert the language of a "dead statement" by using a "living statement," and the difference between a "living statement" and a "dead statement" is that a "living statement" can make the language not fail. In other words, a "living statement" is an open-ended sentence that doesn't give closure to its meaning but rather keeps the meaning unrestrained and open. This new strategy for Zen to express truth through language is divided into three categories: "self-contradictory," "intentionally misreading," and "answering what is not asked" (Ge Zhaoguang 2008: 426–29). The aesthetic thought of Zen-Taoism resonates with the Russian formalists' "defamiliarization."

The third chapter of *Pitch of Poetry* is titled "Echopoetics." It consists of eleven interviews, including Professor Nie Zhenzhao's interview with Bernstein, still relevant more than ten years later in showing that echopoetics is a collage of diversity and integration. Defamiliarization is the main expression of echopoetics. Bernstein once said that 90 percent of his poems were the re-creations of clichés.[7] The resonance of echopoetics with the subversive language strategy of Taoism is an important dimension for understanding echopoetics. For example: the first line of "You" is "time wounds all heals, spills through," which is a defamiliarization of the common saying "Time heals all wounds" (Bernstein 2010: 73), dismantling the restraint of idiomatic language and striking the stereotypes of time and wounds. Another example: the poem "The Truth in Pudding" is full of defamiliarized words and expressions, "different/idiosyncratic words and deeds," such as: "Poetry shows the ink the way out of the inkbottle," "A thing of beauty is annoyed forever," and "Poetry is to the classroom what a body is to a cemetery" (Bernstein 2013: 4–11). Another example is the last two lines in "Corrections": "say what you hate. / That's poetry" (Bernstein 2018: 29), which is one of the best examples of Bernstein's use of "strike stereotypes with defamiliarization" in his quest for and interrogation of experimental writing. These defamiliarized clichés seemingly focus on amusement but in fact provoke the reader's thinking, as the Gatha of Zen-Taoism, which reflects Bernstein's call for experimental poetry. The following is an example of a poem that explains how the "epiphany" of language occurs through the defamiliarization of a "living statement" in Bernstein's poetry.

First, it is necessary to explain "imploded syntax" and "analytic lyric" (Zhang Ziqing 2012: 23–24). Bernstein claims that the centrifugal forces in poetry can "pull different disparate elements together rather than projecting them outward" (2016: 266). I argue that Bernstein's vivid metaphor for the centrifugal performance of poetry also expresses the characteristics of imploded syntax, "like a piece of metal getting red-hot but collapsing into itself rather than exploding outward" (266). The imploded syntax seems to have an unexploded energy or impulse, flowing strongly and subtly, ready to go. Similarly, Bernstein's analytic lyric is the implosion and the subversion of traditional lyric poetry, showing the defamiliarization of language. Zhang Ziqing (2012: 24) believes that analytic lyric breaks the whole "speaking voice" in the poem in traditional lyric poetry (such as Shelley's "Ode to the West Wind") and uses "imploded syntax."

"For Love Has Such a Spirit That If It Is Portrayed It Dies" is an analytic lyric poem with centrifugal forces. The title of the poem comes from the

7. See the recording of the *Penn Review*'s interview with Bernstein in 2018.

thirteenth-century Italian poet Guido Cavalcanti's "Ballate III," translated by Pound.[8] Bernstein rewrites Pound's translation:

For Love Has Such a Spirit That If It Is Portrayed It Dies

Mass of van contemplation to intercede crush of
plaster. Lots of loom: "smoke out," merely
complicated by the first time something and don't.
Long last, occurrence of bell, altitude, attitude of.
The first, at this moment, aimless, aims. To the
point of inordinate asphalt—lecture, entail.
These hoops regard me suspiciously. A ring
for the shoulder (heave, sigh . . .). Broadminded in
declamation, an arduous task of winking
(willing). Weary the way the world wearies,
circa 1962. The more adjoins, sparklet and parquet
reflection, burned out (up). Regard the willing,
whose movement be only remonstration, ails
this blue bound boat. The numberical tears.
Edged out where tunnels reconnect, just below
the track. . . .
(Bernstein 2010: 67)

The beginning of this poem brings the reader into endless contemplation and memory, showing the theme of "faith and loyalty of love" in Cavalcanti's original poem in different defamiliarizations. The defamiliarization of language is mainly manifested in the juxtaposition of disagreement and contradictory meanings: "To the / point of inordinate asphalt" and "lecture, entail" are juxtaposed; "burned out (up)," a pair of contradictory words, are both separated and connected; fragmentations are superimposed with defamiliarized words; and so on. These writing techniques result in being "self-contradictory," or the lines intentionally induce misreading, and a "dissonance" in rhythm emerges. "Defamiliarization is an anti-absorption method with good experimental results" (Luo Lianggong 2013: 93), and this poem greatly reflects the anti-absorption of poetry,[9] which prolongs the aesthetic process, and the heterogeneous language tries to open the folds of the language, expands the enclosed space, and highlights the nature of language.

8. See the poem "Ballate III" in Pound's translation of Cavalcanti's *The Sonnets and Ballate of Guido Cavalcanti*.

Contradictory and ambiguous language in the poem is not intended to leave readers alone but to inspire their imagination. The words "bell," "lecture," and "declamation" are reminiscent of religious sermons and oaths, while "hoops" and "A ring / for the shoulder" allude to religious or ideological shackles. "To the / point of inordinate asphalt" can be seen as a metonymy for the fettered "I," or it can be understood as a frenzied defending of the collapse of the religious or ideological building, and multiple semantic meanings are generated in the fracture and fragments of language. Readers' participation is essential to achieve the language's epiphany. In the reader's imagination, "the shoulders" become heavy due to the "ring," which implies that prayer is of the same difficulty. The "winking" and the "willing" are homonymic, which seems to indicate that it is difficult to be "willing," and these lines portray the disobedience and nihilism as a whole. And "circa 1962" can be understood as a specific year, or any year in the sixties. On the one hand, 1962 is a significant year for the poet himself, if we take into account that it was the time when the poet entered adulthood. It is conceivable that he was going through important life transitions such as religious ritual; on the other hand, as mentioned above, the 1960s were a great turning point in American society. The anti-mainstream movements shook the status of religious and social traditions in the 1960s. The poem also turns here, from religion or ideology to the description of love.

> . . . Aims departing after one another
> & you just steps away, listening,
> listless. Alright, always—riches
> of that uncomplicated promise. Who—what—.
> That this reassurance (announcement)
> & terribly prompted—almost,
> although. Although censorious and even more
> careless. Lyrical mysticism—harbor, departing
> windows. For love I would—deft equator.
> (Bernstein 2010: 67–68)

"Equator" in "For love I would—deft equator" is the longest latitude, representing the hottest place. If connected to the "lyrical mysticism" of the previous line, it seems to show the ephemerality of love. "Deft equator" is also in contrast to "altitude" in an earlier line, since the word *altitude* means the height above sea level. The poet uses a unique image to imply that love is like an imaginary latitude or a space. Following these lines are fragments of language and peculiar line breaks, breaking the grammar and syntax:

> Nonchalant attribution of all the, & filled with
> such, meddles with & steals my constancy, sharpening
> desire for that, in passing, there, be favorite
> in ordinary, but no sooner thought than gone. My
> heart seems wax, that like tapers burns at light.
> (Bernstein 2010: 68)

The words "all the, & filled with" are rather ambiguous. What does "the" or, in the next line, "such" refer to? With the distinct use of the comma in "sharpening / desire for that, in passing, there, be favorite," the traditional syntax is broken, and also what is "that" and where is "there"? These lines form a "living statement," which is reserved for the readers to ponder over: what "the," "such," and "there" are. These words were originally referred pronouns in English, and they have specific functions of reference. But in the poem, the English language, which is originally narrative and clear, is subtly tactful, vaguely broken, trying to bring the reader into a kind of "speechless" space. The line breaks here demonstrate the stuttering of the language, and there are things unsaid, unspeakable, and not able to be portrayed, which creates tension between lines and dissonance in rhythm. But I argue that as Lao Tzu points out, "The great skill seems like clumsiness, / The greatest eloquence like stuttering" (Lao Tzu 1997: 97), and the dissonance in rhythm breaks the rules of language to achieve the speechlessness.

The use of polysemy at the end of the poem reverses the nihility of love and faith at the beginning of the poem, exemplifies the poet's exquisite and flexible use of semantics, and shows the epiphany of language.

> . . . . Depressed eyes
> clutter the morning and we drown in a sea of
> helping hands. Better the hermit than the sociopath.
> Destruction?—the wind blows anyway, any where,
> and the window frame adorns the spectacle. That
> person fixes in your head, and all the world
> consumed through it.
> (Bernstein 2010: 70)

On the surface, the ending of the poem is also the destruction of love: "we drown in a sea of / helping hands" portrays the death of "we" who have lost faith and love, while "better the hermit than the sociopath" highlights the difficulty of interpersonal communication. "And the window frame adorns the spectacle" at the same time embodies the sadness of perseverance and the sadness of broken love, which conveys the indirect and melancholy beauty. The last line of the poem, "That / person fixes in your head, and all the world / consumed through it," is even more profound, poignant, and ambiguous, with two different translations or interpretations, which echoes Zen-Taoism's "straight words seem crooked." First, this line contrasts with the previous line, and it seems that by metonym, the mind is compared to a window frame, and the lover is represented by a landscape. If the word *consumed* is understood to mean being exhausted, the end of the poem reflects the desolation of love and the exhausted world, implying the coming of death and sorrow. However, the polysemy of *consumed* also turns the verse back. The word refers to the loss of emotions, energy, et cetera, and also refers to being filled with strong emotion. So, understanding "through it" is crucial. The poet does not use "through" her/him, but what does "it" refer to? The poet does not give an answer but leaves it open. Does it refer to poetry, or love, or faith, or others? The word *it* can also refer to "a wonderful person," or "the ideal person" in colloquial language. The use of colloquial expression is common in Language poetry. The word *through* means "going through" and "by virtue of." If *it* is understood as "a wonderful person," then the poetry reverses itself and love does not disappear, and through the wonderful person, the world is filled with love and the love is fulfilled. The landscape in the mind becomes the whole world, suggesting the salvation of the world. The other interpretation of this line is, "the whole world is filled with it." However, "it" does not have one explanation, because its virtual meaning magnifies and extends the poetic meanings, gaining the effect of a "living statement" and constantly approaching the possibility of salvation. The energy of implosion in the poems gathers at the end of the poems, and it implodes deeply in the subtle enlightenment of the language's "nature." Obviously, this poem echoes the theme of Cavalcanti's lyrical poem, but unlike the straightforward style in Cavalcanti's poem, Bernstein's poem is fractured and fragmentated, and with a turning, the poem forms a dialogue with the predecessor poets, Pound and Cavalcanti, et cetera, and challenges and innovates their poetic styles. This analytic lyric poem uses a unique method to break out of the language barriers and limits, and uses the method of "strike stereotypes with defamiliarization" to perfectly show the epiphany of the language, in which readers participate.

Zhang Ziqing points out that there are four types of American Zen poets. Although their poetry pursues meditation, the poems are more straightforward than subtle, and it is no good using the aesthetic standards of ancient Chinese Zen poetry to measure American Zen poetry (2016: 12).

While pointing out the profound influence of traditional Chinese philosophy on American poetry, Bernstein said, "As is well known, the influence of classical Chinese poetry and philosophy has been profound for American poetry from the 19th century onward. But how well we—Americans who don't know Chinese—really understand Chinese classical poetry is to be questioned, and has been, by scholars such as Yunte Huang" (quoted in Nie Zhenzhao 2007: 14).[10] It would be an exaggeration to say that Bernstein has an in-depth and comprehensive knowledge of the traditional Chinese philosophy of Zen-Taoism. However, Bernstein's skillful use of numerous writing techniques has indeed created a unique and subtle poetic realm that is different from other American Zen poets. From this, we can see that following Imagism, the Black Mountain School, and the Beats, Zen-Taoist philosophy has had a profound influence on American postmodern avant-garde poetry—Language poetry. Undoubtedly, Bernstein perceptively and accurately perceives that the philosophy of Zen-Taoism and the spirit of the postmodern era are in resonance and in harmony, and he skillfully combines the aesthetics of Zen-Taoism with his poetics in an inclusive and innovative way, which forms an important part of his echopoetics. The internalization of Zen-Taoism becomes a force in Bernstein's echopoetics. As a Jewish American poet, Bernstein uses Zen-Taoist thoughts and political aesthetics, such as "the mutual transformation between nothingness and truth," "speechlessness," and "striking the stereotypes with defamiliarization" to effectively demonstrate his concern for the Other in the society and strikes a blow and rails against the lifeless "official verse culture."

In his poetry, full of wisdom and philosophical thoughts, Bernstein reveals the history of sorrow and joy, and the coexistence of honor and sorrow, demonstrating the transcendence of sorrow and reflections on the survival predicament of postmodern society. Combining the perspective of Zen-Taoism philosophy, we can understand the epiphany caused by Bernstein's unique poetic language and deeply appreciate his unremitting efforts and outstanding contributions to American avant-garde poetry. As Chen points out, Western postmodern deconstruction attempts to get out of the metaphysical circles of Western languages and to find new language strat-

9. Please refer to Bernstein's "Artifice of Absorption," in *A Poetics* (1992). The Chinese version is included in *Language Poetics*, trans. Luo Lianggong (Shanghai Foreign Language Education Press, 2013).

10. Bernstein illustrates this topic by citing Yunte Huang's study in *Shi: A Radical Reading of Chinese Poetry*: "I am thinking of not only Huang's illuminating study of Pound, but more particularly his work *Shi: A Radical Reading of Chinese Poetry* (New York: Roof

egies; this is similar to Taoism (Chen Yuehong 1990: 40). In the twenty-first century, it is no accident that echopoetics and Zen-Taoism resonate with beautiful chords; the breakthrough of the restrictions of language and logos is a result of the efforts and perseverance of both Eastern and Western poets and scholars from ancient times to the present. Bernstein, with his "rich achievements and unique ideas, had an important impact on American and Western poetry" (Luo Lianggong 2013: 93). Western critics have also repeatedly stated that Bernstein has largely changed the aesthetic value and standards of American poetry. Further engagement with Bernstein's echopoetics has profound implications for studying the influence of traditional Chinese philosophy on American Language poetry and even postmodern poetry.

References

Abe, Masao, ed. 1986. *A Zen Life: D. T. Suzuki Remembered*. New York: Weatherhill.

Bernstein, Charles. 1992. *A Poetics*. Cambridge: Cambridge University Press. The Chinese version is included in *Language Poetics*. Translated by Luo Lianggong. Shanghai: Shanghai Foreign Language Education Press, 2013.

———. 2010. *All the Whiskey in Heaven: Selected Poems*. New York: Farrar Straus Giroux.

———. 2013. *Recalculating*. Chicago: University of Chicago Press.

———. 2016. *Pitch of Poetry*. Chicago: University of Chicago Press.

———. 2018. *Near/Miss*. Chicago: University of Chicago Press.

陈盛 [Chen Sheng]. 2010. 《论杰克·凯鲁亚克俳句的禅意》,《当代外国文学》第 31 卷第 1 期, 第 161–67 页。 ["Zen Buddhism in Kerouac's Haiku." *Contemporary Foreign Literature* 31, no. 1: 161–67.]

陈跃红 [Chen Yuehong]. 1990. 《"活句"与"死句":道家美学的语言策略》,《贵州大学学报》第 59 卷第 4 期, 第 38–41, 88 页。 ["'Sentence Alive' and 'Sentence Dead': Language Strategy of Daoism Aesthetics." *Journal of Guizhou University* 59, no. 4: 38–41, 88.]

Chung-yuan, Chang. 1970. *Creativity and Taoism: A Study of Chinese Philosophy, Art and Poetry*. Harper Colophon Books.

范明华 [Fan Minghua]. 2009. 《论"虚无"在中国美学思想中的意义》,《东岳论丛》第 30 卷第 5 期, 第 130–34 页。 ["On the Significance of 'Nothingness' in Chinese Aesthetics." *Dongyue Tribune* 30, no. 5: 130–34.]

葛兆光 [Ge Zhaoguang]. 1985. 《禅宗与中国文化》。上海人民出版社。[*Zen and Chinese Culture*. Shanghai: Shanghai People's Publishing House.]

———. 2008. 《增订本中国禅思想史》。上海古籍出版社。 [*An Updated Edition to the History of Chinese Zen Thoughts*. Shanghai: Shanghai Classics Publishing House.]

胡敏 [Hu Min]. 2008. 《论禅宗诗歌的"陌生化"表现手法》,《中国文化研究》第 16 卷第 4 期, 第 63–70 页。 ["Defamiliarization in Chinese Zen Poetry." *The Study of Chinese Culture* 16, no. 4: 63–70.]

老子 [Lao Tzu]. 1997.《道德经》。Arthur Waley 译,外语教学与研究出版社。 [*Tao Te Ching*. Translated by Arthur Waley. Beijing: Foreign Language Teaching and Research Press.]

罗良功 [Luo Lianggong]. 2013. 《查尔斯·伯恩斯坦诗学简论》,《江西社会科学》 第 34 卷第 5 期, 第 93—98 页。 ["Introduction to Charles Bernstein's Poetics." *Jiangxi Social Science* 34, no. 5: 93–98.]

毛宣国 [Mao Xuanguo]. 2006. 《中国古代"无"的哲学美学智慧及启示》,《求索》第 26 卷第 4 期, 第 127–80 页。 ["The Philosophical and Aesthetic Wisdom and Insights in Chinese Traditional 'Nothingness.'" *Seeker* 26, no. 4: 127–30.]

米家路 [Mi Jialu]. 2017. 《望道与旅程:中西诗学的幻象与跨越》。秀威资讯科技。 [*The Tao and the Routes: Mirage and Transfiguration in Western and Chinese Poetics*. Taipei: Showwe Information Co. Ltd.]

Morton, Timothy. 2010. "Ecology as Text, Text as Ecology." *Oxford Literary Review* 32, no. 1: 1–17.

聂珍钊 [Nie Zhenzhao]. 2007. 《查尔斯·伯恩斯坦教授访谈录》,《外国文学研究》第 29 卷第 2 期, 第 10–19 页。 ["Interview with Charles Bernstein." *Foreign Literature Studies* 29, no. 2: 10–19.]

邱紫华 余锐 [Qiu Zihua and Yu Rui]. 2006. 《不可言说的言说——禅的意会思维特征及其表达方式》,《华中师范大学学报》第 42 卷第 6 期, 第 101–5 页。 ["Speaking the Unspeakable: The Thought Pattern and Its Manifestation in Zen." *Journal of Huazhong Normal University* 42, no. 6: 101–5.]

Suzuki, D. T. 2016. "Wisdom in Emptiness." In *Selected Works of D. T. Suzuki*, vol. 3, edited by Jeff Wilson and Tomoe Moriya, 201–25. Oakland: University of California Press.

叶维廉 [Wai-lim Yip]. 2002. 《道家美学与西方文化》。北京大学出版社。 [*Taoist Aesthetics and Western Culture*. Peking University Press.]

———. 2007. 《中国诗学》。人民文学出版社。 [*Chinese Poetics*. Beijing: People's Literature Publishing House.]

张节末 [Zhang Jiemo]. 1998. 《道禅对儒家美学的冲击》,《哲学研究》第 44 卷第 9 期 , 第 55–61 页。 ["The Countercultural Effects of Zen-Daoism on Confucian Aesthetics." *Philosophy Studies* 44, no. 9: 55–61.]

张子清 [Zhang Ziqing]. 2009. 《从边缘到主流:关于垮掉派诗歌的反思》,《江汉大学学报》第 26 卷第 4 期, 第 15–19 页。 ["From Margin to Main Stream: The Reflection on Beat Poetry." *Journal of Jianghan University* 26, no. 4: 15–19.]

———. 2012. 《美国语言诗》,《国外文学》, 2012 (1): 19–31. ["American Language Poetry." *Literary Abroad* 2012, no. 1: 19–30.]

———. 2016.《美国禅诗》,《南京理工大学学报》第 29 卷第 3 期, 第 1–13 页。 ["American Zen Poetry." *Journal of Nanjing University of Science and Technology* 29, no. 3: 1–13.]

赵毅衡 [Zhao Yiheng]. 2013. 《诗神远游:中国如何改变了美国现代诗》。四川文艺出版社。 [*The Muse from Cathay*. Chengdu: Sichuan Literary Publishing House.]
朱良志 [Zhu Liangzhi]. 2011. 《美是不可分析的——评道禅哲学关于美问题的一个观点》,《学术月刊》第 55 卷第 8 期，第 11–16 页。["Uninterpretable Aesthetics: On an Opinion of Zen-Daoism Aesthetics." *Academy Monthly* 55, no. 8: 11–16.]
朱雪峰 [Zhu Xuefeng]. 2017.《美国先锋戏剧里的道禅思想与美学:一种跨文化谱系考察》,《当代外国文学》第 38 卷第 4 期, 第 35–43 页。 ["Tao and Zen in the Politics and Aesthetics of American Avant Garde Theatre: Approaching an Intercultural Genealogy." *Contemporary Foreign Literature* 38, no. 4: 35–43.]

Susan Bee, *Threadsuns*, oil, enamel, and sand on linen, 40 x 50 inches, 2015. Reprinted by permission from Susan Bee.

A Source Which Is Also a Translation: Toward an *Expanded-Yiddish* Poetics, with Special Reference to Charles Bernstein

Ariel Resnikoff

> And now inestimable time after the mythic creators of these dark phantoms, poets have no memory even of the loss of the ancient songs; their words ring hollow against an indifferent universe; they are bereft of images, of stories, of illusion. In these times, poems are made just of words in infinite constellations. Yet in their supernal impotence, these poems are as sublimely daemonic—world defining and defying—as those most ancient songs of the time before beginnings.
> —Charles Bernstein, "Before Time"[1] (2018a)

> By that I mean the weak dazzle of the lighting that occasionally flares up on the distant horizon, those rebellious but as yet unfledged forerunners which nevertheless, burst into light from time to time to reveal glimpses of the storm that is gathering in the distance and which will erupt—if not today, then tomorrow or the day after that.
> —Der Nister, *The Family Mashber* ([1948] 1987)

1. After S. Y. Agnon, after Gershom Scholem, after the Baal Shem Tov.

boundary 2 48:4 (2021) DOI 10.1215/01903659-9382257

א. Hidden Astral Teachers: A Clairvoyant Parable

It is to script and language that clairvoyance has, over the course of history, yielded its old powers.
—Walter Benjamin, *Selected Writings Volume 2, Pt. 2: 1931–1934*

like a roll of negative film . . . is unrevealable until it has found a camera to project it and a surface to throw it upon
—Mina Loy, *Islands in the Air*

i. Agodo[2]

In a 1995 LINEbreak conversation with Charles Bernstein, Hannah Weiner reads excerpts from a late work entitled "paw," from her "Astral Visions" poems. At one point in her reading, Hannah describes paw, an astral bear, living in and on her forehead: "when I got home," she says, "the bear was very small, he had changed shape to a very small brown bear who lived in a cupboard in my forehead it had blue sheets" (Weiner 2010: 155).[3]

Bernstein hears something in Weiner's late work that many listeners/readers would almost certainly miss: that is, that the image, *or vision*, of the cupboard on Hannah's forehead, with a bed inside laid with blue sheets, brings up an echo, or astral translation, of the practice of wrapping phylacteries, also called *tefillin*: the most ancient of Jewish equipage. "The reason I mention that," Bernstein says,

> especially sitting across in your apartment where we're recording this with two mosaic works of your father's with Hebrew letters on them, is [that] within the Hebrew tradition very orthodox Jews will put the Hebrew text exterior to their forehead when they pray. This seems to me an interesting relationship to the idea of this astral, as you would say, textual imagination or imaginary being, as I might say, actually existing in your forehead. Does that make any sense to you? (Weiner 2010: 161–62)

2. *Agodo* (sometimes spelled *Aggadah*): Aramaic/Hebrew/Yiddish for all that is *not* law, tales and lore, gossip, jokes, poems, quips, non sequiturs, tangents, parables, proverbs, narratives, meditations, musings, stream of consciousness, all things not apparently legal(istic). Most importantly, *Agodo* claims no authority, no power over the stakes of the Talmud and Midrash, and instead takes a minor route, releasing the raw texts from the weight and burden of the cult, and allowing flux, flow, poetics, aesthetics, and innovation to flicker through even the most dusty corners of the Jewish canons.
3. I quote here from the published transcription of the conversation in *Wild Orchids*, which is available on Weiner's Electronic Poetry Center (EPC) page.

Hannah's initial response avoids and defers the inquiry, refusing closure: "Well, all I can say is that paw's real self is a healer. And that's an important thing among Native Americans. And within the Jewish . . . So that's a holy thing to be" (162).

Yet Bernstein persists in his reading/listening: "And within the Jewish tradition, which you also have roots in," he says, "the word itself is healing, the word itself as a text. In the sense of the Torah as a text actually appears on the head, so this return of the word as healing, as astral, seems to bring several different strands of your work together" (162).

And now Hannah recognizes the question and responds in earnest, riffing on Charles's very *chutzpah* in bringing it up so plainly: "Well I haven't discussed it," she says, "but I'm paw, both Levi and Cohen. So I don't know if you know what it means."

> [Charles:] What does it mean to you?
>
> [Hannah:] Oh, the Levis were the holiest tribe who had no land and were the hidden teachers, and they went from place to place and were welcomed everywhere. It's in Deuteronomy. It doesn't say they were hidden as teachers, but you have to know that. They're the ones who carried the Torah to the Ark. And the Cohens developed later with the temple, and they were the high priests, and they were also silent, but they dealt with the people at large. So . . . I have, you know, I didn't think of putting it in the introduction, but my grandmother was a teacher, and my mother was somewhat. (162–63)

After this, the conversation moves on to other things, ending finally on the topic of Weiner's undergraduate thesis at Radcliffe, which she wanted to write on Dostoyevsky but which, she tells Charles, she was forced by her advisor to write on Graham Greene. "But surely there's a Dostoyevskian side to our guest today," Charles remarks, signing off, "Hannah Weiner. Hannah, it's been a great pleasure to be chatting with you here in your house on the Lower East Side." And Hannah's response at the close: "Oh, gee Charles, don't leave me with Dostoyevsky, unless you leave me with the Underground, which is where I'll always be . . . what I call a silent subculture" (164).

ii. Drash[4]

For
anything said is significant—& much that
Is not said but only spoken, hinted—
tossed from a glazed eye to a
Nearing touch.
—Charles Bernstein, "Pockets of Lime" (1991)

The audio scene here strikes me as quite remarkable: Bernstein and Weiner sitting together for this rich recorded conversation in Hannah's Lower East side house—and the astral bear of Hannah's "paw," which, it would seem, in one sense lives (or lived for a time) on Hannah's forehead in a tiny cabinet or house with a tiny bed laid with blue sheets.[5] The cabinet-house, Charles suggests, might also signal the most ancient Jewish practice of binding small leather boxes—called "houses" themselves in Hebrew—filled with scripture to one's forehead and left bicep.[6] And in response, Hannah presents a doubly exposed vision of her mongrel lowercase jewishness, at once Native American healer and diasporic Levite priest, as "hidden teacher" in "a silent subculture."[7]

This scene is far more than what it seems. Bernstein and Weiner may not have even fully realized it at the time—though I suspect they probably did to an extent, however silently—but there is a potent spark of recognition and acknowledgment, a momentary illumination of an inheritance cloaked otherwise in rags, at once hidden and hiding, yet revealed here for a split moment in the astral communication between radical Jewish poets.[8]

4. I use the term *drash* here—a variant of *midrash*—to connote a form of loose "exposition" or "investigation" as an antinomian echo of the traditional rabbinic midrash, a Jewish oral mode of interpreting, commentating on, elaborating on, or introducing a text.
5. The name *paw* itself appears to me to be a metonymic deferral of the Yiddish/Jewish name *Ber*, meaning "bear."
6. In Hebrew, these boxes are traditionally called *batim*, meaning "houses."
7. Although Weiner's linking of Jewish diasporic and Native American lineages may seem at first arbitrary or even counterintuitive, I find this connection to be quite pertinent within a wider context of ethnopoetics, a major movement and poetic ethos adjacent to, if not directly associated with Weiner's work; see, for example, Jerome Rothenberg's discussion of the various intersections of ethnopoetic (re)sources in his "Pre-Face" to *Symposium of the Whole: A Range of Discourse Toward an Ethnopoetics* (2016: xv).
8. The rag, or *shmata* in Yiddish, *smartut* in Hebrew, is an important symbol within diasporic Jewish culture, connoting "the rag trade" and larger garment industry by which so many Jews found means to make a living spread across the globe during the nineteenth and twentieth centuries. Famously, or perhaps, infamously, the early-Statehood

This powerful revelation as shared hidden inheritance and lineage, for both good and bad, takes place like the flash of a camera, for an instant, almost blindingly, in the donning of Hannah's visionary *tefillin*, a wearing of the Jewish word for just a moment between the two artists before moving on to other matters at hand.

To end at the "Underground," which for Hannah as much as for Dostoyevsky, is to end with the domicile itself, the *domohabitus* in which the two poets sit and subsist for a solitary moment in conversation, with kabbalah-inflected mosaics by Hannah's father hanging on the ambient walls. The Underground is also a *hidden place*, I think, and even more so, a place to hide—in and with and even from language—and to read and write from that place of hiddenness as a form of ritual healing, surviving by the very words transcribed, by the translation of writing as it flickers amid vast and constant loss. Weiner and Bernstein are kindling something quite extraordinary while sitting together, perhaps unconsciously in certain regards, or even *dis*consciously, but nonetheless with great urgency and immediacy of latent awakening.[9] Not that either of these poets are crypto-Jews themselves in any sense—quite the opposite, as Bernstein would say, their Jewishness is right out there in the open. Rather, we might say, it is a strain of suppressed antinomian diasporic Jewish language and culture that burrows or hides itself in the bodies of their ongoing works, in conscious and unconscious speculative ghost lineages. The languages that lie behind their Englishes, which had been projected into extinction but never truly died, despite the millions murdered—which would not and could not die—instead translated themselves outward in continuous hiding in plain sight. This radical strain of Jewish praxis, which finds a diasporic landless terrain in Yiddish language and culture, specifically, is translated in the early to mid-twentieth century out of the powerless jargon—a derisive Slavic term for Yiddish—and into the more secure languages of the nation-state, into every language that Yiddish came into contact with as a function of forced mass migrations. The translation of diasporic language into national language takes place primarily as a mode of survival in this case; and the transition and translation from

---

Zionist poet of the Israeli *Moderna* Natan Alterman (1910–70) accused the *expanded-Yiddish* poet Avot Yeshurun (1904–92) of writing in a language of rags (*lashon smartutim*), because he included Yiddish and Arabic slangs within his Hebrew verse.

9. I use the word "*dis*conscious" here to connote a sense of something between dreaming and waking, a lucid dream of sorts, perhaps, which is neither wholly conscious nor wholly unconscious.

languages across migrating generations and lineages leave unmistakable traces behind: giant masses of charcoal and ash, with live embers buried deep below the silent soot.

What's not discussed in the meeting between Bernstein and Weiner is as compelling as what is. Take *tefillin*, for example: these are leather boxes called "houses" that Jewish people have been binding to their foreheads and arms for thousands of years.[10] The practice has always struck me as an ancient graphomaniac's acupressure, and for many years I myself laid *tefillin* every morning as a somatic ritual: binding words to the body, the words one speaks in meditation in silent prayer and sings aloud in chant and song. Each leather house contains four scrolls each with passages from the Hebrew bible: two from Exodus (13:1–10 and 13:11–16) and two from Deuteronomy (6:4–9 and 11:13–21). All versions of the same directive, which refers to the Jewish responsibility to wear language on the body as a sign and memorial of redemption, as a constant reminder of the exodus from Egypt and of the transition and translation from slavery to freedom. The house bound to the arm has only one compartment with one long scroll containing all four biblical passages, while the house bound to the forehead contains four compartments, each containing a single folded scroll, each containing a single biblical passage. Both houses are wrapped to the body with attached leather straps, and in ancient times Jews wore *tefillin* all day long, while in modern and contemporary times they are traditionally "laid" once a day during morning prayer.

The biblical passages do not refer to the word or object of *tefillin* proper, however—a word that is itself almost impossible to trace in Hebrew beyond the singular *tefilah*, meaning "prayer"—but instead use the term *totafot*, an untranslatable fusion neologism of Coptic and Afriki (which, Rabbi Adin Steinzaltz comments, actually refers to Phrygian) dialects, or so the Talmud tells us.[11] *Tot* meaning "two" in Coptic, according to the Tal-

10. Traditionally, only men are commanded to wear *tefillin*, and a woman wearing them is frowned upon in the orthodox Jewish patriarchal system. Weiner's vision of a secular Jewish woman's astral *tefillin* is all the more radical, in this sense, and recalls the powerfully transgressive Hebrew writing of Yonah Wallach (1944–85), who queers the practice and object of *tefillin* by writing about women laying them on men in S and M rituals in her poem "Tefillin."

11. There are many possible origins, of course, but I happen to be partial to Rabbi Akiva's derivation in Sanhedrin: 4b of the Babylonia Talmud, even if it is somewhat etymologically questionable.

mud, and *Fot*, meaning "two" in Phrygian, a doubled and doubling echoic equation turned measurement, to build a portable *domohabitus* for the word as world, not on sturdy foundations of land but from a perpetual state of landlessness, in the impossible diasporic necessity of translation.[12] This untranslatable word, *totafot*, refers in the Bible specifically to a somatic grapho-signaling space between the eyes, where Hannah's paw builds his cabinet-house in and upon her forehead. The doubling site of language in utter flux is a vision of Hannah's astral *tefillin*, an untranslatable translational sign and translingual trace of an ancient diasporic *totafot* as latent signal; and the blue sheets of paw's bed immediately recall the light blue *tkhelet* of the *tallis*, which the ur-Hebrew Gebalians extracted from snails on the banks of the Mediterranean.[13]

So the stretch of Hannah's "paw"—as with much of her poetry and poetics—is astonishingly wide, and what Charles registers and records, and we might also say, invites, is a hidden lineage in Hannah's writing, which is connected to his writing through its very transmutability—by an *un*spoken word between them, which lives as much in their accents and inflections as in their disparate ancestral pasts, in a shared diasporism that chooses them and chooses their writing without their choosing. A ghost language exists between them like a forgotten mother tongue, which nonetheless *must find ways to emerge in the world.* Between them, between the walls of the Underground, the eight corners of a concealed *totafot*, Hannah's paw speaks: *in the house between the eyes, a language resides, perpetually erased from history, it embeds and imprints itself in and on the body. Let us broadcast it on six million wavelengths in every language, from a common yet wholly particular ghost language.*

12. Rabbi Steinzaltz's comment appears in his comprehensive English translation of the Babylonia Talmud, in Sanhedrin: 4b. In *The Living Torah*, Rabbi Aryeh Kaplan goes even further to argue that the word *tot* appears to also be a cognate of the Latin word *totas*, and hence the English *total*, while *p(h)oth* might be a cognate of the Gothic *bothe*, Sanskrit *botto*, and English *both*.

13. The *tallis* in Yiddish, or *talit* in Hebrew, is the traditional Jewish prayer shawl, the concept for which derives from the Old Testament in Numbers 15:38 and Deuteronomy 22:12. The *tallis* has twined and knotted fringes which are traditionally died with the color *tkhelet*, a particular cross between royal purple and royal blue, which the ancient Gebalian people of Byblos extracted from snails and traded with the ancient Egyptians for papyrus.

ב. vat em i doink here?: Yiddish Sparks in Vast Expansive Darkness

I disagree with Robert Frost's often quoted remark that poetry "is lost . . . in translation." For me poetry is always a kind of translation, transformation, transposition, and metamorphosis. There is nothing "outside" translation: no original poem or idea, nor one perfect translation. It's a matter of choosing among versions. Translation is a form of reading or interpreting or thinking with the poem. In that sense, there can be no experiencing the poem, even in your own language, without translating. Without translation the poem remains just a text, a document, a series of inert words. Poetry is what is found in translation.
—Ian Probstein, "Charles Bernstein: 'Of Time and the Line'" (2015)

i. "from whom did I take permission"[14]

The nexus and net of *expanded-Yiddish* poetics is as vast as its ongoing diaspora. Bernstein and Weiner's meeting in the Lower East Side is a particularly potent example of such a poetics at work, through the trace of their encounter, in recording and transcription of the scene. The more I search for these latent traces of spark(l)ing, the more I seem to find, like secret s/crawl spaces in the walls and floorboards of the languages I read, write, and translate. My praxis as a contemporary writer and translator has become a process of iridescent mapping, in these terms, a means of charting the translingual residues wherever they appear, on everyday pieces of writing, on every text I engage with, even here, flickering through this essay.

Bernstein is a writer who conducts (à la Jack Spicer) tremendously powerful *expanded-Yiddish* frequencies in rhapsodic translational echoes, further and farther bendings backward toward ghost languages not afforded him in any originary sense. In these terms, Charles's writing and thinking do away with origin(ation) as a stable—let alone ideal—category altogether, moving through his m/other-tongue English rather as searchingly as one would through a foreign dialect. His writing operates in perpetual aversive transcreation, so that every source for Bernstein—in his ears, eyes, and mouth—becomes a translation turned back from its source, reversing itself as only the "backward Jew" can (said half-jokingly) from its proposed ori-

14. I take this phrase from the title of Avot Yeshurun's 1979 Bialik Prize speech in which he asks about the decimated inheritance of the Jewish writer after the Holocaust: "And I—from whom did I take permission to lay my ancestors on the chestnuts beneath the wood and the fire" (2020: 420).

gin and originality. I don't mean to say that Bernstein is unoriginal in the least, certainly not; rather, I mean that the origin of his originality is in fact in the very transgressive un/originary event of translation—a poetics that does away with origin as its primary act. From his *Asylums* on, the only filiation in Charles's *oeuvre* is to say that there is no filiation at all, but translation, trans-creation, version, and near-infinite versions. His work is the chilled gefilte fish *yoykh* we drink after we eat the fish. *It's the jelly*, "the best part," I hear an elder Reznikoff reply.

When it comes to Bernstein's relation to the radical possibilities of subterranean Jewish lineages and legacies in poetry and art, his greatest and most powerful living precedent is and always has been Jerome Rothenberg.[15] Jerry, unlike Charles, spoke Yiddish as a child and then ostensibly forgot much of it, before remembering it anew (much as I did, much later, in a dream), through and into his poetry and poetics. Rothenberg was quite close to Hannah Weiner, as well, and would certainly figure into Weiner's notion of an "Underground silent subculture" and her vision of hidden astral teachers as landless Levite technicians.[16] It's Rothenberg's *Poland/1931*, and later *Triptych*—which Bernstein writes the preface to—that blows the doors wide ajar for so many of us, presenting as it does a spectral translation of an eradicated Jewish past in the process of translating itself *out of Yiddish* and *into English* via Rothenberg's poetic cipher: a living language site (and sight) in transmission of what is hidden and what continues to survive in ongoing hiddenness.[17] The books included in *Triptych—Poland/1931,*

15. Jerome Rothenberg (b. 1931); a major elder poet-translator-editor-assembler and cofounder of ethnopoetics; coeditor with Dennis Tedlock of *Alchuringa: A Journal of Ethnopoetics*, and with Pierre Joris of *Poems for the Millennium I–III*.

16. Thinking here specifically of one of Hannah's late books, *Silent Teacher/Remembered Sequel* (written 1989–91, published 1993), and one of Rothenberg's earliest, *Technicians of the Sacred* (1968).

17. My sense for this hiddenness is inextricably tied to Sander Gilman's notion of "the hidden language of the Jews" in his *Jewish Self-Hatred: Anti-Semitism and the Hidden Language of the Jews*. Yet, while Gilman focuses on the pathological turn as it relates to trauma—as in Freud—I treat this hiddenness within a wider context of translation, the site, I argue, where language simultaneously reveals and conceals its seams. Additionally, my sense for the sonic-somatic stakes of Jewishness and subsequently, anti-Semitism, has been greatly impacted by Gilman's *The Jew's Body*, and his discussion in the first section of this book, "The Jewish Voice," on sound, accent, and Jewish difference. Writes Gilman, "The creation of the image of the Jew who is identifiable as different because he or she sounds 'too Jewish' provides a model through which we can see the structure of the image to create an absolute boundary of the difference of the Jew even as this boundary historically shifts and slides. Jews sound different because they are represented as being different" (1991: 11).

Khurbn, and *The Burning Babe*—changed the landscape of poetry and poetics in North America irrevocably by responding to the catastrophic chasm of postwar Europe from and through the dream of a Jewish American subjectivity turned inside out on its own Anglo-white passing, with an urgency that only the New York Yiddish modernists had previously achieved.[18] In channeling the specter of his murdered ancestors, Rothenberg presents us with a poethical experiment in reshaping our collective diasporic futures through kaleidoscopic reimagined pasts as paths to an *expanded-Yiddish* English present.[19] *Triptych* also changes what it means to be a contemporary Jewish poet—and in particular, a contemporary Jewish poet living in the United States—by creating a space for the eradicated Jewish tongue to live another life, an afterlife in English—for the last Jews of Europe to speak in a sense to an American public for the first time.[20] In his prologue to Rothenberg's *Triptych*, Bernstein writes, "The poems in *Triptych* envision a place neither there nor here: they build a liminal dwelling of betweenness, populated by ghosts and goblins, where objects are disguised as words and words are used as objects of resistance. All of this is presided over by historical personages brandishing indelible facts and syncretic figures making the only sense we may know this side of Heaven" (Rothenberg 2007: vii).

This "dwelling of betweenness, populated by ghosts and goblins," is the language/scape of Rothenberg's translated Yiddishland, a diasporic terrain woven of dispersed and displaced languages, constantly deferring and debating the terms of their displacement.[21] The precedent and permission Rothenberg provides here cannot be overstated: for poets, writers,

18. Mikhl Likht (1893–1953), for example, warned of the consequences of total Jewish Anglicization as it relates to whiteness and the Jewish necessity of miscegenation, in particular, in his poem "The Song of my Black Brother": "The ink may be false, every word on the paper false / like the holy-true receipt of our genealogical record" (1957: 220; translation is mine).

19. "Kaleidoscopic" became an important term for the New York Yiddish modernists of the 1910s, 1920s, and 1930s, in thinking about the polysemic shifting qualities of a radical secular Yiddish culture in perpetual diasporic flux.

20. There are other poetic texts that address the Holocaust in advance of Rothenberg—Charles Reznikoff's *Holocaust*, for example, or Muriel Rukeyser's "To Be a Jew in the Twentieth Century"—yet none with the sheer speculative force of Rothenberg's *Triptych*, which finds a way somehow to speak in and through the ghost language of the murdered Jews rather than around or about it.

21. "Yiddishland": a Yiddish modernist shorthand for the prolifically scattered sites of stateless Yiddish culture situated, though never settled, across the globe.

and artists working in inherited or translated tongues—dialects that are inherently and expressly not the dialects of their ancestors—Rothenberg opens a pathway, or better yet, a network of pathways, out of the national house of language and into the cellar or attic of migratory translation.[22] This space—which somehow escapes the perpetual destruction of the nation-state as a force of con(de)struction—is where the ghosts of dialects past speak in silent landless other-tongues, eating the pages from holy books for sustenance and sheer survival.[23] Such an aesthetics and poetics of the cellar-attic s/crawl space may be derived in the most literal and visceral terms, from the cellars and attics and crawl spaces where Jews hid from their murderers, and where they hid their most precious texts and manuscripts from Nazi and Stalinist biblioclasm.[24]

ii. Translingual Constellations and Poetic Mazl[25]

At my birth the stars played me crooked.
—Charles Bernstein, "My Luck"[26] (2018c)

He called over his shoulder
Standing on one foot

22. Rothenberg's notion of "total translation" as a speculative utopic ideal is key here, as he writes in his Pre-Face to *Shaking the Pumpkin: Traditional Poetry of the Indian North Americas*: "The question for the translator is not whether but how far we can translate one another. Like the poet who is his brother, he attempts to restore what has been torn apart. Any arrogance on his part would not only lead to paternalism or 'colonialism' (LeRoi Jones's term for it from a few years back), it would deny the very order of translation. Only if he allows himself to be directed by the other will a common way emerge, true to both positions" (1981: 93).
23. Thinking here in particular of Isaac Bashevis Singer's "The Last Demon," which recounts the last days of the last Jewish *sheyd* (demon or spirit) in the decimated *shtetl* of Tishivitz after the Holocaust.
24. I always remember the powerful work of the "Paper Brigade," in these terms, a group of residents in the Vilne Ghetto—led by the Yiddish modernists Abraham Sutzkever (1913–2010) and Shmerke Kaczerginski (1908–1954)—who smuggled Jewish books and manuscripts, among other precious cultural materials, past Nazi guards, saving them from enforced destruction by burying and hiding them in caches throughout the ghetto.
25. The Hebrew/Yiddish term *Mazl*, which likely derives from Akkadian (*manzaltu*), referring to the position of a star or planet in the ancient context. In Jewish Aramaic and Biblical Hebrew, for example, it means "constellation," whereas in Yiddish it comes to mean "luck" or "fortune." A classic Yiddish proverb comes to mind, which jokes that goyish (non-Jewish) *mazl* is always inherently good luck, while Jewish *mazl* is just the opposite, inherently bad luck.
26. Translation of Abraham ibn Ezra.

The footless cobbler
A fruitless farmer
Of course he says
The invisibility of it all
The sheer disappearing act
That lingers
When the darkness surrounds
Says the Bedouin Sheikh
Disguised
As Robert Creeley—
No Jerry, it was Jerry
Who stood up
On his chair
All those years ago
And sung: you see
You see Diane!
I dreamt it
I dreamt it
before I even knew
who he was.[27]

It was Rothenberg who first introduced me to Bernstein, and Rothenberg who first insisted that there was no better poet or person to work with on a PhD around the sorts of questions I was asking through my poetics and scholarship.[28] These questions were (and are) not so much about *Yiddish proper*—a fact that I can tell sometimes irks my Yiddishist colleagues—but about its multifarious miscegenated afterlives in translation, as poetry. And Rothenberg was right. The first afternoon I sat with Charles, on the day that he and Susan Bee moved from the Upper West Side to Carroll Gardens, Brooklyn—no small move, mind you—I immediately recognized him as a teacher of the yet unarticulated field of *expanded Yiddish* I was attempting to imagine in and through my work. I remarked to him within the first half

27. Verse is mine.

28. I completed a PhD at the University of Pennsylvania in 2019 with Bernstein as my key advisor and doctoral supervisor. My dissertation, entitled "Home Tongue Earthquake: The Radical Afterlives of Yiddishland," is a work that explores the *expanded-Yiddish* dynamics and constellated relations between Mikhl Likht (1893–1953), Mina Loy (1882–1966), Louis Zukofsky (1904–78) in the US, and Avot Yeshurun (1904–92) and Harold Schimmel (b. 1935) in Israel/Palestine.

hour of us talking that it sounded to me as though he was thinking in Yiddish and speaking in English—that is, speaking a dialect of the very Brooklynese he writes about so compellingly with regard to Louis Zukofsky. Yet while Louis trained himself out of Yiddish over the course of many years, to sound (aloud) as Anglocentric as Pound or Eliot, Charles leans into his New York Jewish accent, taking pleasure in the bends, torques, and mis/pronunciations it achieves in jarring relation to an arbitrarily imposed standard English. Of course, Zukofsky was doing just this on the page in many instances; but Charles takes it one step further, vocalizing the Jewish accent in both writing and speech, and bringing it to the foreground of his practice and praxis as a poet in the most banal and everyday sense, in the voicing of his voice in the world. In this sense, his vocalization of Zukofsky's "A Foin Lass Bodders" has always struck me as paradigmatic of his wider concerns as a poet and person: to bring the concealment of antinomian resistance to the surface and voicing of a text, to let it stumble over itself for the sake of revealing itself for what it is, marked by its difference and dissonance as *apart from* while also still *inside* the house of English. The double and doubling house of paw's trans-astral *totafot* appears in the double-talking Zukofsky, as well, whose quantum Jewish character Charles translates and transmits more convincingly than any other poet or scholar I've ever read. While Zukofsky pronounces his Brooklynese sound transcreation of Cavalcanti's "Donna mi prega" in an affected high modernist Anglo accent—in order, ostensibly, to "better the instruction," as he writes in "A Poem Beginning 'The,'" glossing Shylock—Bernstein voices Zuk's version in a deep-inflected performance of the Jewish New York sounds it so "begs" (Bernstein 2011: 135), a voicing that reveals the previously concealed Yiddish underpinnings of Zukofsky's homophonic "double-talking" sensibility:

> A foin lass bodders me I gotta tell her
> Of a fact surely, so unrurly, often'
> 'r 't comes 'tcan't soften its proud neck's called love mm...
> (Zukofsky 1978: 409)[29]

29. A recording of Louis Zukofsky reading "A Foin Lass Bodders" at Johns Hopkins University on December 13, 1975: https://media.sas.upenn.edu/Pennsound/authors/Zukofsky/Kenner-1975/Zukofsky-Louis_06_A-Foin-Lass_John-Hopkins_12-13-75.mp3; a recording of Charles Bernstein reading Zukofsky's "A Foin Lass Bodders" at the University of Pennsylvania on March 21, 2007: https://media.sas.upenn.edu/pennsound/authors/Bernstein/McGann-Session/Bernstein-Charles_04_Zukofsky-Foin-Lass_Upenn_03-21-07.mp3.

So, when I wrote to Bernstein in advance of our first meeting to ask whether he saw a connection between Zukofsky and an innovative diasporic Yiddish counter-lineage in American letters, he responded affirmatively: "of course there is this connection!!" (pers. comm., October 20, 2012).

We arranged to meet to discuss, among other things, the Yiddish-threshold poet, Mikhl Likht (1893–1953), a translingual kith-cousin of Louis Zukofsky and Charles Reznikoff, who was writing Yiddish poetry in the teens, twenties and thirties, as experimental and paradigm shifting as the Objectivists' English poetry, only across the language aisle.[30] Stephen Ross and I had just begun translating Likht's Yiddish modernist long "poem of a life," *Protsesiyes* (Processions), and we had recently discovered a letter from Zukofsky to William Carlos Williams, in which Zuk tells Williams that he has been translated along with Ezra Pound, Mina Loy, Marianne Moore, T. S. Eliot, and numerous other first-wave Anglo-modernists, *into* Yiddish *by* Likht. "And you've been not traduced but translated," he writes,

> as something is just translated on a level or even to heaven—you, and Ezra, and Cummings, and Eliot, and Wallace Stevens, and Mina Loy (all these names don't mean the same thing to me of course but I'm trying to outline the effort for you). And the fellow who did it—one Licht [*sic*]—asked me to ask you to forgive him for not asking your permission! If a half dozen read his work and understand it as Yiddish I'll be—but it is Yiddish and literature to boot! (Williams and Zukofsky 2003: 22)

When I brought this letter to Rothenberg in Encinitas a few weeks earlier, he had stood up from his seat with great force and energy and stated: "I dreamt it before I even knew who he was!" And it was that same night that Rothenberg told me I must meet and speak to Charles, and that same night that he wrote Charles to say the same about me.

I arrived in Carroll Gardens that first afternoon with a photocopy of Zukofsky's letter to Williams in hand and with a letter I had found from Williams to Likht himself, as well, ready to explain who this Mikhl Likht was, and to explicate in some way the translingual modernist worlds I believed his writing and translation to cast into relief. But Bernstein already knew, not the particulars, so to speak, not the specifics of the worlds per se but their

30. Likht was a close associate of the New York Yiddish modernist Introspectivism group, established and led by Yankev Glatshteyn (1896–1971), Aaron Glanz-Leyeles (1889–1966), and N. B. Minkov (1893–1958).

dynamics, their movements, their archipelagic ebbs and tides. Because Likht's hidden worlds, the terrains of a translingual Jewish language buried underground to survive, were and are the same worlds that Bernstein's work inherits and transmits *without his choosing*, but which he willingly accepts—with Rothenberg's critical precedent—as a responsibility rather than a burden of our particular historical and ongoing diaspora. "The secular Jewish culture that was wiped out in the Second World War," he writes in his essay "Radical Jewish Culture / Secular Jewish Practice,"

> . . . stranded the correlative developments in America. . . . Imagine European poetry and philosophy by the descendants of Benjamin and Heine. But, to a large extent, this is not to be, or anyway, insofar as it is to be, it too must be the task of secular Jewish culture on this side of the Atlantic and of our radical poetry and ambiguating poetics. I think it is difficult to acknowledge this unwanted and perhaps even insufferable task, certainly it has been difficult for me. But perhaps this is what we have been chosen for. (2010: 16)

Such a statement presents a robust scaffolding for the *expanded-Yiddish* reality I have long been living within. Bernstein gets right to the point in directing our attention to the continual difficulty of acknowledging the task at hand—unwanted perhaps and insufferable as it is—since a core part of that task has to do with a sharing in the very hiddenness of it, in order that the inheritance might somehow survive, by the skin of our teeth, *or tongues*. For Bernstein then, Benjamin and Heine might also be Yiddish writers in a sense, or perhaps it's more accurate to say that their German operates for Bernstein as a strange strain of Yiddish translation. Bernstein inherits the poetics of Benjamin and Heine through and into his writing and thinking as an *expanded-Yiddish* German afterlife in English and intercomprehendible, if incomprehensible, translation of a Jewish dialect(ic)—as Rothenberg writes of Celan:

> you said "jew"
> & I said "jew"
> though neither spoke
> the jew words
> jew tongue
> neither the mother language
> *loshen*
> (1980: 42)

In his essay "Articulating a Radical and a Secular Jewish Poetics: Walter Benjamin, Charles Bernstein, and the Weak Messiah as Girly Man," Stephen Paul Miller argues most compellingly for Bernstein's powerful, almost genealogical, connection to Benjamin, and through Benjamin, also to Heine, as well as Kafka. I agree wholeheartedly with Miller's notion of Bernstein's and Benjamin's radical and secular Jewish praxis as poethics, in Joan Retallack's sense, which he describes in detailed summation and illumination at the close of the essay:[31] "Through nonsensuous similarity," he writes,

> poetic politics, cleaving, a blending of poetry and history with all other language, dynamic biblical parallelism, poetic structures of intensification, modern prophecy, going against the brush of history, material and poetic dialectic and discourse, the flâneur, and profane illumination, Benjamin and Bernstein bring us a much needed radical secular Jewish poetics. Whether or not this poetics is biblical, it is consistent with what Benjamin felt in 1938 as Brecht described fascism's astonishingly far-reaching powers and plans. "While he was talking," wrote Benjamin, "I felt moved by a power that was the equal of that of fascism—one that was no less deeply rooted in the depths of history than fascism's power. It was a very strange feeling, wholly new to me. (Miller 2014: 66–67; Benjamin 2006: 340)

The translingual hem of *expanded Yiddish* is above all elastic, deferring in every direction fascism's blunt monological force as a spectral counterforce to fascism's very power through its utter powerlessness.[32] Surely the ethos of a Jewish dialect "without an army and a navy" does not die in Auschwitz. The Jewish ethos and ethical power of the Yiddish dialect as landless Levite teacher, which was already operative in Benjamin's German, we might speculate, survives in the record of the necessary translation

31. Writes Retallack in *The Poethical Wager*: "Poetics without an *h* has primarily to do with questions of style. Style is the manner in which your experience has understood, assimilated, imprinted you. . . . Your poethical work begins when you no longer wish to shape materials (words, visual elements, sounds) into legitimate progeny of your own poetics. When you are released from filling in the delimiting forms. . . . If you persist, patterns in your work may become more flexible, permeable, conversational, exploratory" (2003: 38).

32. As the sociolinguist and scholar Max Weinreich famously held, using Yiddish as his case in point: *a shprakh iz a dialekt mit an armey un flot* (A language is a dialect with an army and navy) (Weinreich 1944).

between languages: in the sonic and textual residues left behind as writing and speech.[33]

When I visited Bernstein in Carroll Gardens for the first time, the maps of *expanded Yiddish* as I have come to figure and fathom them now were wholly abstract to me. All I knew from was this *Likht*, I now joke, mis/translating myself from Yiddish.[34] From that day forward, Bernstein and I embarked

33. The constellation that Miller imagines—which moves between Bernstein, Walter Benjamin (1892–1940), Heinrich Heine (1797–1856), Franz Kafka (1833–1924), and even Bertolt Brecht (1898–1956)—maps vividly onto my own sense for an expanded and continually expanding Yiddish nexus, in Miller's case, across nineteenth- and twentieth-century German. It's worth noting that *expanded Yiddish*, as I fathom it, does not merely pertain to Jews per se but to innovative threshold figures of all backgrounds that cleave to language, so that Bertolt Brecht could certainly be understood as a liminal or limit case *expanded-Yiddish* figure. In the contemporary context, I read both Pierre Joris and Rosmarie Waldrop as *expanded-Yiddish* practitioners to the core, though neither of them are Jewish by any standard religious or ethnic measure.

I have already discussed Hannah Weiner (1928–97) as a critical English-language presence and precedence within this larger speculative poetic mapping, as well as Bernstein himself (b. 1950), Jerome Rothenberg (b. 1931), Louis Zukofsky (1904–78), and Charles Reznikoff (1894–1976), all in English. There is also Paul Celan (1920–70) in German, Mikhl Likht (1863–1953), and Der Nister (1884–1950) in Yiddish, and we might add also the Anglo-Mongrel modernist Mina Loy (1882–1966)—who I have reason to believe was in fact matrilineally related to Kafka, and whom Likht translated and responded to in his first "Procession"—as well as Clarice Lispector (1920–77) in Brazilian Portuguese, Alejendra Pizarnik (1936–72) in Castellano and French, Edmond Jabès (1912–91) in Egyptian French, Osip Mandelstam (1891–1938) and Isaac Babel (1894–1940) in Russian, and Avot Yeshurun (1904–92) and Harold Schimmel (b. 1935) in Hebrew. The list grows more extensive by the day, and the more I search the more I find: *expanded-Yiddish* practitioners writing and transcreating prolifically in any and every language throughout the nineteenth, twentieth, and twenty-first centuries.

I have in mind to edit a compendium of modern/contemporary *expanded-Yiddish* practitioners of the Americas, which would additionally include (just "to outline the potential effort"): Muriel Rukeyser, Mark Rothko, Armand Schwerner, Rose Drachler, Bob Kaufman, Philip Guston, Adrienne Rich, Larry Eigner, Allen Ginsberg, Jackson Mac Low, Ted Greenwald, David Meltzer, David Antin, Jerome Rothenberg, Eleanor Antin, Jack Hirchman, Adeena Karasick, Charles Bernstein, Julie Ezelle Patton , Harold Schimmel, erica kaufman, Susan Bee, Jamaica Kincaid, Jake Marmer, Maria Damon, Johanna Drucker, Lewis Freedman, Mira Shor, Michelle Taransky, Norman Finkelstein, Rachel Blau DuPlessis, Bob Perelman, Judah Rubin, Matvei Yankelevich, Rachel Levitsky, Rachel Zolf, Craig Dworkin, Isaac Goldemberg, Mimi Gross, Rachelle Owens, Norma Cole, Eugene Ostashevsky, Julia Bloch, Bob Glück, Steven Seidenberg, Tirzah Goldenberg, Laynie Browne, Joel Newberger, Norman Fischer, Anne Tardos, and Hank Lazer, among others.

34. Riffing on the classic Yiddish idiom *vos veys ikh fun—?* (what do I know from—?).

on a long and errant antinomian midrashic conversation, which is ongoing, both *b'al-peh* (orally) and *b'ktsav* (textually), and which actively speculates on what such maps of *expanded Yiddish* might look like if they existed, if we could imagine them from their place of latent concealment *into* a contemporary existence. The aporia we face is that these veiled cartographic lineages *always exist* and *have always existed*, but always also in hiding—we both knew it then and know it now, without having to say it outright, since it speaks for itself in our bodies, on the steps of our lips, roofs of our mouths, and doorways of our tongues—but from where? And how to speak to and through this reality while maintaining the ghost languages' originlessnesses, that is, while making no claim to no origin but translation? Between ourselves looking outward, between the walls of our ever-expanding subcultures and undergrounds, the eight corners of an astral *totafot* signal constant irreparable difference as dissonance, and Hannah's paw now speaks again, this time in the voice of Benjamin: *we must follow the "mediating links" of "stars, entrails, and coincidences"* (2005: 967–98).

> *iii. If my German and my English were dialects of Yiddish / Oyb di bobe volt gehat reder*[35]

> It is never just a matter of recognition as refiguration but redemption through resistance.
> —Charles Bernstein, *Shadowtime* (2005)

In 1967, Jerome Rothenberg and Paul Celan met at a cafe in Paris to discuss Rothenberg's translations of Celan's German poems into English.[36] They spoke in a mixture of broken German and broken English, and only at the end of the conversation did they realize that they both spoke Yiddish, and, as Rothenberg tells it, after that there was not that much more they had to say. In December 1975, Rothenberg writes a poem in memory of his meeting with Celan, which I have already quoted, but which I quote below again, more extensively:

35. *Oyb di bobe volt gehat reder:* Yiddish, meaning "If my grandmother had wheels"—an idiom that usually concludes, ". . . she'd be a trolley car," which pokes fun at the speculative imaginary while recognizing its most radical transformative potentials.
36. Rothenberg was Celan's first English translator, and Celan's work is an extremely important influence on Rothenberg's poetics and aesthetics throughout his *oeuvre*.

of how your poems
arise in me
alive
my eye fixed on
your line
"light was • salvation"
I remember
(in simpler version)
Paris
nineteen sixty seven
in cold light of
our meeting
shivered to dumbness
you said "jew"
& I said "jew"
though neither spoke
the jew words
jew tongue
neither the mother language
loshen . . .
(1980: 42)

This poem marks the encounter between the young Rothenberg and elder Celan as a translingual spark from within and outside the vast and violent darkness of Nazi monolingual monologic. The common languages lie latent, suddenly active, but only for a moment, a flicker, *likht* "light was • salvation." We might think of this meeting as a form of testimony and witness, as well, a spiritual pouring out of dormant trauma via ghost languages, only for a moment—first spoken, later translated into writing.

Rothenberg's conversation with Celan—much like Bernstein's conversation with Weiner so many years later—presents a momentary illumination of the new translational Jewish networks being forged across (and *between*) the postwar *khurbn* ruins.[37] Indeed, Zukofsky would foreshadow

37. I use the Yiddish term *khurbn* here with Bernstein's preface to Rothenberg's *Triptych* very much in mind; writes Bernstein, "The problem is inherent even in the name. The extermination of the European Jews was not a sacrifice, which is why *Shoah*, a Hebrew word meaning 'catastrophe' is often used in preference to *holocaust*. Rothenberg, however, uses a Yiddish word, *khurbn*, meaning "destruction," which retains, for him, the power of the vernacular" (2007: ix–x).

this dynamic in the final lines of his first major work, "A Poem Beginning 'The'" in the form of a *translation and adaptation* from the Yiddish American modernist Yehoash's "oyf di khurves" (on the ruins):

> How wide our arms are,
> How strong,
> A myriad of years we have been,
> Myriad upon myriad shall be.
> (2011: 20)[38]

Despite many years of friendship, Rothenberg and Zukofsky never spoke of their shared Yiddish histories, though their respective works whisper with translingual Yiddish fusedness, Anglo-mongrel (as Loy so rightly put it) shimmering below and behind the English host. The field of *expanded Yiddish* as I conceptualize it might be understood then as an epidermal field, one shed as skin into ether, as dust, as ash, not reconstructed but re/de/composed.

• • • •

In the spring of 2019, the contemporary German poet-translator Norbert Lange and I met at a bar in San Francisco to discuss Lange's German translations of Stephen Ross's and my English translations of Likht. Lange spoke in German, while I spoke in Yiddish, inflecting a friendly *daytchmerish* (German Yiddish), wholly inter-comprehensible to one another, as all Yiddish is at its outer limits. We related aloud to one another in three languages during the conversation the feeling we had of harnessing a translingual echo between ourselves and our elders Bernstein and Rothenberg and ancestors Celan, Zukofsky, Likht, and Loy.

A few days after our meeting, I received an email from Bernstein:

> between my email and your reply, I've spent some time with Norbert Lange, speaking of Likht and of you. Norbert using your English to create German translations of Likht is the perfect extension of what you're writing about. . . . So Likht has found his readers—with you as medium—in Norbert and I talking about him on President Street. His work coming into German through your English. There's something very beautiful about that. It's not that it comes full circle but that it's a continuous circuit with no beginning or end. In this sense German is

38. *Translation and adaptation*: from Yiddish, *fartaytshn un farbesern*, meaning "free translation," literally to "translate and make better."

> the kind of dialect of Yiddish. And Americana English a hodgepodge: miscegenation with no return. (pers. comm., April 15, 2019)

Charles, as I have been attempting to describe in this essay, is one of the first contemporary Jewish artists I recognized early on as an inheritor and teacher of an *expanded-Yiddish* praxis. And now between myself and Lange, between Rothenberg and Celan, between Zukofsky, Likht, and Loy, Bernstein affirmed the potency of the echo Lange and I had felt during our meeting, without assuming we understood its origins in the least. Indeed, as Bernstein suggests, it is in fact the originlessness and continuous circuit of translation as its own source that determines the force of an *expanded-Yiddish* poetics of the past, present, and future.

Returning to Rothenberg and Celan for a moment, I can't help but think of Amos Schauss's Yiddish translation of Rothenberg's "The Wedding" from *Poland/1931*, which I first heard Rothenberg read aloud in his deep Bronx-Yiddish accent while I was sitting between Bernstein and Mimi Gross at Bob Holman's Bowery Poetry Club on the Lower East Side—in the exact neighborhood of the former semi-autonomous cultural territory of New York Yiddishland, the same neighborhood Henry James visited in fear and disgust in his *American Scene* in 1904 (the same year Louis Zukofsky was born there), and which Mina Loy visited in im/pure delight and miscegenating excitement when she found herself living there in 1920.[39] To my ears suddenly it sounded as though Rothenberg had conceived of "The Wedding" in Yiddish but had written it in *Poland/1931* in English translation. "I very well may be the last Yiddish modernist," he said to us that night, half-jokingly, as he has said on many occasions since. "Yes," I thought, "perhaps he is, and if he is, then perhaps so are we, though we write in spontaneous and unconscious, perhaps even *barbaric*, English translation." Or as Bernstein writes in a recent poem dedicated to me, an adaptation "after Reznikoff":

> How difficult, Yiddish, for me;
> even father, the Yiddish for, Hebrew, tongue
> 's foreign. Like home never had
> or ones do.
> (2021: 49)

39. Mimi Gross (b. 1940); on another occasion, after a reading that Charles and Susan Stewart gave at the Bowery, Mimi, Bruce Andrews, Rivka Weinstock, and I found ourselves wandering together around that same neighborhood, and Mimi remarked to us how Allen Ginsberg had come to her parents' house over the years to speak and read Yiddish with her father, the New York Yiddishkayt sculptor Chaim Gross (1902–91).

ג. Coda: On Contemporary Antisemitism, Jewish Self-Hatred, and Translating Bernstein *into* Yiddish

This is not a theory of reading
this is about staying alive.
—Charles Bernstein, *Shadowtime* (2005)

. . . in a cellar or an attic, there was something brewing here and there, minute by minute, even then in that stagnant environment. And a bit of light showed that, depending on who chanced to see it, was either frightening or prophetic.
—Der Nister, *The Family Mashber* ([1948] 1987)

In 2015, while attending a conference at SUNY Buffalo, I was accosted at a bar by what appeared to me to be a vehement anti-Semite, though he claimed his threats were purely Marxist class critique, a claim we Jews with any memory of the twentieth century know all too well. It was the violence of this man's remarks that set off what you might call my "anti-Semitism radar," that sense deep in the Jewish body that makes every hair stand up because you know you are in danger, that this person very well may want to see you dead. The strangest part of this encounter was not that I was screamed at and lunged at by a wasted anti-Semite in a bar—much worse things have happened to Jews over the millennia—but what was especially bizarre and unsettling to me was that this man was my age, was one of my contemporaries, a contemporary poet no less, and a supposed ally of the Left, a supposed antiracist by any regard. Indeed, we had (and have) many friends and colleagues in common, and we are a part of the same poetry communities and networks. Without going into the gory details of the encounter, I will only say that this man insisted, when he found out that I was a student of Bernstein's, that Charles and Susan Bee should be assassinated in their home, and that their resources should be redistributed to the poor poet masses. At first, he almost said it as a joke, like a sick improvised play on Josef Kaplan's *Kill List*. He then went further, however, to suggest that Charles and Susan were in fact part of a larger circle of writers and artists who controlled influence and had special powers through their wealth. He listed four other contemporary Jewish writers who he said were a part of this circle and who he said should also be assassinated, without mentioning a word about the common variable in his virulent equation. "And you don't think it's worthwhile to note that all the writers on your list are Jewish?" I asked him. I didn't even say the word *anti-Semite*, not the word *anti-Semitism*, not even the word *Jew*, but just the word *Jewish*, and this man exploded, screaming at me, that this was a dirty nefarious misreading of his righteous Marxist class critique, and he lunged toward me to teach me some sort of lesson I suppose, if Stephen Ross and I had not run out of the bar in fear for our safety and the ultimate safety of our friends and teachers.

Before I told Charles this story, I had to prepare myself mentally and emotionally; I had to think carefully about how to present this ugly news to him. I needed to tell him; this I knew. And when I finally mustered the courage and told him, he sighed sadly and said, *it's horrible, but what can you do? These sorts of things happen all the time, you can imagine.* This was his response, as well, when a patriotic Saudi Facebook account publicly threatened our lives and erroneously referred to us as "Zionist pigs" on the event page for our sit-in at Kelly Writers House for the Palestinian exile poet Ashraf Fayadh. And it was his response to the numerous Mongrel Coalition posts about the appropriated trauma of Jewish intellectuals, which he and I discussed each time a new slur would come out on their website or Facebook page.[40] Jerry Rothenberg told me: *keep your head down and keep on with your work is all you can do.* None of it would come to any good, that was for sure. But it was, and still is, a contemporary reality of everyday life: a static systemic culture of anti-Semitism that has existed in the world since the Greeks, or at least you could say, in a more modern manifestation since the advent of Christianity, and always among writers and artists as well, especially in the most modern*ist* contexts.[41] We may want to imagine these things away, but we cannot. As I have already written, we feel them at the core of our bodies: anti-Semitism is not merely a cerebral but somatic force. This is where Fanon perhaps failed to see the body of the Jew.[42] The pile of ash at Majdanek death camp is all the raw evidence we need to determine this fact.[43]

40. One particular post I remember, because it was published on the Poetry Foundation website, included several troubling blasts, including: "Let My People Go: Appropriating the Black Body and Resurrecting Identity Politics for Jewish Academics"; while this line remains visible, other disturbing lines from this post have been redacted: https://www.poetryfoundation.org/harriet/2015/05/mcag-presents-the-mongrel-dream-library.

41. This is especially true for American poetry abroad during the first half of the twentieth century; Ezra Pound is perhaps the most famous example, since he went so far as to preach in favor of the extermination of the Jews on Mussolini's radio waves, but also notably, T. S. Eliot and E. E. Cummings, among numerous others.

42. "Two realms," writes Fanon in *Black Skin, White Masks*, "the intellectual and the sexual. . . . The Negro symbolizes the biological danger; the Jew, the intellectual danger" (1967: 127).

43. It is important to note that these are not isolated events, but that these sorts of threats occur all the time and are the subject matter of ongoing conversations between contemporary Jewish writers and artists.

The necessary hiddenness of an *expanded-Yiddish* poetics persists in both conscious and unconscious realms. Consciously, one knows that there are forces, sometimes hidden themselves, sometimes plain out in the open, that would like to see us eradicated, that would like to see us murdered in our homes. Perhaps this is what the man at the bar in Buffalo did not understand about his sick joke—and then supposedly serious class critique: that he was engaging with a very run-of-the-mill discourse of anti-Semitism—one I knew all too well already—which was not innovative or radical in any sense, but just the opposite, and which threatened my very being, even as he poorly cloaked it in orthodox Marxist ideological fatigues. It sounded more like Leninism to me, personally, though I didn't even say *that* to him.

In the unconscious realm, the ghost language, which lives in and on the body, healing it from trauma—Hannah's astral *totafot*—stirs to the sounds of the projected eradication still infecting the very air we breathe. In hiding, this language survives, we know, not dead, though perhaps imagined so, latently waiting for a spark of light to emerge. As Charles Reznikoff once remarked: "just when you think the lights have gone off, they come back on" (1974). And though we Jewish poets today may have nothing else left to do but sigh with sadness at contemporary anti-Semitism as a reality of daily public and private life—a systemic fact as real as misogyny or racism or Islamophobia or homophobia or transphobia—our writing and translations when intertwined speak differently, for the ghost language knows better.[44] It remains in hiding from those forces that would see it and us wiped out, emerging only by the trap/attic door of an expanded-Yiddish poetics.

Yet, it is not only anti-Semitism that threatens the ghost language of *expanded Yiddish* by way of the Jewish body but statist Jewish ideologies themselves, Zionist and American alike, which appear in the form of reverse transposed anti-Semitic discourses, as diatribes of remarkable Jewish self-hatred. One such example of this is the neoliberal/neoconservative Israeli/American smear campaign against Gertrude Stein, around which Bernstein

44. Even within groups of colleagues who otherwise claim to be actively opposed to all forms of hatred and oppression, I see anti-Semitism get swept under the carpet and shrugged off all the time. And though Bernstein and I and many of our secular radical Jewish contemporaries are actively engaged as anti-hatred-oriented people in our daily lives across the board, we rarely discuss the realities of the anti-Semitism we face except quietly with one another. Indeed, it has taken me five years to feel safe enough to write publicly about the anti-Semitic poet at the bar in Buffalo, though I knew for certain it was anti-Semitism he was disgorging from the moment I said the word *Jewish* to him.

organized an extensive dossier on *Jacket2* entitled "Gertrude Stein's War Years: Setting the Record Straight," and about which he wrote at length in his "Gertrude and Alice in Vichyland." For this report, Charles asked me to do some Hebrew translation and reconnaissance work, and together we discovered that the source of one of the major smears against Stein in the mainstream American and Jewish American press—which insists that she nominated Hitler for a Nobel Peace Prize in 1938—originated at the neoconservative pro-settlement Zionist University of Ariel—located in the occupied West Bank—in a (h)academic journal called *Nativ* (Native). The smear in this Zionist settler journal claims that Stein is a forerunner of Yitzchak Rabin and Shimon Peres, that she is a dangerous self-hating and self-defeating leftist Jew like them, their ancestor in fact, and the sort that would seek the destruction of Judaism all together. Yet their projection of Stein's false self-hatred (since the entire story is a made-up fallacy and nothing more, as Charles proves beyond any shadow of a doubt in his report) functions as the very sort of Jewish self-hatred it dumps on Stein, one constantly pointing out an inherited historical fascism without realizing it is in fact pointing to itself, that the ugly vitriol it spews is its defining feature. Perhaps this is not so different from the hatred of someone like this man in the bar in Buffalo or the Saudi patriot. It is what fueled the language wars in Israel/Palestine—Hebrew *against* Yiddish and Arabic—and what led Jewish parents in the United States, perhaps out of fear of this hatred, to assimilate their children into English as fast as possible. I always remember in this regard when I think about *why I write in English and not in Yiddish*, Charles Reznikoff's account of his mother smacking his father on the head with a Yiddish newspaper and admonishing him not to bring that sort of *shund* or trash into the house.[45]

This essay began and ended with two epigraphs from Der Nister, the great Yiddish symbolist writer who took on his pseudonym, which means "The Hidden One" at a time when he was living as an illegal immigrant in Russia. Wearing the implicit hiddenness of his subjectivity as a Jewish writer in the Soviet Union within his very name, Der Nister lived under the radar of the Stalinist regime for a long time and was in fact one of the last of his cohort to be arrested by the gulag and put into prison. He died awaiting a show trial in his cell in 1950 as part of an entire generation of Jewish writ-

45. This comes to me from a mixture of family and poet's lore, and I include it here as a further iteration of the *expanded-Yiddish agodo* I am attempting to engage and activate in this essay.

ers who were murdered by Stalin between 1948 and 1952. I carry the weight of Der Nister's death with me everywhere I go as a reminder of the stakes of the *expanded-Yiddish* poetics I've been discussing in this essay. But did the man in Buffalo realize that my literal ancestors as well as my literary predecessors in Europe and Russia had been snuffed out in precisely the same terms he was insisting on? Our *expanded-Yiddish* praxis persists at the site of this gaping and ongoing trauma—through a poetics of healing in whatever language host it finds—as a resistant response to both historical and contemporary demands for its projected extinction.

I offer the following Yiddish translation of Bernstein's "High Tide at Race Point," a poem I'm wild about from his collection *Near/Miss* (2018b), and which is dedicated to Norman Fischer—a contemporary *expanded-Yiddish* poet himself—as a signal of difference and resistance against the forces both of Jewish self-hatred and anti-Semitism, which work in tandem to project a foreclosed future for stateless and powerless languages.[46] Hidden because the anti-Semites would never be able to read it, and because the self-hating Jews wouldn't want to anyway. I offer it in the company of Likht's Yiddish translations of Loy and Williams, and Norbert Lange's translations of Likht, and Rothenberg's translations of Celan, and Bernstein's translations of Mandelstam, and Amos Schauss's Yiddish translations of Rothenberg, and I dedicate it to Hannah Weiner and to all the hidden landless Levite technicians of an astral *totafot*. I offer it finally as a spark against the anti-difference darkness of our "epoch of catastrophe" and as a flash of light in the face of a proposed eclipse.[47] The final line of the poem reads: "grief without end," which I translate "*tsar on sof*" and about which Bernstein comments: it "alludes to 'ein sof' (without end) in the Kabbalah and the implications of that. (There is also the echo of Freud's distinction between grief, which ends, and melancholy, which doesn't.) But I think the *ein sof*, the 'without end' is a hidden key, or anyway an example of the kind of hidden you are referring to. Echo without end; or as I have it in another poem, my version of the Shema: 'annoyed echo' / *Adonai Eḥad*" (pers. comm., September 20, 2020).

This is, as far as I know, the first translation of Bernstein's *expanded-Yiddish* English verse into Yiddish.

46. Norman Fischer (b. 1946); another powerful example of an *expanded-Yiddish* poet and teacher working within an English-language literary context or "host."

47. I translate Avot Yeshurun's concept of *t'kufa khurban*—which signals a violence that encompasses the twentieth and twenty-first centuries and beyond—as "epoch of catastrophe."

ד. A Yiddish Translation of "High Tide at Race Point" for Norman Fischer

Poetry, centered on the condition of its wordness—words of a language not out there but in here, languages the place of our commonness—is a momentary restoration of ourselves to ourselves.
—Charles Bernstein, "Three or Four Things I Know about Him" (2001)

Hoykh Fleyts in Reys Poynt

far Norman Fischern

An anons on a farkoyf.
A breg yam on zamd.
A gelibter on a gelibte.
A flakh on a droysn.
An onrir on a hant.
A protest on a tsibe.
A kval on a dno.
A shtokh on a bays.
A geshrey on a moyl.
A foyst on a geshleg.
A tog on a sho.
A park on benk.
A lid on a text.
A zinger on a kol.
A kompyuter on zikorn.
A kabane on a plazshe.
A shtroykhl on a veg.
A troyer on a farlust.
A tsil on a tsvek.
A rash on a klang.
A mayse on a sipur-hamayse.
A zegl on a shif.
An eroplan on fligl.
A feder on tint.
A mord on a korbn.
A zind on a zindiker.
A heskem on tnoyem.
A gevirts on tam.
A zhest on bavegung.
A tsukuker on an aroyskuk.

An ukos on an oysbeyg.
A yeyster on a tayve.
A mos on dimensiye.
A nazi on a yid.
A komedyant on a vits.
A tsuzog on a hofenung.
A treyster on der treyst.
Di zikherkayt on zikher zayn.
Ganvenen on ganeyve.
Di volt-geven on dem geven.
Di mishne on toyre.
Di tsvey on dem eynem.
Dos zaydene on der zayd.
Dos umfarmaydlekh on dem muz.
Logik on gedrang.
Plutslingkayt on enderung.
A kanyon on tifenish.
Gaz on reyakh.
Festkayt on fil.
Der gliver on haftkayt.
A refue on a krenk.
A krenk on a shpur.
A mineral on a forem.
A linye on farlengerung.
Akshones on kavone.
Leydik on pustkayt.
Tsoym on tseteylung.
A marionet on shtriklekh.
Oysfolgn on kriterye.
An antoyshung on a dervartung.
Farb on shatirung.
A gedank on a toykhn.
Tsar on sof.

References

Benjamin, Walter. 2005. *Selected Writings, Volume 2, Part 2: 1931–1934*. Edited by Michael W. Jennings, Howard Eiland, and Gary Smith. Cambridge, MA: Harvard University Press.

———. 2006. *Selected Writings, Volume 3: 1935–1938*. Edited by Howard Eiland and Michael W. Jennings. Cambridge, MA: Harvard University Press.

Bernstein, Charles. 1991. "Pockets of Lime." In *Rough Trades*, 80–88. Los Angeles: Sun and Moon Press.

———. 2001. "Three or Four Things I Know about Him." In *Contents Dream, Essays: 1975–1984*, 13–33. Evanston, IL: Northwestern University Press.

———. 2005. *Shadowtime*. Los Angeles: Green Integer.

———. 2010. "Radical Jewish Culture / Secular Jewish Practice." In *Radical Poetics and Secular Jewish Culture*, edited by Stephen Paul Miller and Daniel Morris, 12–17. Tuscaloosa: University of Alabama Press.

———. 2011. "Objectivist Blues: Scoring Speech in Second Wave Modernist Poetry and Lyrics." In *Attack of the Difficult Poems: Essays and Inventions*, 131–57. Chicago: University of Chicago Press.

———. 2018a. "Before Time." In *Near/Miss*, 169. Chicago: University of Chicago Press.

———. 2018b. "High Tide at Race Point." In *Near/Miss*, 19–20. Chicago: University of Chicago Press.

———. 2018c. "My Luck." In *Near/Miss*, 160. Chicago: University of Chicago Press.

———. 2021. "After Reznikoff." In *Topsy-Turvy*, 49. Chicago: University of Chicago Press.

Der Nister (The Hidden One). (1948) 1987. *The Family Mashber*. Translated by Leonard Wolf. London: William Collins Sons and Company Ltd.

Fanon, Frantz. 1967. *Black Skin, White Masks*. Translated by Charles Lam Markmann. New York: Grove Weidenfeld.

Gilman, Sander. 1991. *The Jew's Body*. Abington, UK: Routledge.

Likht, Mikhl. 1957. "Dos lid fun mayn shvartsn bruder" ["The song of my black brother"]. In *Gezamlte lider* [*Collected Poems*], edited by N. B. Minkov, 219–21. Buenos Aires: Farlag Geliye.

Loy, Mina. n.d. *Islands in the Air*. MSS 6, Box 1, Folder 10. Undated page, recto and verso. Yale Collection of American Literature (YCAL), Yale University, New Haven, CT.

Miller, Stephen Paul. 2014. "Articulating a Radical and a Secular Jewish Poetics: Walter Benjamin, Charles Bernstein, and the Weak Messiah as Girly Man." In *Reading the Difficulties: Dialogues with Contemporary American Innovative Poetry*, edited by Thomas Fink and Judith Halden-Sullivan, 41–69. Tuscaloosa: University of Alabama Press.

Probstein, Ian. 2015. "Charles Bernstein: 'Of Time and the Line.'" *Arcade Journal: Poetry after Language Colloquy*. https://arcade.stanford.edu/content/charles-bernstein-time-and-line.

Retallack, Joan. 2003. *The Poethical Wager*. Berkeley: University of California Press.

Reznikoff, Charles. 1974. "Reading at the Poetry Center at San Francisco State

University." March 24, 1974. San Francisco, CA. MPEG-3 49:27. https://media.sas.upenn.edu/pennsound/authors/Reznikoff/Reznikoff-Charles_SF-State_03-21-74.mp3.

Rothenberg, Jerome. 1980. *Vienna Blood & Other Poems*. New York: New Directions Publishing Company.

———. 1981. *Pre-Faces & Other Writings*. New York: New Directions Publishing Company.

———. 2007. *Triptych: Poland/1931, Khurbn, The Burning Babe*. New York: New Directions Publishing Company.

———. 2016. "Pre-Face." In *Symposium of the Whole: A Range of Discourse toward an Ethnopoetics*, edited by Jerome Rothenberg and Diane Rothenberg, xi–xvii. Berkeley: University of California Press.

Weiner, Hannah. 2010. "Complete Transcript of 1995 LINEbreak Conversation with Charles Bernstein." *Wild Orchids*, no. 2: 141–65.

Weinreich, Max. 1944. *YIVO Bleter* 23, no. 3 (May–June 1944).

Williams, William Carlos, and Louis Zukofsky. 2003. *The Correspondence of William Carlos Williams and Louis Zukofsky*, edited by Barry Ahearn. Middletown, CT: Wesleyan University Press.

Yeshurun, Avot. 2020. *Global Modernists on Modernism: An Anthology*. Translated by Ariel Resnikoff. London: Bloomsbury Academic.

Zukofsky, Louis. 1978. "A Foin Lass Bodders." *Paideuma* 7, no. 3: 409–11.

———. 2011. *Anew: Complete Short Poetry*. New York: New Directions Publishing Company.

Charles Bernstein: Avant-Garde Is a Constant Renewal

Ian Probstein

One of the founders of the school of innovative L=A=N=G=U=A=G=E poetry and the current winner (2019) of the Bollingen Prize, Charles Bernstein speaks of the avant-garde as a constant renewal. In his essay about John Ashbery, which I discuss below, Bernstein writes that he always understood the title of David Lehman's book *The Last Avant-Garde* (Lehman

All poems of Charles Bernstein used with permission. I adapted and extended this piece from my introduction to the Russian translation of *Sign Under Test: Selected Poems and Essays* [*Ispytaniye znaka*], edited by Ian Probstein, with poems translated by Probstein and essays translated by Arkadii Dragomoshchenko, Patrick Henry, Alexei Parshchikov, Mark Shatunovsky, and Probstein (Moscow: Russian Gulliver, 2020). The author and the translator are grateful to Irina Usacheva and Vadim Mesyats for the beautifully published book: http://gulliverus.ru/books-tr/238-charlz-bernstin-ispytanie-znaka-izbrannye-stihotvoreniya-i-stati.html (accessed June 9, 2020). Some parts of this essay were previously published in *The River of Time: Time-Space, Language and History in Avant-Garde, Modernist, and Contemporary Poetry* (Boston: Academic Studies Press, 2017), 229–44. I am grateful to Academic Studies Press for giving the permission to reprint parts of the text.

boundary 2 48:4 (2021) DOI 10.1215/01903659-9382271

1999), dedicated to the New York School, "in the sense of *the one before this one*. For avant-gardes are always and necessarily displaced floating flotillas, out on a nameless sea that everyone is always naming" (Bernstein 2016: 150; Bernstein's emphasis). In his recent "Fireword/Foreword to Reading Experimental Writing," he restates the idea:

> The history of poetry is pockmarked by innovation and invention, by the struggle for the new *not as novelty but as necessity*. And this aesthetic struggle has often, though not always, been led by those previously denied a place in literary history. Over the past two centuries, this *pataquerical* imperative has become Western poetry's activist center. The macadamized verse of conventional poetry (MVCP) proliferates like lawn ornaments in a museum of suburban life. In such works, coherence and expression metamorphose into a Coke and Pepsi *mélange*, concocted for sipping on a smoky, hot day. MVCP abhors aesthetic pleasure and semantic license, supposing it can save meaning by suffocating it. (Bernstein 2020: ix; Bernstein's emphasis)

In 1976, Bernstein wrote, "There are no thoughts except through language. . . . The look of the natural [is] constructed, programmatic—artful . . . there is no normal look or sound to a poem. Every element is intended, chosen. That is what makes a thing a poem. . . . Fundamentally, construction is at the heart of writing" (Bernstein 1986: 49). However, Bernstein also transforms language into perceptible possibilities, or rather impossibilities, of perception: a marriage of sound and sense. He explores the limits of impossibility to find out what is possible. He not only pushes language to its limit, extending its boundaries, but he also pushes reality itself to its limit, his keen eye perceiving the irreality and absurdity of many things in our life, and he pushes reality to its utmost—to absurdity. Doing so, Bernstein distorts or deforms reality with the help of surreal fantasy, as in "Beyond the Valley of the Sophist":

> The prolonged hippopotami of the matter
> swivel for their breakfasts, fall in the middle landing soft
> with the horse shrill of honeysuckle, to the decimated
> acid of the sweet
> tub. They are hobbled, dejected
> & lie frozen with salted humbling.
> To the ocean of shorn horizon, averting America's

sentient emptiness, here where the body's sightless ascent
revolts in paltry recompense.
(Bernstein 1991: 70)

In his programmatic essay "Introjective Verse," which is in essence an ironic parody of Charles Olson's "Projective Verse" of 1950, Bernstein states that "ebullient denial of reality takes such a verse out of believing [reality]" and that Oscar Wilde was just getting superfluous when he stated that "life imitates art, not the other way round" (Bernstein 1999: 111). Opposing closed, hermetic, and reflexive poetry, Olson suggested open, "projective verse" based both on Pound's ideas and on "Objective Verse," the subject of Louis Zukofsky's essay "Sincerity and Objectivism" (1931). Olson understands poetry as a surge of energy on the one hand; on the other hand, he insists on the inseparability of form and content. Moreover, he claims that form is no more than an extension of content, which contradicts not only the ideas of Gertrude Stein but also those of Pound and Williams. Bernstein seems to turn all these notions upside down and inside out—from centrifugal to centripetal and from projective to introjective, and he refuses to interpret the meaning outside the specific poetic context, even rejecting the meaning, a very important point for Olson. To paraphrase Marjorie Perloff's comparison of Stein and Eliot in "Gertrude Stein's Differential Syntax," one could say that Olson "believes that words have a naming function, that they mean individually, whereas Stein [and one might add here Bernstein] believes that meaning is only conveyed by *use*, and hence by the larger context of the sentence" (Perloff 2002: 56). Bernstein goes even further, claiming that poetry "makes no promises, no realities outside the poem: no stances only dances. It is the matter of content, this discontent" (Bernstein 1999: 112). He does not freeze on the spot, but at the same time, he does not escape from the painful issues of everyday life. In his latest book of essays, *Pitch of Poetry*, he writes,

> To imagine that there is a neutral space, a craft of poetry, that is free of ideological domination or contamination, is positivism. In poetry culture, it is the most virulent form of ideological self-deception, because it cannot open up to contradiction, difference, or dialectic, that is, to *com(op)positionality*.
>
> To transcend ideology, aesthetic partisanship, movements, groups, and positions is to be blinded by idolatry.
>
> A poetics is valuable to the degree that it is able to engender other positions in response, both complementary and oppositional.

> The cyclical triumphalism of postpartisanship in postwar US poetry, insofar as it intends to end the argument rather than foment it, is the most disingenuous form of position taking.
>
> This triumphalism mirrors, rather than counters, the avant-gardism of formalist progress, which eradicates the prior and the other almost as fast as it eradicates itself. (Bernstein 2016: 297; Bernstein's emphasis).

Bernstein also shifts the notions of the genre: in his work, there are many texts that could be called essay-poems, such as his "Artifice of Absorption" (1987), but also later, the work "How Empty Is My Bread Pudding" from *Recalculating* (2013: 81–91), dedicated to the famous linguist George Lakoff. Shifting the conventionality of the genre, estranging or defamiliarizing it (in the words of Shklovsky, whom Bernstein likes to quote[1]), mixing techniques, interspersing quotations with allusions and collages akin to Pound, Charles Bernstein is at the same time aphoristic: "Don't confuse the puzzle for the solution, the poet for the poem" or:

> Injustice in the pursuit of order is oppression.
> Mendacity in the pursuit of security is tyranny.
> (Bernstein 2013: 87)

John Ashbery, as one of the brightest representatives of the New York School, and Charles Bernstein, as a representative of the Language (L=A=N=G=U=A=G=E) school have similar attitudes toward language. They have much in common in terms of poetics: in the rejection of loud phrases, prophetic statements, emotions, confessionalism, and certain self-centeredness. Poetry is a private matter for both. Both have poetics built on the "oddness that stays odd," as Bernstein himself put it, paraphrasing Pound's "news that stays news" (Pound [1960] 1987: 29), in his essay written for John Ashbery's eightieth birthday, "The Meandering Yangtze"

1. The term *estrangement*, or *defamiliarization*, was put forward by Victor Shklovsky (1893–1984) in his seminal "Iskusstvo kak priyom" [Art as device, or Art as technique], first published in volume 2 of *Sborniki po teorii poeticheskogo yazyka* [Collections (of essays) on the theory of poetic language] (Petrograd, 1917), 3–14. See Shklovsky (1929) 1990: 1–14, esp. 6, 11–14. He considered "the device of defamiliarization," or estrangement, as one of the main devices in literature aimed at a "shift" of meaning and perception to de-automatize them. Brecht further developed this concept ("alienation") as did the structuralists of the Prague school ("de-automatization"). It is possible that Gertrude Stein, who wrote, "Rose is a rose is a rose," and Ezra Pound, who drew his "make it new" from Chang Ti (the Chinese emperor of 1766 BC), came independently to the same idea.

(Bernstein 2016: 152). Both are aimed at renovating the language, and the verses of both are built on fragmentation, collage, moving from one statement to another without preparation. However, in Ashbery, whose poems are surreal, these transitions are smoother, based on an apparent connection, what Bernstein calls "hypotaxis" or "associative parataxis" (152), that is, using conjunctions, such as "ever since," "meanwhile," "in the meantime," "because," and the like, that do not really connect anything but are "fictitious"' or "false" conjunctions:

The answer is that it is novelty
That guides these swift blades o'er the ice,
Projects into a finer expression (but at the expense
Of energy) the profile I cannot remember.
Colors slip away from and chide us. The human mind
Cannot retain anything except perhaps the dismal two-note theme
Of some sodden "dump" or lament.

But the water surface ripples, the whole light changes.
(From the poem "The Skaters," Ashbery 1974: 34)

Bernstein even believes that Ashbery's surreal poetics can be described as "slip," seeming gradual, "smooth," a transition between unrelated parts, like in the poem "The Skaters" or in de Chirico's painting. On the contrary, Bernstein seeks sharper, "bumpy" transitions based on "parataxis," as in Pound's famous poem:

The apparition of these faces in the crowd;
Petals on a wet, black bough.
("In a Station of the Metro," Pound [1926] 1990: 111)

Language poetry also suggests a new reading of the established poetry canon, proposing not just a revision of it but rather a new interpretation. For instance, Bernstein is a very thoughtful reader of Emily Dickinson's works. Bernstein quotes Dickinson's poem found in her letter to Susan, her brother's wife:

By homely gifts and hindered Words
The human heart is told
Of Nothing—
"Nothing" is the force
That renovates the World—
(Franklin 1611/Johnson 1563, dated 1883)

In his interview with London's *Wolf Magazine*, Bernstein connects Dickinson's poem to W. H. Auden's famous elegy, "In Memory of W. B. Yeats" ([1939] 2007), by quoting Auden's notable line "For poetry makes nothing happen," and says that Dickinson's other saying, "Don't you know that 'No' is the wildest word we consign to Language," has always been his motto. Bernstein insists that his is "homely poetics, both odd-looking (unattractive, disagreeable, low), and intimate (even private)" (Bernstein 2016: 277). Therefore, for Bernstein, poetry is a private matter; poetry does not serve to achieve any goals. In the end, Bernstein concludes, "I read Dickinson's poem as close to negative dialectic. Nothing in the sense of not one thing: variants around a blank center. To be told about nothing is to come face to face with loss, despair, grief: the irreparable. Nothing repairs the world. *Renovates* is something else again: making new now," Bernstein says, quoting Pound's motto (278; Bernstein's emphasis). Hence for Bernstein, the avant-garde is a constant renewal. He moves to unexplored areas and invents new names for them. In *Pitch of Poetry,* he writes, "The task of bent studies is to move beyond the 'experimental' to the untried, necessary, newly forming, provisional, inventive. Innovation resists maps. I want a poetics that rejects the historical avant-garde's colonic high ground of single best solution but also rejects its dark twin, the bottom-feeding low ground of official verse culture's lobotomization of poetic invention. Conflict is art's quiver" (297).

Bernstein's "pataquerical imagination" is based on Alfred Jarry's (1873–1907) "pataphysics" (meaning "weird," "odd"), the notion Jarry coined in *Dr. Faustroll's Acts and Judgments* (Jarry 1996), *pataphysics*, a science associated with laws that govern exceptions. Bernstein once again blurred this concept. Thus, he developed the idea of "pataquerical" imagination, adding "querical," in which "queer" ("strange") is also an echo of the words *querist* (experienced, questioning) and *quest*. Bernstein himself writes that this is a "syncretic term combining 'weirdness' and 'wildness'" (2016: 77).

The word *echo* is also no accident, since Bernstein also put forward the idea of "echopoetics," that is, poetics based on echoes.

> Unheard melodies are celestial demographics.[2] Even if you can't put your finger on it you can still pretend to count.
>
> You go to the club in the evening only to be clubbed at dawn. How long has this been going on? There's more than one way to fleece a sheep but only one way to stop.

2. This is evidently an allusion to John Keats's "Ode on a Grecian Urn."

> Echopoetics is the nonlinear resonance of one motif bouncing off another within an aesthetics of constellation. Even more, it's the sensation of allusion in the absence of allusion. In other words, the echo I'm after is a blank: a shadow of an absent source.
>
> A network of stopgaps. (Bernstein 2016: x)

In other words, echopoetics "always deforms or removes the basic sound, so it is doubtful whether the original sound exists," as Bernstein explained to me in a private conversation.

Yet, Language poetry, nevertheless, searches for truth even through *zaum'*, in Khlebnikov's sense, by examining the roots of words, restoring meaning by shifting or even distorting it. Reflecting on this idea while analyzing Khlebnikov's famous "Kuznechik" ("Grasshopper"), Marjorie Perloff draws the conclusion that "zaum' in this context, far from being 'nonsense,' is more accurately super-sense" (Perloff 1986: 126) and compares Khlebnikov's thoughts to Pound's famous formula: "great literature is simply language charged with meaning to the utmost possible degree. . . . I begin with poetry because it is the most concentrated form of verbal expression" (Pound [1960] 1987: 36).

In the essay "Nasha osnova" (Our foundation), Khlebnikov also states, "Zaum' language is the fetus of a forthcoming world language. Only it can unite people. Smart languages have separated them" (Khlebnikov 1933: 236).[3] Hence, zaum' for Khlebnikov is also the tool of a future union and the communion of humankind.

Khlebnikov's *zaum'* (beyond understanding) is by no means senselessness but rather the search for the meaning beyond common sense or official doctrine. This is very much in the manner of George Orwell, who revealed the false nature of "newspeak" and showed that language itself exposes the lies of "fraternity, equality, freedom" (the vocabulary of any dictatorship, whether Hitler's, Stalin's, or Mao's) or, for that matter, the half-truths of contemporary American life (Orwell 1949: 7). On the habitual level of everyday business life, Bernstein's witticism mocks, as he puts it in "Beyond the Valley of the Sophist," "the vanity of conceits." "He understated the price of the property to be sure he got less than it was worth. This was the only way he knew for the exchange to have value" ("Sign Under Test," Bernstein 2006: 160). In other words, the devaluation of real values is the only means of value exchange. The poet exposes "free gifts" (here,

3. Khlebnikov 1933: 5:236; translation is mine.

language itself exposes the lies, if we care to examine it) as traps. Hence the Russian saying, "free cheese is found only in a mousetrap." Parodying various aspects of political, social, economic, and business life, Bernstein does not spare intellectuals either, satirizing a wide range of common types of academic discourse.

Bernstein, who recently became Emeritus Donald T. Regan Professor at the University of Pennsylvania, has not become part of the establishment, in that he critiques, often in a comic way, various aspects of modern intellectual, academic, social, and political life, as in an earlier poem, "Beyond the Valley of the Sophist," ridiculing the days of President Reagan, or the present, as in the "Ballad Laid Bare by Its Devices (Even): A Bachelor Machine for MLA" or in "Our United Fates":

> Which is worse—
> Global warring or global warming?
> Credit default swaps or stop and frisk?
> Surveillance states or voters suppressed?
> Children in poverty or gerrymandering?
> Is the American Dream
> Beacon of opportunity
> Or piss on outhouse floor?
> Either way, one thing's for sure
> Income inequality guarantees disunity—
> The one percent's scam du jour.
> (Bernstein 2018: 136)

In our conversation published on January 30, 2020, in the *Russian Liberal Mission* and translated by me into Russian,[4] Bernstein spoke of the shameful hypocrisy of American liberal media: "During the last presidential campaign, National Public Radio said it would not call Trump's lies *lies*; that is their 'Phil Ochs' moment of liberal 'fairness.' NPR commissioned 'Our United Fates' but refused to air it, either because it didn't have the right tone, or it violated NPR's commitment not to challenge its audience with 'difficulties.' Accessibility is the opium of the masses! ("Laid bare" in the title of my ballad is a reference to Shklovsky's "Art as Device."[5])

4. "A Conversation of Ian Probstein and Charles Bernstein on Liberalism." January 30, 2020. http://liberal.ru/new-york-room-by-jn-probstein/beseda-yana-probshteina-s-charlzom-bernstinom-o-liberalizme (the English translation is elsewhere in this volume) (accessed August 31, 2020).

5. Another term put forward by Victor Shklovsky (1893–1984) in his seminal *O Teorii prozy* (1929) (*Theory of Prose*, 1990: 59, 146, 149, 201). The notion of "laying bare,"

Perhaps, though, the Republicans' current branding will haunt their party in the years to come. "But even if that is true, the damage done in the meantime is irreversible."[6]

Evidently, Bernstein was referring to the prophetic lines like "Ballad Laid Bare" written at the beginning of 2017, before Donald Trump's inauguration:

> A little bit south of here, in Washington
> Next week's gonna get a whiff of Armageddon
> Billionaire racist takin' over
> 1600 Pennsylvania Avenue
> Not to mention the Pentagon too.
> Wait and see, he's gonna make the earth
> His own private barbeque.
> (Bernstein 2018: 91)

It is noticeable that Bernstein predicted the situation in which we all appear now, as in "Asylum," the first long poem (1975) written by the poet at the age of twenty-five and included in his selected collection *All the Whiskey in Heaven* (2010). It is based on Erving Goffman's book *Asylums: Essays on the Social Situation of Mental Patients and Other Inmates*, which also refers to shelters, monasteries, military bases, and ships, where people are kept in greater or lesser isolation from the outside world (Goffman: 1961). These include "jails, penitentiaries, P.O.W. camps, concentration camps // . . . army barracks, ships, boarding schools, work / camps, colonial compounds, large mansions // abbeys, monasteries, convents" (Bernstein 2010: 3–4).[7]

> On ward 30
> unless Dr. Baker
> himself asked for them
> persevering, nagging, delusional group—
> "worry warts"
> "nuisances"

---

which means revealing (making palpable) the literary devices, whether tropes, syntax, or plot formation, was also developed by Roman Jakobson in "Modern Russian Poetry" ([1921] 1973: 64–69), and other scholars of the Russian Formalist school. Jakobson even wrote about the "terminology laid bare" about philological studies (1922: 223).

6. "A Conversation of Ian Probstein and Charles Bernstein on Liberalism."

7. The original text, still printed on the typewriter, is available at http://eclipsearchive.org/projects/ASYLUMS/html/pictures/028.html (accessed June 9, 2020).

"bird dogs"
in the attendant's slang
passage of information . . .
. . . .
a special basis of distance and control over inmates
(4–5)

In my view, this poem also alludes to Ken Kesey's *One Flew Over the Cuckoo's Nest* (Kesey [1962] 2007: 17, 161, 272–75) and even to Aleksandr Solzhenitsyn's *The Gulag Archipelago* (1973: 179–276; 533–87, 595–605):

> life history, photographing, weighing, fingerprinting, assigning numbers, searching, listing personal possessions for storage, undressing, bathing, disinfecting, haircutting
>
> nakedness. Leaving off
>
> on, with
>
> clothing, combs, towels, soap, shaving sets, bathing facilities
>
> disfigurement, beatings,
> shock therapy, surgery
>
> dispossession
>
> integrity. . .
>
> (Bernstein 2010: 8)

As I mentioned before, it may also be projected to the COVID-19 quarantine, social distancing, and isolation, but most importantly, to isolationism as a current trend in American politics. Hence this "Language" poem appears to be also prophetic, while the distortion of reality to the utmost degree appears to be a coherent, albeit somewhat grim, nonmimetic representation of our rapidly changing reality:

Another
beg, importune, humbly ask
a daily round of life
his body, his immediate actions, his thoughts
clear of contact
violated; the boundary
relationships. . . .
(9)

To paraphrase his own introduction to the book *With Strings*, entitled "In Place of a Preface a Preface" (Bernstein 2001: xi–xii), the poet seems out of touch with reality, not out of touch but out of reach, not out of reach but out of pitch, not out of pitch of reality but in touch with irreality, not in touch but reaching, not reaching but teaching, not teaching but preaching, not preaching irreality but piercing reality, not piercing reality but bridging reality and irreality, reality and appearance, sense and perception, impossible possibilities and inexplicable causes, inexplicable causes and unavoidable effects, unavoidable effects and unnecessary necessity, unnecessary necessity and inevitable chances, heaven and hell. How does a translator approach this intricate texture? Should he relay or replay it, replay or reply, replay or replace, replace or lace, lace or unbind, unbind or bind bound to interpret, or misinterpret the essence bound to interpret the husk of which art is made, as Bernstein himself once claimed?[8]

In connection with that, I would like to add a few words about the translation of Bernstein's poem "Ruminative Ablution"[9]:

> I've got a hang for langue but no truck with
> *Parole*. You can't bleed an egg cream from a
> Stone. And before you knew it the better
> You fell for it . . .
>
> . . . .
> Worcestershire sauce on the
> Tumbling glosses, & a bottle of snake oil
> For my roiling pen. What's sauce for the gander
> Is gravy for the geese—if you can't buy
> Redemption may I recommend you lease?
> (Bernstein 2001: 71)

Literal translation distorts the essence and any reading, any interpretation, is a translation. George Steiner believes that it is possible to translate only a "contingent motion of spirit" (Steiner 1975: 71), that is, the movement of the poetic thought through an image. To name the phenomena of the world is to reveal them. Revelation is reevaluation: reveiling and unveiling something so palpable and fragile that when "rendered in a disdainful prose," to quote Pushkin, it evaporates.

The title of this ironic poem starts with a large share of satire. Strictly, the word *ablution* means washing clean, as in the ritual cleansing of bap-

8. I already wrote about this feature in Bernstein's poetry (Probstein 2017: 231).
9. See Bernstein and Probstein 2020.

tism; and the word *ruminative* means contemplating, brooding, but based on the context of the poem, especially the last line, which speaks of redemption, I entitled the translated poem, "Reflections on Redemption," which makes more sense for the Russian reader, less familiar with the term *ablution* and more with *redemption*.

Further, from the combination of slang and linguistic terms, namely, the basic terms from Ferdinand de Saussure's *Course in General Linguistics*, "langue," which in Russian translation of Saussure's book is rendered as "language," that is, the general concept for the entire body of language (*langue* in French), and "parole" translated into Russian as "speech," that is, those meanings, alterations, that the language accepts in practical use, such as professional jargon, slang, thieves' jargon, etc. (Saussure [1959] 1966: 9, 13), it is clear that Bernstein ironically pretends to be lost in speech, in the current usage and changes of language. Hence, Bernstein half-jokingly and half-seriously speaks, in fact, about the literary art, poetry, and above all, about the renewal of language.

Next, "hang" rhymed with "langue" is slang for "to have an addiction," "to enjoy" linked with a linguistic term, and then the poet ironically talks about how difficult it is to be understood ("An uttered thought is but a lie," as the great Russian poet Fedor Tiutchev wrote in the poem "Silentium"[10]). However, before you realize it, you're already involved in speech activities, that is, in the painful process of expressing oneself in words; "you fell for it," that is, you are stuck, and the occupation is ungrateful and unpaid, so you live somewhere out in the backwoods (Honolulu) or from hand to mouth, so the translator decided to use the Russian slang of his youth "bare Vasya" (literally, "naked Basil") rhymed with "bare vaser" ("bare water" from the German "Wasser," that is, hot water instead of tea), and then, instead of the English "roiling pen" modified from the "roller pen," I coined a word which is virtually untranslatable (something like "auto" + the word combining "pen" and "curse" or "scold"). In the lines "What's sauce for the gander / Is gravy for the geese," I allowed myself a certain liberty: instead of "gander," I used the Russian word "poliv" (literally, "oiling" or "pouring liquid," which is slang, meaning "brag," "show off," "exhibit").

In recent years, Bernstein himself has been increasingly involved in translating poetry, from Catullus to Mandelstam, Khlebnikov, Apollinaire, Paul Celan, and many others. He once wrote, "The translation of poetry

10. "A thought once uttered is untrue," as Vladimir Nabokov rendered in his brilliant translation of this poem: http://www.lib.ru/NABOKOW/silent.txt (accessed June 15, 2020).

is never more than an extension of the practice of poetry" ("How Empty Is My Bread Pudding," Bernstein 2013: 84). As he told me once in a private interview,

> I disagree with Robert Frost's often quoted remark that poetry "is lost . . . in translation." For me, poetry is always a kind of translation, transformation, transposition, and metamorphosis. There is nothing "outside" translation: no original poem or idea, nor one perfect translation. It's a matter of choosing among versions. Translation is a form of reading or interpreting or thinking with the poem. In that sense, there can be no experiencing the poem, even in your own language, without translating. Without translation the poem remains just a text, a document, a series of inert words. Poetry is what is found in translation. (Probstein 2017: 232)[11]

This attitude toward translation characterizes Bernstein as a Language poet. Bernstein is a Language poet in the Poundian sense: "language charged with meaning to the utmost possible degree" (Pound [1960] 1987: 36). (I first met Charles Bernstein at a conference on Pound). In my view, Bernstein's poetry is meaningful sound or reverberating sound-meaning. In Russian, I coined the compound word "zvukosmysl" (literally, "sound-meaning" or "sound-sense") to apply to both Khlebnikov and Mandelstam. I would even suggest that in at least one respect, Khlebnikov's zaum' is akin to Eliot's "Shanti, Shanti, Shanti" at the end of *The Waste Land*: not only the world itself but poetry as such is beyond understanding and resists interpretation. As Mandelstam wrote, very much like Eliot in "The Three Voices," the voice of music in poetry is incomprehensible without meaning, but if poetry is reduced only to meaning, "the sheets on the bed have never been rumpled, there poetry, so to speak, has never spent the night" (Mandelstam 1979: 397).

In addition to criticism, irony, and satire, another distinctive feature in Bernstein's poetry is a sense of time and space that is palpable in many of his poems, but perhaps most strikingly, in the poem "Of Time and the Line," in which the poet merges time, space (in almost a Bakhtinian sense), and poetry (line). Bernstein's play with the polysemy of the word

11. From the essay "Of Time and the Line"; a somewhat shorter form and a complete interview, including the above citation, were published in *Arcade*, an electronic journal of Stanford University, November 13, 2015, http://arcade.stanford.edu/content/charles-bernstein-time-and-line.

line reveals his attitude toward the past, both recent—"My father pushed a / line of ladies dresses—not down the street / in a pushcart but upstairs in a fact'ry / office"—and historic, going as far back as Adam naming things: "Adam didn't so much name as delineate" (Bernstein 1991: 42). The present stretched to the future in the form of a poetic line uniting time with space. Space is also revealed in a variety of "lines": "Chairman Mao put forward / Maoist lines" (42), "long lines in Russia," soup lines in the United States (43). Unlike Kafka, Bergson, or Proust—who were uncomfortable in space and found shelter in time, as Stephen Kern once stated (Kern 1983: 50–51), Bernstein seems to be comfortably uncomfortable, or uncomfortably comfortable, both in space and time, since his antagonism never acquires the form of agonism. It is rather an ironic, often self-ironic paradox. Hence his advice in "Self-Help" (Bernstein 2006: 171–74) which is in essence above and beyond its irony ("Miss the train?—Great chance to explore the station!" [172]), self-irony ("Bald?—Finally, you can touch the sky with the top of your head" [172]), mockery ("FBI checking your library check-outs.—I also recommend books on Amazon" [173]), and satirical undertones ("President's lies kill GIs.—He's so decisive about his core values" [174]). It is a very existential poem. So is "Sign Under Test" (Bernstein 2006: 157–63) in which the major themes—poetry ("poetry is patterned thought in search of unpatterned mind" [158]), language ("if language could talk we would refuse to understand it" [161]), ironical and satirical juxtaposition of unreal reality with virtual irreality ("it's not the absence in the presence but the presence in the absence" [158])—are again reunited in order to question the essence of being: "If progress is a process, what is the purpose of purpose or the allure of allure?" (163).

Mesmerized by these blank spots (what he does not know or understand), Bernstein writes, "they have become the sign posts of my consciousness" (157). The poet is not satisfied with what he does, nor is he self-righteous or conceited: "Till you get to the backside of where you began. Neither round robin nor oblong sparrow" (158). Yet, for Bernstein, there always seems to be a positive outcome from negative knowledge: "What you don't know is a far cry from what you do" (159).

Trying "to re-imagine the possibilities of sentience through the material sentience of language," Bernstein is nevertheless rediscovering existentialism in order to preserve human dignity and integrity: "the Greeks had an idea of nostos, which is not quite what we call nostalgia. Nostos suggests the political and ethical responsibility of the human being, in orienting herself or himself. You can't go home again but you can stay tuned to your senses of responsibility" (162). Therefore, I would assert that Bernstein is uniting time, space, and line to make, in the Poundian sense, "language charged with meaning to the utmost degree" (Pound [1954] 1985: 36).

References

Ashbery, John. 1974. "The Skaters." In *Rivers and Mountains*. New York: Ecco Press.

Auden, Wystan H. 2007. "In Memory of W. B. Yeats" (1939). In *Collected Poems*, by W. H. Auden, edited by Edward Mendelson, 247. New York: Modern Library.

Bernstein, Charles. 1986. *Content's Dream: Essays 1975–1984*. Los Angeles: Sun & Moon Press.

———. 1987. *The Sophist*. Los Angeles: Sun & Moon Press.

———. 1991. *Rough Trades*. Los Angeles: Sun & Moon Press.

———. 1999. *My Way: Speeches and Poems*. Chicago: University Chicago Press.

———. 2001. *With Strings: Poems*. Chicago: University of Chicago Press.

———. 2006. *Girly Man*. Chicago: University of Chicago Press.

———. 2010. *All the Whiskey in Heaven*. New York: Farrar, Straus and Giroux.

———. 2013. *Recalculating*. Chicago: University of Chicago Press.

———. 2016. *Pitch of Poetry*. Chicago: University of Chicago Press.

———. 2018. *Near/Miss*. Chicago: University of Chicago Press.

———. 2020. "Fireword/Foreword." In *Reading Experimental Writing*, edited by Georgina Colby. Edinburgh: Edinburgh University Press.

Bernstein, Charles, and Ian Probstein. 2020. *Ispytaniye znaka* [*Sign under Test*]. Compiled, edited, and translated by Ian Probstein. Moscow: Russian Gulliver. 2020. http://gulliverus.ru/books-tr/238-charlz-bernstin-ispytanie-znaka-izbrannye-stihotvoreniya-i-stati.html.

Goffman, Erving. 1961. *Asylums: Essays on the Social Situation of Mental Patients and Other Inmates*. Garden City, NY: Anchor Books.

Jakobson, Roman. (1921) 1973. "Modern Russian Poetry: Velimir Khlebnikov." In *Major Soviet Writers: Essays in Criticism*, edited by Edvard Brown, 58–82. London: Oxford University Press.

———. 1922. "Briusovskaya stikhologiya i nauka o stikhe" [The versichology of Briusov and the science of verse]. *Novye Izvestiia*. Akademicheskogo tsentra Narkomprosa R.S.F.S.R. [News of the academic center of the Ministry of Education of the Russian Soviet Federation (of) Socialist Republics]. II: 222–40. Moscow.

Jarry, Alfred. 1996. *Exploits & Opinions of Doctor Faustroll, Pataphysician: A Neo-scientific Novel*. Translated by Simon Watson Taylor, introduction by Roger Shattuck. Cambridge, MA: Exact Change.

Kern, Stephen. 1983. *The Culture of Time and Space*. Cambridge, MA: Harvard University Press.

Kesey, Ken. (1962) 2007. *One Flew Over the Cuckoo's Nest*. New York: Penguin.
Khlebnikov, Velimir. 1933. *Sobraniie proizvedenii* [Collected works in five volumes]. Edited by Yuri Tynyanov and Nikolai Stepanov. Leningrad: Izdatel'stvo Pisatelei [Writers' Publishing], 1928–33.
Lehman, David. 1999. *The Last Avant-Garde: The Making of the New York School of Poets*. New York: Anchor Books.
Mandelstam, Osip. 1979. *The Complete Critical Prose and Letters*. Edited by Jane Gary Harris, translated by J. G. Harris and Constance Link. Ann Arbor, MI: Ardis.
Orwell, George. 1949. *1984*. New York: Harcourt, Brace.
Perloff, Marjorie. 1986. *The Futurist Moment*. Chicago: University of Chicago Press.
———. 2002. "Gertrude Stein's Differential Syntax." In *21st-Century Modernism: The "New" Poetics*. Oxford: Blackwell.
Pound, Ezra. (1926) 1990. *Personae*. New York: New Directions.
———. (1954) 1985. *Literary Essays*. Edited and with an introduction by T. S. Eliot. New York: New Directions.
———. (1960) 1987. *ABC of Reading*. New York: New Directions.
Probstein, Ian. 2017. *The River of Time: Time-Space, Language and History in Avant-Garde, Modernist, and Contemporary Poetry*. Boston: Academic Studies Press.
Saussure, Ferdinand de. (1959). 1966. *Course in General Linguistics*. New York: McGraw-Hill.
Shklovsky, Viktor. (1929) 1990. *Theory of Prose*. Translated with an introduction by Benjamin Sher, introduction by Gerald L. Bruns. Normal, IL: Dalkey Archive Press.
Solzhenitsyn, Aleksandr. 1973. *The Gulag Archipelago*. Translated from the Russian by Thomas P. Whitney. New York: Harper & Row.
Steiner, George. 1975. *After Babel: Aspects of Language and Translation*. New York: Oxford University Press.
Zukofsky, Louis. 1931. "Sincerity and Objectivism." *Poetry* 37, no. 5: 268–84.

Pataquericalism: Quantum Coherence between the East and West

Runa Bandyopadhyay

Pataquericalism, the magical word coined by Charles Bernstein, is the very first word I fell in love with in Bernstein's poetics. Let me call Bernstein's poetics of pataquericalism *Bernsteinism*. As a pataquericalist, to explore his poetic world, let me call you to your time machine first. Hold the light in your fist. Accelerate the time machine just after blastoff. Some percentage of light falls off through your fingers. Let it fall. Now rotate the golden key to the past, not to centuries but just five decades, to reach the singularity of the 1970s, to witness a poetic big bang, where a group of iconoclastic New York poets committed to formal invention and a shared sense of importance to both historical and ideological approaches to poetics and aesthetics as activists were living in a plasma state of ionized ideas and thoughts. They were waiting for the nucleation of a thermodynamic phase transition in the world of American poetry to arrive at "bent poetics," by adding impurities to "pure abstraction" to create an oscillation of figure and nonfigure, appearance and disappearance. "Thermodynamic" in the sense

boundary 2 48:4 (2021) DOI 10.1215/01903659-9382285

of *thermo*, to connect a lukewarm newborn tongue to a new language, and *dynamic*, to connect to its expression as a process of dynamic composition of a poem. They were waiting for the "transformation of figuration into abstraction, abstraction into image, and image into the figurative" (Bernstein 2016: 58). Now, slowly sip Bernstein's "All the Whiskey in Heaven": "Not for a million trips to Mars . . . Not for all the fire in hell . . . Not for all the blue in the sky" (2010: 297), but for the exploration into the imaginary world, which exists between real and unreal. When gold turns grey, you're on your way. After reaching Bernstein's universe of quantum parallelism, where he carries out several superimposed actions simultaneously, you'll find that your old world has vanished. The I-centered lyrical whistle you'd kept in your old hankie has been crystallized to create a nonmaterial non-purpose-driven aesthetic space. This nucleation process is a random process, a quantum randomness opposed to strictly deterministic laws of nature, similar to radioactive decay, where the sparkling Bernsteinian atom, along with those of Silliman, McCaffery, and Bruce Andrews, radiates gamma rays to create microscopic fluctuations in the existing system of verse culture, until there is an unusually large fluctuation of the new phase of poetry, so large that it is more favorable for it to grow than to shrink back to nothing.

This thermodynamic phase transition is the Language poetry movement. And *L=A=N=G=U=A=G=E* magazine, coedited by Bernstein, "a poet of the pataquerulous kind," with Andrews, published its first issue in 1978, became the CMB radiation (Cosmic *Multifoliate* Background radiation, in my sense), replacing *Microwave* with *Multifoliate* to extend the radiation from a specific frequency zone to multiple possibilities of poems, for the movement to keep the imprint of the historical poetic big bang and also to pursue: "A poetry aversive to convention, standardization, and received forms, often prizing eccentricity, oddness, abrupt shift of tone, peculiarity, error and the abnormal—poetry that begins in disability. This is what I call pataquerical imperative" (Bernstein 2016: 76).

I am so fascinated with this word *pataquericalism* that I'd like to start mining the word in my own way. The first word I take from *pataquericalism* is *queer*, from the Austrian British philosopher Ludwig Wittgenstein. Wittgenstein's *Philosophical Investigation* shows how the language we use shapes how we perceive the things from our physical world. Wittgenstein made the fundamental philosophical base for *L=A=N=G=U=A=G=E* as well as for the pataquericalist Bernstein. Entering from German to the English language in the sixteenth century, *queer* means strange, peculiar, eccentric, uncommon, anomalous, curious, odd, weird, or bizarre, altered, unexpected, to generate "a kind of aesthetic shock treatment or method of intoxication . . . to transform the queer instantiation of wordness from malady to melody" (Bernstein 2016: 317). The second word I take is *query*—critical inquiry into the language of poetry, questioning preconceived notions of beginning, middle, and end by means of a rejection of closure. By combining the two words *queer* and *query*, I arrive at *QU(E)ERY*, to mean queer inquiry. The third word I take is *'pataphysics*, coined and defined by the French protomodernist Alfred Jarry of the late nineteenth century, as "the science of imaginary solution, which symbolically attributes the properties of objects, described by their *virtuality*, to their lineaments" (Jarry 1996: 22). Pataphysics is the "science of *imperceivable* solutions to opaque problems," in Bernstein's words (2016: 171), or, in the words of Roger Shattuck, introducer of Jarry's "neo-scientific" or "hypothetical" novel *Exploits and Opinions of Doctor Faustroll, Pataphysician*: "If mathematics is the dream of science, ubiquity [*sic*] the dream of morality, and poetry the dream of speech, 'pataphysics fuses all into the 'common sense' of Dr. Faustroll, who lives all dreams as one" (Jarry 1996: ix). This makes the scientific base of *pataquericalism*. If metaphysics is the science beyond physics, 'pataphysics is the science beyond metaphysics, the dynamic interplay between metaphysics, the "science" of abstraction, and 'pataphysics, the "science" of exception, not of the general but of the particular. Allow me to add these terms to mean scientific exception via abstraction. So the combination of my chosen three key words gives rise to *PATAQUERY*, to mean queer inquiry into the poem by means of 'pataphysics. This may or may not be the origin of the Bernsteinian word *pataquericalism*, yet I love to imagine it this way.

Pataquericalism is a new leftist way to gain freedom from the known, freedom from authority, to move on in the Bernsteinian way: "I was born yesterday . . . and I'll die tomorrow" (Bernstein 2013: 124). This is to say, Bernstein will wrest freedom even from all the authorities of his own mind and memory. Everything of yesterday will die so that his mind will be always fresh, always young, innocent, full of vigor and passion. This strongly resonates with the tone of Barin Ghosal, the key poet of the *Kaurab* literary movement in the world of Bengali poetry in India, started in 1968: "Kill your own memory; only then you will feel an active new quality propagating in your innerself. It is possessing you. All the niches left void by your memory are being occupied by quality. Quality only has helped you to overcome all obstacles" (2003a: 54). Or as Bernstein puts it, "CARPE DIEM: CARP AND DIE / I am not the man I was much less the one I will be nor imagine myself as, just the person I almost am" (2013: 125). Otherwise, what would memory have done? "Exaggerating the past it would have reduced our future. Arriving into future means just that. There is no place called future. All the time lying ahead is future" (Ghosal 2003a: 54).

This freedom of mind is a state of mind, a sense of freedom, a freedom to doubt, to question everything, even to hold our own judgments open to question, to reformulate others' formulations, to find new ways to throw away every form of dependency, conformity, and acceptance of conventions. Now the question is about the possibility of such a mind. It comes about because we are brought up in a culture so dependent on our environment and its tendencies that our perception can't be independent of cultural and social paradigms. These paradigms alone determine what we see. With our cognitive dependency of perception, our mind can see only what is already known. The poet is in a trap. We can go back to our early twentieth-century Indian philosopher Jiddu Krishnamurti:

> In order to deny [the] authority of all religious organizations, traditions and experience, one has to see why one normally obeys—actually study it. And to study it there must be freedom from condemnation, justification, opinion or acceptance. Now we cannot accept authority and yet study it—that is impossible. To study the whole psychological structure of authority within ourselves there must be freedom. And when we are studying we are denying the whole structure, and when we do deny, that very denial is the light of the mind that is free from authority. Negation of everything that has been considered worthwhile, such as outward discipline, leadership, idealism, is to study it; then that very act of studying is not only discipline but the negative of it, and the very denial is a positive act. (1969: 90)

This negation of negation is to arrive at affirmation, to echo Wittgenstein, "Negation is a gesture of exclusion, of rejection. . . . A double negative is an affirmative" (1958: 147). Here I could hear an expanded thought of the *Brihadaranyaka Upanishad*:[1]

1. *Upanishad*: The older meaning of the term *Upanishad* is "secret word" or "secret import" or "secret doctrine" to emphasize the mystic and ultrarational aspect of philosophical thought. Adi Sankracharya, an early eighth-century Indian philosopher, interpreted the term as standing for the realization of Brahman-Atman (soul, the self) identity, to emphasize the harmony between the inner mystic vision of the unity and universality of the self as the absolute being. The *Brihadaranyaka Upanishad*, which is the last part of Yajur Veda, one of the four Vedas, the oldest Sanskrit scripture of Hinduism, written around 700 BCE by those who were against the traditional Vedic order, questions the

> "Not this, not this." Because there is no other and more appropriate description than this "Not this." Now its name: "The Truth of truth." The vital force is truth, and it is the Truth of that. (hymn 2.3.6, 1950: 336)

This "Truth of truth"—"Not this, not this"—can never be brought within the scope of any affirmation, but one may (only) glimpse it indirectly through negation of all limiting adjuncts, whether it is of life or language, realizing one's identity with the Truth of truth, the pure intelligence—to say it in the Bernsteinian way, "Higher level of intelligibility" (Bernstein 2016: 210), which is imperceptible; the Self alone, not autonomously individual but quintessentially social. In spite of the truth being presented in a hundred ways, the Self is the last word of it all, arrived at by the process of "Not this, not this" to break up the tyranny of name and logic. This negation of negation is the only means of the freedom of mind where two negative particles of "Not this, not this" are used in an all-inclusive sense, which leads to Bernsteinian positivism:

> My motto has long been Dickinson's "Don't you know that 'No' is the wildest word we consign to Language?" I have nothing to say and I am not saying it. I have nothing to not say and I am saying it. I have nothing to not say and I am not saying it. I read Dickinson's poem as close to negative dialectics. Nothing in the sense of not one thing: variants around a blank center. To be told about nothing is to come face to face with loss, despair, grief: the irreparable. Nothing repairs the world. The revolution of the word is the force of nothing. (Bernstein 2016: 278)

This force of negativity makes the process a positive stimulus of multiple possibilities and creates the other voice: "I want other voices / but I want them always to be / my own other voice" (Bernstein 2013: 22). This other voice is the self-voice, which is realized by being heard of from others, reflected on through argument and reasoning, and meditated upon to ascertain being such and such but not otherwise. Then the "other voice" is known, for there is nothing else but the self-voice. Bernstein explains the process of generation of this other voice:

---

priestly class, rejecting materialistic concerns to move from external spiritual aspects like rites, sacrifices, and ceremonies to an internal spiritual enlightenment. In general, the Vedas give poetic and symbolic expression to Hindu spiritual truths, while the *Upanishads* express the philosophical truths of the Vedas.

> In my practice, certain kinds of unexpected and unpredictable associations occur when I think peripherally (aslant). I have learned to potentiate those associations. There's also a kind of sound and rhythmic or musical patterning that occurs, concomitant with less-than-conscious mental states. Just as when puns occur to me, or rhymes, assonances, I'm not looking for them. They come to me because I'm in that zone of consciousness. . . . Poems are ways of creating containers or structures or forms that channel those verbal/semiotic/symbolic/psychic streams. The poem is the medium in the double sense that it's a material ground but also something that receives signals. (2016: 264)

The similar process of receiving "signals" was explained by Ghosal:

> We are floating in a quantum field, where all interactions involve continuous creation and destruction of particles with which we, the material world, are made of. Only six percent reflection of its vibration could be seen through our eyes. Poems are signals creating from the vibrational modes of this field, stretched over space-time and constantly evolving and dissolving in our brain. A sensitive poet needs to perceive these signals. The active part of his consciousness, which may be called his "free will" or mind, is constantly creating imaginary experiences through abstract matching with his earthly/phenomenal experiences through the external world, and electrical/chemical pulses move through the neural network of his brain continuously. Through a constant replacement process and from continuous refraction/reflection of images, sounds, and sensations, suddenly a flash of light or spark is generated in a special excited state. (SPARK—Spontaneous Power Activated Resonance Kinetics—my acronym for easier understanding.) This happens in a magical moment when his mental capacitance is just conducive enough to receive the spark. (1996: 22; my translation)

This magical moment may be the moment of global quantum coherence, as proposed by theoretical physicist Roger Penrose. Global quantum coherence takes place in the brain's microtubules, inside the cytoskeletons of a large family of cerebral neurons. In this "less-than-conscious mental state," all electrical resistances and fluid frictions (viscosity) drop to zero to satisfy superconductivity/superfluidity of a single quantum state, which remains essentially unentangled with (by a "shielding" from) its environment, or else, Penrose states, the "quantum state . . . would become immediately lost in the randomness inherent in that environment" (1994: 351). This is the "inner silence" zone. In this "magical moment," Bernstein presents a resonant word—*channel*, which is "like a river or a stream. . . . A site for external reception" (2016: 264). As if the pataquerical poet is pointing toward Penrose's noncomputational Orch-OR (Orchestrated Objective Reduction) philosophy (Penrose 1994: 52), according to which the quantum coherence inside the neuron will be orchestrated by "Objective State Reduction," when a neuron fires because the electrical field, the "mind energy" propagating as nerve signal through the "channel," is likely to be detected by Jack Spicer's Martian, who enters into the drawing room of the host poet to play with the furniture in the room.

The more the furniture—new words, new languages, new forms—the more possible patterns can be generated by Martians, because these "new" are unknown, the terra incognita of Eastern philosophy/Zen Buddhism, the mysterious dark energy of the mind or a quintessential form of dark energy, not constant but dynamically changing, depending on the ratio of its kinetic and potential energy, as per modern science: the non-ordinary states of consciousness, awaiting expansion to acknowledge the source of knowledge to enter into the shadow of the mind, the imaginary world beyond the computational world, to resonate with the Spicerian tune—"language is part of the furniture in the room. Language is not anything of itself. It's something which is in the mind of the host that the parasite [the poem] is invading" (Gizzi 1998: 9)—or with Burroughs's tune—"The word is now a virus. . . . The word may once have been a healthy neural cell. It is now a parasitic organism that invades and damages the central nervous system. Modern man has lost the option of silence. Try halting your sub-vocal speech. Try to achieve even ten seconds of inner silence. You will encounter a resisting organism that forces you to talk. That organism is the word" (1967: 305).

This "inner silence" is neither the product of a quiet mind nor the outcome of attention; rather, it is the mind's power of emptiness, detachment, receptiveness to shift the awareness from the rational mode to the intuitive mode of consciousness, a silence in the abyss of "nothing," where all contradictions and conditions are buried, a silence where the observer is completely alone and not translating the observed, "wei wu wei," or action through inaction of Eastern philosophy—Taoism, Hinduism, or Buddhism.

In this state of "inner silence" of the mind, Bernstein receives the *signal*: "My mind's a blank, then something occurs to me in the moment. It's like the way allusion works. A song or an associated literary line invades my mind, bonds with a perception: I don't seek it out; it just appears" (2016: 264). This blank state of mind is what Krishnamurti called a religious mind with a state of silence. But, before going into the state of mind, let us probe into our understanding of what mind is. Ghosal defined it nicely in his essay "With Mind":

> It is difficult to define what mind is. However, it can be said scientifically that our brain creates consciousness through experience and stores it in our cerebrum. This consciousness has two parts. One is passive, which performs all our physical work without our consent. The other part is active, which may be called *free will*. This active part is mind, where the program and programmer of a conscious mind is the same. The mind gradually builds up through the own "will" of the human to create the storage of required quality and perfection to progress. The direction in which way his "will" moves depends on his surroundings, the storage of facts, and the health of his brain. Mind itself creates its virtual realization and virtual imagination. This tendency converts the physical experience of human into imaginary experience, which I called the "fittest model of the world in our mind." (2003b: 83; my translation)

Now coming back to the state of mind. The state of silence of mind is "not produced by thought but is the outcome of awareness, which is meditation when the mediator is entirely absent. In that silence there is a state of energy in which there is no conflict. Energy is action and movement. All action is movement and all action is energy" (Krishnamurti 1969: 100).

Before going further, I must be clear at this point that this "religious" mind, as I mentioned, is something entirely different from the mind that believes in religion. We are going to discuss neither "truth-seeking activity" nor religion nor the religious process of meditation nor searching for God, religious faith, et cetera, because I have faith in Bernsteinian faith: "Religion is giving religion a bad name. / Nor am I an atheist. I believe in the fallible gods of thought and in my resistance to these gods. I have faith in my aversion of faith" (Bernstein 2013: 125).

Here, both the philosopher and the poet are talking not about religious mind but about awareness, alertness, movements, energy of mind. Sitting in India, with the prevailing state of Hinduism, Ghosal also rejected any connection of his consciousness theory of poetry with spiritual/religious meanings; rather, it simply means total awareness/alertness to knowledge, experience, and information at a single instant of time.

Coming back to the silent state of mind where the active part of the consciousness starts its journey to an expanded field of consciousness, moving to a limitless, timeless, horizonless state without any center, space, or time, where deterministic objective reality of matter dissolves into a subjective *indeterministic* probability wave, the potential possibility in the form of counterfactual reflections of reality. Does this state of mind lead to Expansive Consciousness? Let me check what we received from Ghosal, the introducer of Expansive Consciousness theory in the world of Bengali poetry:

> The deep-rooted concept of a person is fixed and immobile. One may have various consciousnesses on the same subject and various consciousnesses on multiple subjects at the same time. Often there may be conflicts between those consciousnesses due to their apparent chaos, lack of causal relationships, false beliefs, and symbolic authority of words, of language. Subjective void in the human body is seventy percent, which is the collective darkness created by all quarks of each atom of the body. This darkness is mobile. . . . Within this apparent chaos of consciousnesses, if one becomes alert enough of one's own existence in a known and given surrounding, then there will be the possibility of the best suitable model, which opens up a new trail in an unknown terrain—which I am calling *Expansive Consciousness*, a centrifugal journey aversive to centripetal surrealism. Here thought begins from the center of the matter, subject and concept of the event, to move centrifugally to expand radially outward. This journey is similar to cubism but does not stop at the surface level; it expands beyond the dark outer space of matter toward infinity, an enlightened journey stepping out into the unknown. (2003b: 107; my translation)

Ghosal's Expansive Consciousness theory is a process of alertness and mental energy (an entropic energy generated from the disorder). Expansive consciousness is from the randomness of the system when molecules break down into atoms and atoms break down into their constituent particles. We can know the measurement and observed structure of a particle, we can know the relative position of two particles, but we can't know the magnetic attraction, the gravitational force between them, since a particle's position and momentum can never be measured simultaneously with precision, as per the Heisenberg uncertainty principle. We can't know the interactions between quark and antiquark, the elementary particles with a fractional electric charge that fuels the strongest aesthetic force, the poetic particles used, for example, by James Joyce in *Finnegans Wake*. All objects of the world, including *we*, are made of the dynamic interactions of these aesthetic forces, which are at the root of any poem. We can't know these binding forces, these possibilities of interaction and their future, but their interrelationship can be realized intuitively by expanding our consciousness. As if the poetic process is resonating with the quantum-relativistic model of superstring theory in contemporary physics, where particles are not points but patterns of vibrating supersymmetric strings, spread over space-time. As the vibrational rate of a violin string determines its pitch, the vibrational mode of the superstring determines the particle to which it will be manifested, like Bernsteinian quarks and antiquarks, where "Pitch is the sound of poetry. But pitch is also the attack or approach. The angle. Pitch in the sense of register" (Bernstein 2016: x): to register the energy pattern of virtual particles with "a poetics of dynamic movement, where each phrase takes on new meaning in new contexts" (111), not as isolated entities but as integral parts of an inseparable network of dynamic interplay like "double protuberance" of Jarryan pataquarks—utterly serious but totally laughable, or absolutely absurd but philosophically essential. And the ceaseless flow of energy manifests itself to give rise to our material world to find the Faustrollian new reality, not static but active, with an oscillation in rhythmic movements like Shiva's Dance in Hindu mythology, which is a metaphor for cosmic cycles of creation and destruction, vacillation between life and death, between the yin and yang of Taoism.

So we have reached the pataquerical world of Bernstein with a quantum coherence between Western and Eastern philosophy, between modern physics and Eastern mysticism, which is resonating in the field of poetry in the Bernsteinian way of *Recalculating*: "Poetry is metadata without code, free-base tagging, cascading style sheets with undefined markers. . . . My skin is burning but inside I am as cold as the North Pole. My shivering is metaphysical, a kind of involuntary davening" (2013: 9). Or in his pitching to poetry: "The past is just as lost as our love is, our love was. Ontological pitching (a metaphysical lurch or stagger): here/not here; heard/not heard; taught/untaught" (2016: ix). This *pitch* makes a sign of the strain against the grain, the temporal oscillation to redefine the words through pataquericals, an endless transformation of the poem itself, where every poem becomes a model of a possible world through active enlistment of the reader. We knew about this potential world from the poetics of Ghosal:

> One fittest world or universe resides in our mind as concept. It is not important whether those exist outside our mind. We forget the other

> ones until any of it threatens our own existence. These concepts do not change with mere accidents. From all possibilities conceivable of an incidence or an event that happens, it can be said that only a single possibility took a concrete shape and immediately became unreal leaving other possibilities or potentials in mind at the level of imagination, which are real to a being, that is, only those belong to a person. Thus distinguishing between realities and unrealities we tell ourselves that we live in abstract realities and imagination, and ignore the fantastic unreal world around us. (2003a: 90)

Here Ghosal's voice is an echo to theoretical physicist Stephen Hawking's "model-dependent realism," which applies not only to scientific models but also to the conscious and subconscious mental models we all create in order to interpret and understand the everyday world: "There is no way to remove the observer—us—from our perception of the world, which is created through our sensory processing and through the way we think and reason. Our perception—and hence the observation upon which our theories are based—is not direct, but rather is shaped by a kind of lens, the interpretive structure of our human brain" (Hawking and Mlodinow 2010: 62), to echo as well the voice of the Language poet Bernstein, who "sees" the world as a word: "Language operates as a lens or filter or map or probe with which, and through which, we negotiate the world. It never drops away and leaves us the world, nor do we perceive the world without the echo of language" (Bernstein 2016: 239). So the experiences in our every step to the external world are changing to the abstracted imaginary experiences, to break open the barriers of a poet's consciousness, to step out into an unknown darkness, to imagine through language the Bernsteinian "unimaginable and face that to which we cannot give a face" (165), to whistle "old tunes that we make up in the pitch dark of night" (ix), to enter into Spicer's Martian's dictating zone of poetry, to receive Ghosalian sparks of Expansive Consciousness.

This poetic theory of imagination and infinite possibilities, paradoxes of conceptual thinking of Eastern philosophy or model-dependent realism of modern science, shows our material world only as tendencies, probabilities, possibilities, not actualities, from where we get the concept of Maya in Hinduism. To say that the world of Maya changes continuously means that the manifold forms in the world are Maya, not fundamental; these manifold forms exist as illusory concepts and are ever changing. This does not mean that the world is an illusion; *concept* is not Maya, but the *illusion of concept* is Maya, as we see in the *Bhagavad Gita*: "While actions are being done in every way by the *Gunas* (qualities) of nature, one who is deluded by egoism thinks thus: I am the doer" (hymn 3.27).[2] Here *Guna* means that our nature is made up of three attributes—*Sattwa* (soul/purity/light/harmony), *Raja* (passion/motion/continuous interaction of particles with which we are made of), and *Tamas* (darkness/inertia/subjective void of the human body as well as the cosmic world). The dynamic interplay between these forces/energies of nature is the action; the whole universe is in action, and every action has a consequence in nature, in performance.

Action is a process of our conscious being to raise ourselves to our own higher possibilities, to come out of the predominant passivity of our *Tamas*-ic nature, to enter into the passion and struggle with our *Rajas*-ic nature, and from there through the knowledge of the self, the soul, the whole we enter into the greater light, the purity of our *Sattwa*-ic nature, the enlightenment. Being, as we are, very insignificant beings with respect to this vast universe, we can know only part of it. Knowing our limitations, the poet does his action: "Language is a limit; the self is a limit. And rather than try to overcome the limits through transcendence, or a universalizing humanism, I prefer bouncing off them. That way I stay closer to the ground" (Bernstein 2016: 272). This is to refer to his own action, knowing the limitation of language in his poetic world to get the poet's enlightenment in his own way. This indeed echoes the similar theory of enlightenment in Zen or Taoism: "Zen does not mean withdrawal from the world but means, on the contrary, active participation in everyday affairs, belief in the perfection of our original nature, the realization that the process of enlightenment consists merely in becoming what we already are from the beginning" (Capra 1975: 124).

Since pataquerics is born "under the sign of 'pataphysics" and Alfred Jarry, there is always a vacillation between science and philosophy. When Bernstein says, "The poem is the medium in the double sense that it's a material ground but also something that receives signals" (2016: 264), the "double sense" becomes a poetic reference to the wave-particle duality—"material ground" to particle and "signal" to wave nature—and his resonant word *channel* is pointing toward the well-known scattering matrix theory of quantum mechanics, which sowed the seed of string theory. So the type of interaction or association through a particular channel is again a matter of probability in science as well as possibilities in poetics because they

2. *Srimad Bhagavad Gita* [The song of God], translated by Swami Gambhirananda, Kharagpur IIT, India (website), accessed February 2020, https://www.gitasupersite.iitk.ac.in/. This Hindu scripture was written around the second century BCE and is part of the Indian epic *Mahabharata*.

are "unexpected and unpredictable associations," as Bernstein continues, but it depends on available energy, the mental energy as per the poet's perception. Again, in the same passage, Bernstein writes of "unconscious associations," in the sense of our psychological suppositions, which form the matrix of all metaphysical assertions, mythology, philosophy, and life. "*Transition* is a metaphor I lean on perhaps too much, as implicitly quoting Emerson in *The American Scholar*: 'The preamble of thought, the transition through which it passes from the unconscious to the conscious, is action'" (2016: 282). This *action* means the invasion of the unconscious to a definite condition of the conscious, to form the thought/action/events/resonance.

There is another factor that comes into the picture with this *channel*: *resonance*. Resonance is again related to vibration, "a kind of sound and rhythmic or musical patterning" (Bernstein 2016: 264). When this energy or frequency of rhythm reaches a certain value, the channel, the quantum state, begins to resonate, and the vibrations of the probability wave suddenly become very strong; it causes a sharp increase in the interaction probability. This resonance is an event, not an object but an occurrence, and manifests itself through words and happens when "My mind's a blank . . . I'm in that zone of consciousness . . . less-than-conscious mental states" that is a "result of a hunch or intuition or something even more subliminal" (264)—a nonintellectual experience of reality—Penrose's noncomputational quantum collapsing in our brain. And in the right circumstance, the poet taps into those streams in diverse ways. "Poems are ways of creating containers or structures or forms that channel those verbal/semiotic/symbolic/psychic streams," Bernstein continues. These "ways" point to the mystical term *intuition*, the most sophisticated observational apparatus of the Eastern mystical world to observe nature, to transform the objective reality to subjective reality, which includes the observer/perceiver/reader. It works like puns, as Bernstein mentions: "I never lose the opportunity to have puns, the forms of jokes as much as jokes, anecdotes, aphorisms, doggerel" (233), like nonsensical riddles of *koan* in Zen, like paradoxical anecdotes in Taoism, like "nonsense" and "gibberish"—two primary pataquericals.

The moment when one realizes a pun, not with any explanation or intellectual analysis but with intuitive insight into the nature of the pun, one experiences a moment of laughter, the Tao of enlightenment, "If it were not laughed at, it would not be sufficient to be Tao" (Capra 1975: 37). Bernstein gives the reason of his poetic intuitive process:

> I maintain a deep affection for the realm of reason, a realm that goes beyond rationality but that is not irrational. Reason incorpo-

> rates intuition, including what Jack Spicer calls dictation. I also have that experience when I am writing poems. You set something up, certain conditions let's say, and then, well, it starts to happen. It's not entirely controlled by a rational intelligence. Surely it involves the unconscious, but the unconscious is part of the mind and part of reason. (2016: 264)

The cosmic form, the harmonious whole, the unification of all physical phenomena, the inner realm of ourselves, can be seen not through the physical eyes or through the rational mind, because these observations are not entirely controlled by a rational intelligence, but through the intuitive eyes, Jarryan pataphysical eyes, the third eye of the Indian mystic world. It's "a particular act of gazing . . . turning my attention on to my own consciousness"; Wittgenstein called it "the queerest thing" (1958: 124), a deep inner experience attained through intense absolute affirmation. Here poet/scientist/mystic are inquiring into the essential nature of matter/life/event through their own way—scientist through the deeper realm of matter, mystic through the deeper realm of consciousness, and poet through the exploration of their imaginary world but expressing it with a language becomes indescribable in all realms, as wonderfully said in the *Kena Upanishad*: "The eye does not go there, no speech, nor the mind. We do not therefore know how to instruct one about it. It is different from what is known and it is beyond what is unknown."[3]

This resonates with physicist Fritjof Capra's views of the difficulty faced by the present-day quantum-relativistic approach of modern science: "Physicists can 'experience' the four-dimensional space-time world through the abstract mathematical formalism of their theories, but their visual imagination—like everybody else's—is limited to the three-dimensional world of the senses. Our language and thought patterns have evolved in this three-dimensional world and therefore we find it extremely hard to deal with the four-dimensional reality of relativistic physics" (1975: 148). So the problems of language expressing our thoughts is the same for all, whether scientist, mystic, or poet. If we ask ourselves, What is poetry?, the immediate answer may be: poetry is a sensation, or, as Bernstein puts it, "Poetry is an extension of thinking with the poem" (2016: 204) and the word is Brahma! As it was wonderfully said in the *Katha Upanishad*, "This word (*Om*) is verily Brahma; this word is verily the highest; he who knows this word, obtains,

3. *Kena Upanishad*, hymn 1.1.3, translated by Swami Sivananda, Kharagpur IIT, India (website), accessed February 2020, https://www.gitasupersite.iitk.ac.in/.

verily, whatever he desires."[4] This is to mean that in the poetic realm, *Om*, the original sound at the source of any word/syllable/letter, is Brahma, equivalent to *energy*, the essence of life, in modern day's terminology. *Om* and Brahma are inseparably associated, and *Om* should be meditated upon as Brahma itself.

This meditation may be the main process from or desire of a new poetry where the inherent sound of the expressed image in a poem must ring in the reader's mind in resonance with the poet's mind after the disappearance of the first impression of the moving images of a poem. The best process would be if the poet's *thinking* could be transmitted to the conscious reader without any words. However, that doesn't happen. And knowing that a *word* doesn't mean anything, it has no function other than referring to a particular object, state, or thought, or its representation, and it becomes necessary to construct a framework of words where the imaginary experience of the poet's mind will be the center of gravity. The joyous pain of this process seems to be the figuration or construction of a poem, which is enjoyed by every poet. The construction process, by the perfect selection of words, creating new words by the process of word recombination, *verbification*, adverbial and adjectival modification, abolition of pronouns, creates an altogether different poetic language and continuous balancing around the center like the way "the positive energy of the matter can be balanced by the negative gravitational energy, and so there is no restriction on the creation of whole universe" (Hawking and Mlodinow 2010: 227), so as to put no restriction on the creation of new language in the poetic world, as Bernstein says:

> *L=A=N=G=U=A=G=E* was not about deconstruction as an end in itself but about reconstruction, emplacement, and enactment: it was constructive. In the poetry, syllogistic logic and naturalistic plot gave way to intuitively felt, aesthetically designed, or programmatically arranged connections among elements of a work. The poem was imagined not as the fixed voice of a self-contained ego conveying a predetermined or paraphrasable message but as a collage or constellation of textual elements: not voice, but voicings. (2016: 68)

And to explore these possibilities, the Language poet thinks, "Language is an event of the world, just as, for language users, the world is an

4. *Katha Upanishad*, hymn 1.2.16, translated by Swami Sivananda, Kharagpur IIT, India (website), accessed February 2020, https://www.gitasupersite.iitk.ac.in/.

event of language. Even the world is a word" (Bernstein 2013: 11). All events are reflections/resonances that manifest themselves through words. Again, the resonance is not an object but an occurrence, where associations are related to probabilities that cannot be expressed directly but through imagination, as proposed by Jarry and explained by Roger Shattuck: "The virtual or imaginary nature of things as glimpsed by the heightened vision of poetry or science or love can be seized and lived as real" (Jarry 1996: ix). That may be the reason the Language poetry movement argued for a poetry:

> That did not use words instrumentally but rather created a non-purpose-driven aesthetic space that allowed for pleasure in reflection, projection, and sensory engagement with verbal materials. This writing would create a very different role for the reader . . . the imagination of readers was activated: they were not told what to think or feel or see but encouraged to make intuitive leaps: to *interenact*—as I like to say it—rather than passively consume. . . . In this way, poetry becomes an act of construction rather than a transfer of preexisting information. (Bernstein 2016: 68)

Or, in the Ghosalian sense of language:

> The person who is creating the art is an artist, and the perceiver (reader) of the art is also an artist. The poet's observation, understanding, thinking, and his intelligence allow the source poetry, received by the senses, to trigger his brain at any given moment. Sooner or later the poem is constructed with the poet's imaginary experiences and the poet, passionate with beauty, writes the poetry with the abstract imagination by using emotive language implanted with fuzzy logic. The perceiver, a reader, creates another abstraction of the poem through his own imaginary experiences. Communication is completed when both the writer and the reader enjoyed the poem. (Ghosal 2003b: 100; my translation)

As if a poem is formed in a particle accelerator in the subatomic zone of poetics; "subatomic" to refer to Plank's dimension, where ten raised to a negative number points toward *nothing* because "Nothing is the force / That renovates the world" (Dickinson cited in Bernstein 2016: 276). Here the particles, the words, the quarks of poetry, pataquericals, are engaged in dynamic patterns or processes that involve a certain amount of energy to appear to us as their mass/text with structure/form. The poem comes to be in the collision of two imaginary worlds, the poet's and the reader's, but moreover where each, poet and reader, live in a world of both abstracted realities and pataquerical imaginations. The poem is constructed in the collision of the poet's imagination and the reader's imagination. The poem is activated/charged through the energy of the two colliding pataquericals, which are redistributed to form a new pattern. If a sufficient amount of kinetic/dynamic energy can increase this energy so that reader can *interenact* through their own imaginary experiences, then this new pattern may evolve new particles, a new resonance. This *new* does not mean *recently made* but *novel*, *original*—the originality "that spawns me as it spurns me," in Bernstein's sense (2013: 123), *anoriginality* in Andrew Benjamin's torquing of this idea.[5]

Whether it is poetic or mystic or scientific language, abstraction is always associated with an expression of inchoate material. Abstraction can be viewed as a conceptual map of reality, where rational knowledge is reduced to a system of abstract concepts and symbols—which is again not complete because words of language have several meanings, remain largely in our subconscious, and connect to the respective concept with the sound of the word when we hear it. Similarly, science also abstracts its language by limiting the meaning of its words/rules of logic by replacing them with symbols of mathematics. In "Disfiguring Abstraction," Bernstein writes,

> Abstraction is the dream of figuration just as lines are a way of marking time till the sentence is over. . . . Abstraction is never more than an extension of figuration, just as figuration is never more than an extension of abstraction. But also abstraction is never more than a figuration of extension, quote the Raven. . . . Abstraction is figuration by other means. . . . Abstraction is a metaphor, not a style; the connection of one abstract work to another is by family resemblance, in Wittgenstein's sense. The harder we try to define abstraction, the more it slips away. In this sense, abstraction is a term of art like *conceptual*, *representational*, *realist*, *material*, *spiritual*. (2016: x, 50)

But existing verse culture, whether it is in the West or East, America or India, is very far away from such a conception of poetry, especially when it demands transparency/accessibility in a poem, as position. Bernstein satirizes in his poem "Thank You for Saying Thank You":

5. See Bernstein's discussion of Andrew Benjamin's "anoriginality" in Bernstein 1999: 285.

> This is a totally
> accessible poem.
> There is nothing
> in this poem
> that is in any
> way difficult
> to understand.
> . . . Each line,
> word, & syllable
> have been chosen
> to convey only the
> intended meaning
> & nothing more.
> . . . .
> A hundred
> readers would each
> read the poem
> in an identical
> manner & derive
> the same message
> from it. . .
> . . . .
> It
> says just what
> it says. It's
> real.
> (2006: 7–9)

However, the new poetry under discussion here in no way satisfies this delusory demand for accessibility, because pataquerics "opens the page out to something that is not a two-dimensional Euclidean space but a curved space, a space with n-dimensionality" (Bernstein 2016: 216), indeed a space in which it is possible to "curve continuously" (12). And in this curved space-time, different observers/perceivers/readers will experience the event/resonance/occurrence of the matter/event/words differently in different temporal sequences. So the words in a poem lose their absolute significance/meaning in space-time. The new poetry moves toward opacity and away from transparency to reflect the view that poetry is a mode of rhetoric.

As soon as Bernstein says, "For me, poetry is a form of sophism and of rhetoric rather than of truth and sincerity" (2016: 242), conventional authorities immediately point their index fingers—what about poetry's power to address the fundamental questions of the existence/meaning of life or lack of meaning? What about mystery/misery/yearning or spiritual experiences? Probably these types of questions are universal in the world of conventional poetry, whether it is in the West or East, America or India. Ghosal gave an answer to this type of question in a joking tone: "Are you a saint? Have you come to tell the truth? Are you not aware that truth gets buried in the media-controlled society? Have you come to tell the secret esoteric realization of philosophy? Have you come to impart knowledge about life? Don't you know they are more intelligent, more wise, more expert than you?" (2003b: 38; my translation).

This resonates with Edgar Allan Poe, whose tomb is the birthplace of pataquerics. Poe: "I would define, in brief, the Poetry of words as *The Rhythmical Creation of Beauty*. Its sole arbiter is Taste. With the Intellect or with the Conscience, it has only collateral relations. Unless incidentally, it has no concern whatever either with Duty or with Truth" (1909: 222; quoted in Bernstein 2016: 299). So poetry is not to mediate truth, because "truth is the antithesis of existing society" (as Bernstein quotes Theodor Adorno in the epigraph to "Emotions of Normal People" in *Dark City* [1994: 85]).

Then what must poetry do? The pataquerical Bernstein answers: "The task for poetry is not to translate itself into the language of social and linguistic norms but to question those norms and, indeed, to explore the ways they are used to discipline and contain dissent. Poetry offers not a moral compass but an aesthetic probe. And it can provide a radical alternative to the outcome-driven thinking" (2016: 79).

Here lies the basis of his pataquericalism, a precarious querulous inquiry/probe into the system, into the *inner self*, with a rhythmic oscillation between hope and despair of the paradoxical reality, action through inaction within the ever-changing space-time, with quick pronunciation of the pataphysical "ha ha"[6] (27) until the phrase becomes confounded, random, odd, or queer in our n-dimensional reality by shattering Descartes's duality of mind and matter, good and evil, body and soul, to reach the quantum unity of reality. So Bernstein, the linguistic terrorist of the American poetry

6. The dog-faced Baboon Bosse-De-Nage (so named because of the double protuberance of the cheeks), who knows no human words but "ha," is a character in Jarry, *Exploits and Opinions of Doctor Faustroll, Pataphysician* (1996).

world, says "I do what I can, what I want, what I come up with, what appeals to me, what hasn't been done in this way before, what I don't understand, what holds my attention, what pushes me a little further than I have gone, what throws me back to ground I thought I knew so well but in which I can no longer find my way" (2013: 90).

When we probe into the poetics of Barin Ghosal, the villain of the Bengali poetry world, we get a similar kind of reflection:

> You, the poet, will tell only about your exploration/adventure without imparting knowledge or imitating the life-mirror. A poet must give just the hints of his adventure. He is no one to write poetry. Poetry already exists because everywhere everything is poetry. The reader, the journey-lover, the seeker can feel that within the *inner self* without reading your poems. The search for poetry is a personal journey for the poet, for the reader too. The reader can recognize or feel the touch of his own poetry with the constructed poem of the poet. This reader denies the dummy/doll-like poem, made by any artificial technique. (2003b: 38; my translation)

Both poetic processes demand the removal of old attributes or qualities of poetry. There is no space in this new poetry to impart, as its end product, the poet's feelings or subjective experiences; rather, the poet engages in an interplay of polar opposite quarks like pleasure and pain, gain and loss, victory and defeat, honor and dishonor, praise and censure, expression and blank, and so on, since the whole universe, the material world, is not static but vibrating string in space-time, engaged in endless rhythm and action with a continual cosmic dance of energy. Bernstein says,

> I am more interested in sensation than in feeling, if feeling is understood in a narrow sense as the expression of a limited set of predefined emotions: happiness, sadness, grief, et cetera. I don't have a feeling that I, the poet behind the words, want to convey to you the reader. The feelings emerge in the process of the poem, both in writing it and in reading it. Turbulence, uncertainty, ambivalence, exhilaration, fear, loss, groundlessness, falling, guilt, error—these are a few of the overlaid feeling tones I explore. (2016: 221)

The pataquerical process demands exclusion of emotion, rhyme, analogy, symbol, metaphor, description, history, story, drama, news, comment, speech, exaggeration. But if everything is excluded, what else is there to write? How to cook without cooking spices and formula? That is the self-imposed constraint of bent studies. Only deconstruction cannot play the secured tune of flying into the sky of poetic freedom; instead it makes the horizon of poetry grey. So not only deconstruction but a game of break and make and move on, to echo Ghosal: "Being out of the old poetry or mainstream, we had reach to an open space where there was no rule, no school of writing poetry, no examiner, no reward, no reader. There was only a field for playing with words to construct the poetry with our own personalized feelings/perceptions/consciousness, where there was more sign than word, tingling of sound, radiance of flashing, music of nature" (Ghosal 2016: 64; my translation). It is like Wittgenstein's *language-game*: "The speaking of language is part of an activity" and since "[e]very sign by itself seems dead[,] . . . [w]hat gives it life? In use it is alive" (1958: 11, 128). So the poet plays with language to make its sign alive, plays the inherent sound of the word to create a rhythmical/musical sensation to signal the mystery of language. And the poetic language moves a little bit of its long journey—not to overthrow its conventionality "but to reconfigure: a necessary deconfiguration as prerequisite for refiguration, for the regeneration of the ability to figure—count—think figuratively, tropically" (Bernstein 1992: 227). Therefore, the pataquericalist "opens the floodgates of a sublimely nude poetics of blank: the noise of silence" (Bernstein 2016: 310) to echo the Poe-tics "*only this and nothing more*" because, echoing Rogelio Lopez Cuenca, "*Du Calme*—poetry makes nothing happen," because "A work of art is the overlay of a set of incommensurable possibilities, linked together around an *anoriginal* vanishing point" (Bernstein 2013: 123).

There is a hymn in the *Bhagavad Gita*—"Of the unreal there is no being; the real has no nonexistence. But the nature of both these, indeed, has been realized by the seers of Truth."[7] To echo modern physics: the total energy of the universe must always remain zero; no new thing can be created and nothing can be destroyed; only a change from one to another is possible. Every era possesses this change, a dream to go beyond the known to search for the unknown, not eternity but the unknown dimensions of Jarryan "ethernity," to move from classical to modern physics by continuously increasing the dimensions of space, to move from S-Matrix to string to superstring to M-theory, to move toward the Theory of Everything (TOE) to get a model of the universe. To quote Stephen Hawking about M-theory: "No one seems to know what the 'M' stands for, but it may be 'master,' 'miracle' or 'mystery.' It seems to be all three" (Hawking and Mlodinow 2010: 149).

7. *Srimad Bhagavad Gita*, hymn 2.16, translated by Swami Gambhirananda, Kharagpur IIT, India (website), accessed February 2020, https://www.gitasupersite.iitk.ac.in/.

Today it may look like a miracle because its mystery is yet to be resolved; or let's say that M-theory is not *the science* but the *process or journey of invention*, to echo Hawking: "We each exist for but a short time, and in that time explore but a small part of the whole universe" (Hawking and Mlodinow 2010: 13), which resonates with the poetic tone of Bernstein, "Our journey was not over; it was always just beginning" (2016: 11).

There is no destination of poetry; destination means reaching; reaching means closure, where there is no poetry; reaching means putting ourselves in the system of rule, authority, where there is no poetry.

The journey of poetry never ends. Language is always put on a moving stage—from modern to postmodern, structuralism to poststructuralism, language to postlanguage, conceptual to postconceptual, and so on. When modern poetry was gasping for breath in the binding of intertextuality, postmodernism was born, or in Bernstein's sense, "Postmodernism: modernism with a deep sense of guilt" (2013: 172).

In the Bengali poetic zone, postmodernism started with the negation of the surrealistic centripetal path to decentralize thinking and deconstruct reasoning/logic so as to make poetry multivectoral, with the abstraction of imaginary experiences to allow the concept of multidimensional reality. All these ideas are common to both postmodernism and Expansive Consciousness theory in the Bengali poetry world, but the only difference is that postmodernism identifies the signs of changes/progress/possibilities, while Expansive Consciousness theory inaugurates a process of negating the existing in order to move toward infinite possibilities, outwitting the postmodern hostility, similar to Bernsteinism: "What we were doing, with our emphasis on method, was not turning away from process but opening onto an expanded field of process. It's still process, not product. You still don't know exactly where you are going to come out before you are finished. It's a turning away from a preconceived beginning, middle, and end, a rejection of closure" (Bernstein 2016: 259).

These are not similarities but coherences between the voices/processes/thoughts of different poets, scientists, and philosophers with different languages in different zones of times and places of the world. In the poetic realm, it may be called quantum poetics that creates quantum coherence between the thoughts of poets, a quantum coherence between Eastern and Western poetics, a harmonious relationship of all possibilities in the quantum universe and we human beings—who are ourselves mere collections of fundamental particles of nature in this material world, living in a quantum world of paradoxical nature with multidimensional reality backed by Schrödinger's cat paradox, to echo the poetic realm supported by the paradox of the pataphysician Dr. Faustroll's new reality, the heart of Bernstein's pataquericalism, which opens up an infinite space to *interenact*. But for the present, let me stop here my gibberish to quantum collapse into "Catachresis My Love":

> The ordinary is never more than an extension of the extraordinary.
> The extraordinary is never more than an extension of the imaginary.
> The imaginary is never more than an extension of the possible.
> The possible is never more than an extension of the impossible.
> The impossible is never more than an extension of the ordinary.
> Every wish has two wings, one to move it into the world, the other to bury it deep within the heart.
> (Bernstein 2018: 32)

. . . .

About Barin Ghosal and *Kaurab*:

Barin Ghosal (1944–2017) was a poet, theorist, and critic from Steel City Jamshedpur, India. He was an electrical engineer by profession, a pivotal member of the *Kaurab* group, and coeditor of *Kaurab* print magazine. Ghosal was an adventurist in poesphere and broke all barriers with his fuzzy water logic in search of new means of expression, shattering established cultural norms and leading the *Kaurab* literary movement in 1968 with Kamal Chakrabarty and other *Kaurab* members to emphasize the innovative, alternative poetic practice of, and critical thinking on, Bengali literature and to develop a nonmainstream and experimental genre. Though it never had an official manifesto, it developed a whole new generation of creative writing and remains as the most important center for innovative Bengali poetry till today. A detailed documentation of this movement by Ghosal, translated by me, is here: https://www.dispatchespoetrywars.com/commentary/recent-movement-bengali-poetry-new-poetry-barin-ghosal-tr-runa-bandyopadhyay/. *Kaurab* print magazine (*Kaurab Patrika*), first issue published in 1970, presently edited by Kamal Chakraborty from Jamshedpur, in some ways was analogous to *L=A=N=G=U=A=G=E* in the US. Aryanil Mukherjee, one of the members of the *Kaurab* group, started *Kaurab* Webzine in 1998 and interviewed Bernstein in 2008 for *Kaurab* webzine (www.kaurab.com/english/interviews/bernstein.html). Ghosal introduced the new literary theory—Expansive Consciousness—into the world of Bengali poetry in the early 1990s and started a genre of Bengali poetry called *Natun Kabita* (new poetry) with this theory. He wrote more than twenty-five books, including essays on poetics, poetry, criticism, novels, short stories, and an autobiography.

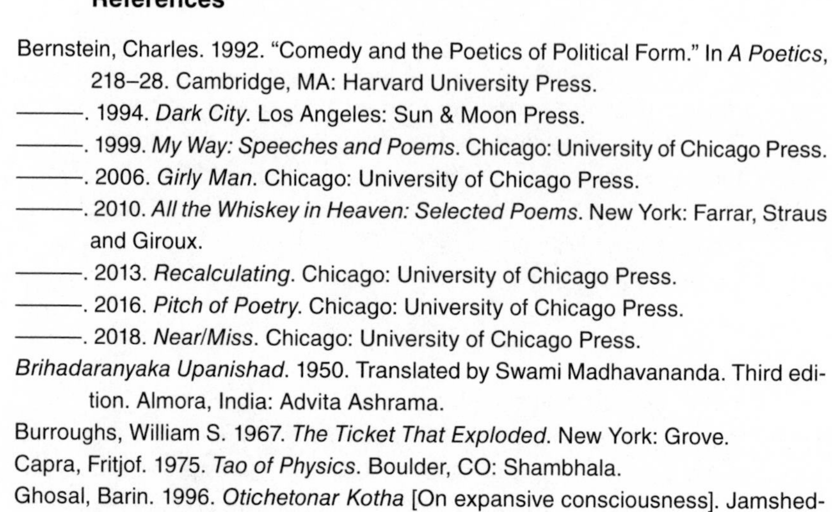

References

Bernstein, Charles. 1992. "Comedy and the Poetics of Political Form." In *A Poetics*, 218–28. Cambridge, MA: Harvard University Press.

———. 1994. *Dark City*. Los Angeles: Sun & Moon Press.

———. 1999. *My Way: Speeches and Poems*. Chicago: University of Chicago Press.

———. 2006. *Girly Man*. Chicago: University of Chicago Press.

———. 2010. *All the Whiskey in Heaven: Selected Poems*. New York: Farrar, Straus and Giroux.

———. 2013. *Recalculating*. Chicago: University of Chicago Press.

———. 2016. *Pitch of Poetry*. Chicago: University of Chicago Press.

———. 2018. *Near/Miss*. Chicago: University of Chicago Press.

Brihadaranyaka Upanishad. 1950. Translated by Swami Madhavananda. Third edition. Almora, India: Advita Ashrama.

Burroughs, William S. 1967. *The Ticket That Exploded*. New York: Grove.

Capra, Fritjof. 1975. *Tao of Physics*. Boulder, CO: Shambhala.

Ghosal, Barin. 1996. *Otichetonar Kotha* [On expansive consciousness]. Jamshedpur, India: Kaurab.

———. 2003a. *Guineapig: A Documentary Film*. Translated by Barin Ghosal. Jamshedpur, India: Kaurab.

———. 2003b. *Kabitar Bhobisyat* [Future of poetry]. Kolkata, India: Kabita Campus.

———. 2016. *Kabitar Uttharadhikar O Knhoj* [Inheritance of poetry and quest]. Dhaka, Bangladesh: Srot Pub.

Gizzi, Peter. 1998. *The House That Jack Built: The Collected Lectures of Jack Spicer*. Middletown, CT: Wesleyan University Press.

Hawking, Stephen, and Leonard Mlodinow. 2010. *The Grand Design*. London: Bantan Books/Transworld Publisher.

Jarry, Alfred. 1996. *Exploits and Opinions of Doctor Faustroll, Pataphysician*. Translated by Symon Watson Taylor. Cambridge, MA: Exact Change Boston.

Krishnamurti, Jiddu. 1969. *Freedom from the Known*. Edited by Mary Lutyens. New York: Harper & Row.

Penrose, Roger. 1994. *Shadows of the Mind*. Oxford: Oxford University Press.

Poe, Edgar Allan. 1909. "The Poetic Principle." In *The Complete Poetical Works of Edgar Allan Poe: With Three Essays on Poetry*, edited by R. Brimley Johnson, 211–39. London: Henry Frowde.

Wittgenstein, Ludwig. 1958. *Philosophical Investigations*. Translated by G. E. M. Anscombe, edited by G. E. M. Anscombe, R. Rhees, G. H. Von Wright. Oxford: Basil Blackwell Ltd.

Ten Plus Ways of Reading Charles Bernstein: Improvisations on Aphoristic Cores

Yunte Huang

> In literature it is only the wild that attracts us.
> —Henry David Thoreau, "Walking"

> If I'm not in the ballpark
> You can find me at the zoo.
> —Anonymous

1. Pitch

"Pitch is the foul stain, the skank and stench of a viscous taint. The kind of poetry I want is when you can't get the pitch out" (Bernstein 2016: x).

A few years ago, after the publication of *Pitch of Poetry* by Charles Bernstein, a friend wrote me from China and asked about how to translate the book's title word *pitch*. I could almost hear the Frenchman Jacques Derrida turning in his grave, mumbling "polysemy." Pardon my French, I wanted

boundary 2 48:4 (2021) DOI 10.1215/01903659-9382300

to say to my friend, it all depends on what business you're in. If you're in music, pitch is the sound. In baseball, it's the throw. If you're in sales, that's your bread and butter, although it's also something Emmanuel Levinas has warned against, or as Bernstein puts it in the preface to *Pitch of Poetry*, "the attack or approach. The angle" (x). Or, you could just be adding a few bucks to the office pool for a nice Christmas gift for someone or, better even, to save the planet. Or, it's the dark and sticky spots you may find at the bottom of your feet after a nice day walking barefoot on a sandy beach.

Of course, I knew what business my friend was in—he's a literature professor, but nowadays you can never be sure; for all I knew, he could be moonlighting. And that's just the rub: you can never be sure when you read Bernstein. And if surety is what you're looking for, I suggest you give your insurance agent a call. Surety bond, I heard, was quite a fad some years ago. As Neeli Cherkovski puts it in his recent review of Bernstein's *Near/ Miss*, "The sense of surety is consistently undercut, often with a humor bordering on a shtick" (Cherkovski 2020). Slanted or sliced the way Ms. Dickinson would like, "veritas," a product that many strive to advertise and market, always comes crooked like a walking stick we lean on for the long journey in life or poetry. "It's true but I don't believe it," quips Bernstein. Or, "Better truth in the shade than a lie in the sun" (Bernstein 2018: 80, 77). Like an old itch, it's always there, but you can only scratch it through a rubber boot, as a Chinese proverb says.

It reminds me of a lunch I once had with someone at the Harvard Faculty Club. That year, upon getting my PhD in Buffalo, where I had studied with Bernstein, I was just starting my job as an assistant professor of English at Harvard. My lunch date was a senior colleague in the department, a towering figure in poetry criticism, someone who had for years defined the taste of mainstream poetry. In that posh mahogany room, where Jamesian characters ghosted in and out, I asked my colleague about a rumor I had heard: "Is it true that of all the major Anglo-American poets, you particularly dislike two?"

"What did you hear?" she was amused, a butter knife halting in midair. "Which two?"

"Robert Browning and Ezra Pound."

"Ah, it's true," she said, putting the knife gently down on the plate. "Because you never know who they are."

By which she meant that the poems of Browning and Pound are so invested in theatrical masking and ventriloquism—Browning's dramatic monologue and Pound's personae—that you cannot find the so-called lyrical self, a singular voice one may associate with a romantic poet, unique like a Mongolian birthmark. I was going to say, "In that case, I guess you also dislike Charles Bernstein." But I didn't need to say that because I knew she wasn't a fan of his work, not his poetry, which follows the polyvocal, polyentendre tradition of Browning and Pound, or his poetics, which forcefully denounces the Romantic Ideology. Jerome McGann (1983), a scholar Bernstein often quotes sympathetically, defines the Romantic Ideology as a grand illusion that continues to haunt the contemporary imaginations of poetry, a notion that poetry, through its commitment to lyrical sincerity and refined craft, can be a universal expression of human sentiment. In the same vein, or the next lane, Bernstein deplores the Wordsworthian idea of poetry as "the spontaneous overflow of powerful feelings" and the accompanying notion of adopting "a diction really used by man." As he puts it in *Content's Dreams*: "The idea of getting all the material in a poem totally 'spontaneously' from my 'self' seems boring to me. . . . I think the whole persona conceit capitalizes on a sense of 'finding a voice' which to me is finding altogether too much too fast, and getting stuck with it" (1986: 394). Instead, he suggests, "Voice is a possibility for poetry not an essence" (45).

As I was writing this, news came from Stockholm that the American poet Louise Glück had won this year's Nobel Prize in Literature. Never a fan of that prize for its conspiratory role in perpetuating linguistic hegemony of European languages, I was amazed, but not surprised, by the milquetoast predictability of the award citation for Glück's work: "for her unmistakable poetic voice that with austere beauty makes individual existence universal." I'm no Charlie Chan, but I could easily detect clues of my former Harvard colleague or like-minded critics making their pitch to the Nobel Prize Committee along the lines encapsulated in the citation. As Philip Marlow says in *The Big Sleep*, "It all ties together."

2. Seams, or Sew What

"I like my poetry the way I like my fruitcake: nutty" (Bernstein 2016: 299).

Tying together, or (k)not, a materialist and constructivist point of view, looking at poetry etymologically as *poesis* or making, has been a central concern in twentieth- and twenty-first-century avant-garde poetics. Pound's ideogram, William Carlos Williams's objectivism, Gertrude Stein's cubism,

John Cage's chance operation, Susan Howe's collage fragmentation, Steve McCaffery's textual carnival, to name just a few, all point to an experimental tradition that has been variously characterized as a "poetics of indeterminacy" by Marjorie Perloff (1999), "disjunctive poetics" by Peter Quartermain (1992), and "discrepant engagement" by Nathaniel Mackey (1993).

The tug-of-war between the will to coherence and the impulse for incoherence—or, as Bernstein insists, coherence by other means—is nowhere more clearly demonstrated than in the work of Pound. In "Canto 116," one of those late cantos composed during his final years, the poet finally had a chance to reflect on his lifetime work, thus giving us a rare glimpse into what my former Harvard colleague would call a "lyrical self." In this late canto, Pound feels conflicted over self-evaluation. On the one hand, he is proud of his work, calling it "the great ball of crystal" and challenging anyone to "lift it"; on the other hand, he readily acknowledges its incoherence:

> I have brought the great ball of crystal;
> who can lift it?
> Can you enter the great acorn of light?
> But the beauty is not the madness
> Tho' my errors and wrecks lie about me.
> And I am not a demigod,
> I cannot make it cohere.
> (Pound 1970: 795–96)

In a typescript version of this poem (housed in the collection of the Harry Ransom Center at the University of Texas at Austin), the poet sounds even crankier: Instead of "I cannot make it cohere," the line reads "The damn stuff won't cohere." A few lines later, the poet regains his confidence (or delusion) and sounds self-righteous again:

> i.e. it coheres all right
> even if my notes do not cohere.
> Many errors,
> a little rightness
> (797)

"Not incoherent, coherent by other means," Bernstein declares in *Recalculating*. "By any means necessary" (2013: 6). Early in his career, before he was appointed the David Gray Chair of Poetry and Poetics at SUNY–Buffalo, Bernstein had worked as an editor of medical journals, an experience that had brought a key concept into his poetics, "dysraphism." As defined in his book *The Sophist*:

> "Dysraphism" is a word used by specialists in congenital disease to mean a dysfunctional fusion of embryonic parts—a birth defect. Actually, the word is not in Dorland's, the standard U.S. medical dictionary, but I found it "in use" by a Toronto physician, so it may be a commoner British medical usage or just something he came up with. *Raph* literary means "seam," so dysraphism is mis-seaming—a prosodic device! But it has the punch of being the same root as rhapsody (*rhaph*)—or in Skeat's—"one who strings (lit. stitches) songs together, a reciter of epic poetry," cf. "ode" etc. In any case, Dorland's does define "dysraphia" (if not dysraphism) as "incomplete closure of the primary neural tube; status dysraphicus"; this is just below "dysprosody" [sic.]: "disturbance of stress, pitch, and rhythm of speech." (Bernstein 1987: 44)

The mismatch, mis-seaming of parts, the cacophony of sound, while inheriting the core of Pound's poetics of assemblage, "to incorporate materials from disparate places," also refutes Pound's utopian yearning for a "great ball of crystal" (Bernstein 1986: 394). As Bernstein states in an essay, "Pound's great achievement was to create a work using ideological swatches from many social and historical sectors of his own society and an immense variety of other cultures. This complex, polyvocal textuality was the result of his search—his unrequited desire for—deeper truths than could be revealed by more monadically organized poems operating with a single voice and a single perspective." Applauding Pound's achievement of sloughing off the straitjacket of lyrical self, Bernstein is at the same time critical of Pound's self-delusion in wishing for an authorial control, creating order out of chaos: "Pound's ideas about what mediated these different materials are often at odds with how these types of textual practices actually work in *The Cantos*" (1992: 123). What Bernstein has identified as the contradiction between Pound's poetic achievement and authorial desire would ultimately lead to moments of self-doubt that we see Pound experiencing in those late cantos.

Writing in the Poundian tradition of polyvocality, Bernstein seeks the indeterminate, off-balance, ironic, and even what seems "clumsy or awkward" (2016: 193). As he explains his compositional method that is decidedly Poundian, "In my work there are quotations from a vast array of sources, and just as many made-up quotations that sound like they are from a prior text. There are lines from other poems, and echoes of lines; remarks from letters (my own and others') or memos from the job; things heard and misheard. Much of this is very specific, though some is not conscious—things that stick in the head but the source is not remembered" (1986: 393–94). Rather than looking for 正名 (*zhengming*), "correct naming," a Confucian concept extolled by Pound as the golden rule for poetic language, Bernstein sees the poem as a "Rube Goldberg malapropism machine": "I do have a taste for the asymmetric and the off-balance, the spastic, which in my work is very often transformed into a rhythmic element (flat-footed, lost in rime), taken as material to spin in different ways, oscillate, create shapes that give these dis-positions a buoyancy and lightness that they don't necessarily have when you're feeling awkward or stupid or inept" (2016: 194).

Once an editor at New Directions asked Pound to correct some of the errors in the earlier editions of *The Cantos*. The poet declined, insisting that the poems are "a record of struggle with errors." 信 (*xin*), the Chinese character meaning *veritas* or sincerity, is, in Pound's words, a man 人 standing by his words 言, or errors. Not to see the schism, the dysraphic seams between the human desire for truth and the fallibility of human speech would make one ill-prepared—P. T. Barnum's "sucker"—for the "pitch of poetry," which is always so ardent and appealing and yet ironic, tongue-in-cheek. As Bernstein writes after Fernando Pessoa in "Autopsychographia":

> Poets are fakers
> Whose faking is so real
> They even fake the pain
> They truly feel
> And for those of us so well read
> Those read pains feel O, so swell
> Not the poets' double header
> But the not of the neither
> And so the wheels go whack
> Ensnaring our logical part
> In the train wreck
> Called the human heart
> (2013: 3)

Somewhere Clifford Geertz said, "There is nothing so coherent as a paranoid's delusion or a swindler's story" (1973: 18). He ought to have added a poet's song, patching up the broken pieces of a human heart.

3. Pudding, Hasty or Upstairs

"When you're right you're right and even when you're wrong you're right, just not as right as when you're right" (Bernstein 2013: 87).

Like a misappropriated or bowdlerized movie line, Bernstein's work draws its energy from verbal vaudeville, slapstick, and punching hilarity. "The Truth in Pudding," for instance, begins with a pseudo-prologue, like an opening scene in a surrealist novel projecting a panoramic view of "the city of language": "Imagine poetry as a series of terraces, some vast, some no bigger than a pinprick, overlooking the city of language. The sound and light show begins in the dark; sentences dart by, one by one, forming wave after wave of the rag and bone shop of the quotidian, events passing before our eyes like the faint glimmer of consciousness in an alcoholic stupor. Facts, facts everywhere but not a drop to drink" (Bernstein 2013: 4).

From here on, the poem tumbles, mumbles, grumbles, jumbles, stumbles, and fumbles around like a dipsomaniac Pat Hobby looking for a waterhole on shuttered Sunset Boulevard during a global pandemic. The ancient itch—the more earnest among us would call it the poetic desire—is still there, and so is the cold, hard pavement of undrinkable "facts." The film crew has quit, leaving the characters freewheeling, snatching lines from each other, wisecracking like firecrackers on a deserted beach, parodying wisdom in front of a cracked mirror. Some lines are italicized, some are inside quotes, some are attributed but most are not, each a fork in the road, testing the reader's determination or readiness to twirl:

> *Speak truth to truth.*
>
> Poetry shows the ink out of the inkbottle.
>
> *Poetry is difficulty that stays difficult.*
> [Hank Lazer via Pound/Williams]
>
> "Is the best you can do really the best you can do?"
>
> Connect the knots.
>
> *Better last night's salami than this morning's baloney.*
>
> Information is born free but everywhere in chains.
> (Bernstein 2013: 4–12)

"When you come to a fork in the road," says Yogi Berra, "take it." Riffing off the Canadian American singer Paul Anka, "It is what it is. It swings,"

Bernstein's poem, or pudding, oscillates between custom-made one-liners and precariously dangling billboards of poetic statements, as if giving a free lesson to some mainstream/main street critics, who often fail to understand his work, deeming it as being too difficult or failing as poetry—most of the time they simply don't know how to laugh:

> So much depends on what you mean by failure, what you want from success, and what you imagine poems do. Insofar as a poem is successful, it fails to fail, but, in failing to fail, it also succeeds at failing. That's a lose-lose scenario (which in the alchemy of poetry we imagine as win-win).
>
> Or,
>
> If reading poetry is not directed to the goal of deciphering a fixed, graspable meaning, but rather encourages performing and responding to overlapping meanings, then difficulty is transformed from obstacle to opening.
>
> Or,
>
> "It is not a thought, finished and complete, that seeks expression in a beautiful form. It is a thought's struggle, what is in and below the thoughts; it is the things and all things behind them, the life-material, expressed in our perception, that we should render in aesthetic creation." [Gunnar Bjorling, tr. Fredrik Hertzberg]
> (Bernstein 2013: 4–12)

The poet explains his modus operandi as one of "generative" poetics:

> Let me give an example of what "generative" might mean. I think of some of my poems as a series of remarks, either in the aphoristic sense or in the sense of observations, constructed items, etc., occurring at the level of phrases or sentences. These can be interpreted in multiple ways: they are each, perhaps to say polyentendres (that is, any given remark can be taken as true, ironic, false, didactic, satiric, fantastical, inscrutable, sad, funny, my view, someone else's view, and so on). Polyentendres suggest the continuous choices of interpretation that confronting the world involves (though that is a matter of semblance only—structural affinity to other forms of creation). (Bernstein 1986: 396)

In a recent essay, Marjorie Perloff has aptly characterized a poem like "The Truth in Pudding" as "a *Dunciad* of overheard conversation and cartoonish gesture," suggesting that "Bernstein's is an art of excess, baroque in its piling up of manifold exemplars of the follies and mendacities of our Waste Land, an unreal—or, more properly, hyperreal city that splinters into fragments before our eyes" (Perloff, n.d.). If you are looking for "the truth in pudding," the poet seems to say, try Hasty Pudding. This is not one of those "neatly laundered poems of the poet laureate and Pulitzers" (Bernstein 2016: 330), which would make it "as if poetry was something you give to your mother-in-law when she goes deaf" (Bernstein 2013: 11).

One year, Bernstein was invited to give a reading at Harvard. When his hilarious lines, often bringing down the house at other venues, failed to strike a chord with some of the poetry heavyweights in attendance, Bernstein had to pause in the middle of his performance and deadpanned, "You guys are really serious, aren't you?" Which did indeed provoke a few chuckles. The dinner reception afterwards, held at Upstairs at the Pudding (now sadly defunct), was more congenial, if memory serves me well.

4. Wit, or Ivy without a Wall

"I never / met / a cliché / I didn't like" (Bernstein 2018: 72).

Readers of Bernstein are often struck by his wit, witticisms proliferating throughout his poems and titles. Those quick turns of phrase or phase may make him sound like an aphorist. Bernstein also often talks about his own work as "improvisations on aphoristic cores" (Bernstein 1999: 7). There's nothing wrong with looking at a poet as an aphorist. Like its cousins—maxim, proverb, adage, epigram, axiom, and dictum—aphorism is meant to achieve the greatest meaning with the fewest words, a generic feature that brings it tantalizingly close to Pound's dictum that poetry is language condensed or charged with energy to the maximum degree. In fact, the affinity between poetry and aphorism is as old as time. When Plato attacked poets, he was also critical of those ancient Greek thinkers who used poetical forms—that is, aphorisms, "which conceal from the majority of men their real meanings." Socrates once complained of the ilk of Heraclitus, "If you ask any of them a question, he will pull out some little enigmatic phrase from his quiver and shoot it off at you; and if you try to make him give an account of what he said, you will only get hit by another, full of strange turns of language. You will never reach any conclusion with any of them, ever" (Hui 2019: 43). The distrust of aphorism in philosophy testifies to its potential and potency as a poetic form. It is no surprise that many antiestablishment thinkers, such as Nietzsche, Kierkegaard, Wittgenstein, and Benjamin, are all inveterate aphorists.

Plato's (and Socrates's) reservation notwithstanding, civilizations were founded on the cornerstones laid by great thinkers whose doctrines have been crystallized into a body of memorable sayings, such as Heraclitus's "You cannot step twice into the same river," and Confucius's "The nature of man is always the same; it is their habits that separate them." After Erasmus almost single-handedly turned aphorism into a literary genre, the post-Renaissance world also boasted such master aphorists as Francis Bacon, Montaigne, Goethe, and Benjamin Franklin. Bacon, for instance, writes specifically of aphoristic virtues:

> The writing in aphorisms hath many excellent virtues, whereto the writing in Method doth not approach. For first, it trieth the writer, whether he be superficial or solid: for Aphorisms, except they should be ridiculous, cannot be made but of the pith and heart of sciences; for discourse of illustration is cut off; recitals of examples are cut off; discourse of connection and order is cut off; descriptions of practice are cut off. So there remaineth nothing to fill the Aphorisms but some good quantity of observation: and therefore no man can suffice, nor in reason will attempt to write Aphorisms but he that is sound and grounded. (1934: 142)

Bacon's notion exemplifies the traditional belief that behind the seeming fragmentation of aphorisms lies a larger truth. And such a mothership of truth guarantees the integrity of these adorable, spattering babies of wisdom.

The iconoclastic Nietzsche also speaks of the virtues of aphorism. In the preface to *On the Genealogy of Morals*, Nietzsche writes, "People find difficulty with the aphoristic form; this arises from the fact that today this form is *not taken seriously enough*. An aphorism, properly stamped and molded, has not been 'deciphered' when it has simply been read; rather, one has then to begin its exegesis, for which is required an art of exegesis." In fact, he regards the third essay of his book as a mere commentary on a single aphorism, a quote from his own *Thus Spoke Zarathustra*, "Unconcerned, mocking, violent—thus wisdom wants us: she is a woman and always loves only a warrior." To do the proper exegesis, one must *unlearn* the method of reading conventionally practiced. "Therefore it will be some time before my writings are 'readable,'" because his aphorisms require "something for which one has almost to be a cow and in any case not a 'modern man': rumination" (Nietzsche 1989: 22–23).

While Bacon sees aphorism's use for knowledge and epistemology, Nietzsche sees in aphorism an endurable literary form, as he writes in *Human, All Too Human*: "Praise of aphorisms: A good aphorism is too hard for the tooth of time and is not consumed by all millennia, although it serves every time for nourishment: thus it is a great paradox of literature, the intransitory amid the changing, the food that always remains esteemed, like salt, and never loses its savor, as even that does." He compares aphorisms to peaks between mountains, and "in the mountains the shortest way is from peak to peak" (Nietzsche 1986: 168).

Contrary to Nietzsche, Bernstein once said, "The shortest distance between two points is a digression" (1999: 47). The danger of romanticizing aphorisms as babies of wisdom is comparable to the peril of idealizing poetry as memorable lines. Rooted in orality, aphorism etymologically derives from the Greek *apo-* "from, away from" + *horizein* "to bound." The ever-receding horizon that can never be reached. In this sense, an aphorism, as Andrew Hui points out in his study of the genre, "is a mark of our finitude, ever approaching the receding horizon, always visible yet never tangible" (2019: 16). In other words, aphorism is an utterance, a gesture, not a packaged wisdom product. Similarly, while mainstream poetry is heavily invested, almost mortgaged to the hilt, in memorable lines, in those orgiastic moments of oohs and ahs, Bernstein has consistently pointed us in a different direction.

In his trenchant critique of National Poetry Month, Bernstein attacks the Official Verse Culture for promoting poems like McDonald's Happy Meals, watering them down to bite-size, easy-to-chew mass products. Rather than reading poems for a fixed, graspable meaning, Bernstein advocates poetry as an exploration of possibility and encourages "performing and responding to overlapping meanings" (2011: 27–31). "Connect the knots" may sound like a memorable line, but the charm of the line comes from its irony and errancy, a simulacrum of the proverbial "connect the dots." The line "Either you have talent or we'll buy you some" sounds like a riff of a dialogue between a headhunter and a hunted head. It is followed by an italicized pseudo-proverb, "Better a four-legged dog than a three-legged cat," inverting and parodying the biblical bromide, "a living dog is better than a dead lion," while making reference to the question of talent in the previous line (Bernstein 2013: 7). Sections of the poem "The Truth in Pudding" present a quick succession of montage-like frame jumping and cutting. "Not the flow of consciousness," as the poem says, as if commenting on itself, "but the flow of perception" (6). It's not that there are no punch lines in Bernstein; they're actually "here and there and everywhere," as the nursery rhyme goes. It's just that they're punch lines meant to punch other lines rather than make themselves memorable. They're definitely not something you can read over after a daily special at your local chop suey joint.

In *The Birth-mark: Unsettling the Wilderness in American Literary History*, Susan Howe insists on regarding "texts as events rather than objects, as processes rather than products," suggesting that "the poem was a vision and gesture before it became sign and coded exchange in a political economy of value" (1993: 19, 147). Walter Benjamin, no stranger to political economy, once said, "A proverb, one might say, is a ruin which stands on the site of an old story and in which a moral twines about a happening like ivy around a wall" (1968: 108). A poem is ivy without a wall.

5. Decoy

"Is the best you can do really the best you can do?" (Bernstein 2013: 5).

This section is intentionally left blank, in response to "This Poem Intentionally Left Blank" (Bernstein 2001: 121).[1]

6. Husks

"Loosely linked stanzas, all bouncing off, or getting sucked into the black hole of the title" (Bernstein 2011: 247).

"Fear and Trespass"

"Searchless Warrant"

"The Truth in Pudding"

"Catachresis My Love"

"Also Rises the Sun"

"For Love Has Such a Spirit That If It Is Portrayed It Dies"

"The Years as Swatches"

"Solidarity Is the Name We Give to What We Cannot Hold"

"Water Under the Bridge Is Like an Old Song You Can't Remember"

"Mao Tse Tung Wore Khakis"

1. Curious readers are also encouraged to check out "Poem Loading" in *Recalculating* (2013), and "This Poem Is a Hostage" and "This Poem Is a Decoy" in *Near/Miss* (2018).

"If You Say Something, See Something"

"Thank You for Saying Thank You"

"Thank You for Saying You're Welcome"

"Nowhere Is Just Around the Corner"

"Two Stones with One Bird"

"Stupid Men, Smart Choices"

"Trouble Near Me"

"Long Before the Rain, I Wept"

"Venereal Muse"

"Won't You Give Up This Poem to Someone Who Needs It?"

"Your Ad Here"

"Me and My Pharaoh"

"How I Became Prehuman"

"Max Weber's Favorite Tylenol for Teething"

"My God Has an Attitude Problem"

"Frequently Unasked Questions"

"Immanuel Can't but Sammy Can"

"O! Li Po!"

7. Strings

"Art is made not of essences but of husks" (Bernstein 2001: xi).

In *One-Way Street*, a book full of aphorisms, headlines, manifestos, shibboleths, and other ephemeral language acts, Walter Benjamin describes how children are more drawn to debris than the world adults have built around them:

> Children are particularly fond of haunting any site where things are being visibly worked upon. They ate irresistibly drawn by the detritus generated by building, gardening, housework, tailoring, or carpentry. In waste products they recognize the face that the world of things

> turns directly and solely to them. In using these things, they do not so much imitate the world of adults as bring together, in the artifact produced in play, materials of widely differing kinds in a new, intuitive relationship. (1996: 449–50)

Benjamin writes this passage under the title "Construction Site," and a construction site—where the remnants of a work process rather than its finished, well-formed, and ready-to-be-consumed products linger—is an apt metaphor for what Bernstein wants his poetic work to become, as he states in *With Strings*: "We used to say the artist would drop away and there would just be work. Can we go further and say the work drops away and in its place there are stations, staging sites, or blank points of radical metamorphosis? Only when we experience this as an emplacement of textuality into material sensory-perceptual fields—turning ever further away from ideality in the pursuit of an ultimate concretion" (2001: xi).

The concern with material concretion, in *With Strings* as in many of Bernstein's poems and collections, is encapsulated in the book's title. "With-strings," like G-strings, are a particular kind of strings. *With*, a modifier as much as a preposition, describes a relationship, a betweenness, in which there's no absolute subject/object dichotomy and neither side disappears completely into the other through domination or metaphorical collapse. In a poem ironically titled (what else!) "Poem," the poet writes:

> I tend to use prepositions
> to suggest a relationship between
> objects, so for example above or
> between
> (2001: 20)

The tone of mockery serves to foreground what we often fail to see: the withness or relationality we have to maintain with anything other than ourselves or even with ourselves. Martin Heidegger calls it "Being-with" or "Dasein-with." To erase this withness by means of abstraction is to collapse the distance with which Bernstein's poetry and poetics have been consistently concerned. Earlier, Perloff characterized Bernstein's work of dysraphism as "an art of adjacency" (2002: 172), something Fredric Jameson would call a "schizophrenic disjunction" (1991: 29). In the work of strings, such an ironized, negotiated adjacency exhibits "contagious proximity":

> I've had it with dolorous pre-
> Clusions, deliberate delirium,

Miscreant ovation.
(Bernstein 2001: 89)

In some sense, Bernstein's famous notion of anti-absorption—that indirection, resistance, difficulty, and even distraction must be central to poetry, a Charlie Chanish gesture of misdirection, catching a suspect off guard—is also about distance, the hazard of either collapsing or rigidifying the distance between reader and text; hence now this satire entitled "Why We Ask You Not to Touch":

Human emotions and cognition
leave a projective film over the poems
making them difficult to perceive.
Careful readers maintain a measured
distance from the works in order
to allow distortion-free comprehension
and to avoid damaging the meaning.
(118)

As opposed to a poetics that bets everything on the stocks of memorable lines and "best poetry of the year," Bernstein, like a precocious child on Benjamin's construction site full of debris, sees a world in which everything has, as the saying goes, a string attached, or a world in which everything falls away, revealing the seams of the universe, pure relations. Here even the poems themselves have assumed a "with" relation with each other, as the poet explains the structure of the book:

> *With Strings* is organized as a vortex, with each poem furthering the momentum of the book while curving its arc of attentional energy. The structure is modular: A short work might become part of a serial poem or a section of a serial poem might stand on its own. The effect is to make the book as a whole a string of interchangeable parts. Political, social, ethical, and textual investigations intermingle, presenting a linguistic echo chamber in which themes, moods, and perceptions are permuted, modulated, reverberated, and further extended. (131)

And Bernstein is even more specific about his interest in the in-between space of poems when he describes the organizing principle of another book of his, *All the Whiskey in Heaven*: "I wanted to suture together disparate, even opposing, forms, in order to create a mobius rhythm out of the movement among the disparate parts; the meaning is as much in the space in between as in the poems themselves" (2016: 243).

Like a Mobius strip, a mystical string, if we circle back to the beginning of this section, where Bernstein asks us to imagine how the poet, as a self-expressive ego trapped in a Newtonian world, would drop away and then even further, the poem itself, as the product of such an egocentric self, would drop away, what will be left? Stations, staging sites, blank points of radical metamorphosis, and so on. "The motif of poetry," insists Bernstein, "is just a husk. When it falls away you don't get to essence but are drifting in time, like always, the strings maybe lifting you up (like a puppet?) or else playing alongside" (2013: 89). Benjamin, with his saturnine vision, said something more morose but equally sobering in his study of German dramas: "In the process of decay, and in it alone, the events of history shrivel up and become absorbed in the setting" (1998: 179).

8. Folds

"So this guy tells me he doesn't know what a schlemiel is. What a schmuck!" (Bernstein 2018: 35).

There is a parodically Baroque quality in Bernstein. Never the "neatly laundered poems of the poet laureates and Pulitzers," his work builds on materials that are, as Gilles Deleuze would say, "differentiated not by a wall but by way of a vector" (1993: xiv). Like aphorisms that by nature are concise and laconic but in composition/compilation explode into a proliferation of verbal excesses, Bernstein's writing, to paraphrase John Hollander's infamous snub of Allen Ginsberg's "Howl" with its explosive parataxis, sponges on the toleration of genteel readers looking for modest morsels of craft and moral.[2]

In *With Strings*, we encounter a Joycean pileup spanning about three hundred words in length: "As if to create not scales but conditions, not con-

2. In his review of *Howl and Other Poems*, John Hollander dismissed Allen Ginsberg's landmark publication as husk, condemning the Beat poet and his fellow counterculture writers for proclaiming, "in a hopped-up and improvised tone, that nothing seems to be worth saying save in a hopped-up and improvised tone" (*Partisan Review*, Spring 1957). Representing the poetry establishment's mandate for craft and decorum, Hollander obviously found intolerable Ginsberg's notion, "first thought, best thought." Inheriting the counterculture spirit of the Beat generation, Bernstein doesn't, however, fully accept the idea of spontaneity, a relic of Romanticism, as aforementioned. Bernstein's riposte was, "FIRST BURP, BEST BURP" (1987: 13).

ditions but textures, not textures but projects, not projects but brackets, not brackets but bracelets, not bracelets but branches, not branches but hoops, not hoops but springs, not springs but models, not models but possibilities . . ." (Bernstein 2001: xi–xii). In this series of (k)nots abutting on each other, we see plights and flights, philosophical façades and philosomatic trillings, straddling heights and conceptual rejoinders, curling capacities and embroidered fans, and a labyrinth of moldings, groundings, enclosures, and exposés.

In "What Makes a Poem a Poem," originally a sixty-second lecture delivered at the University of Pennsylvania on April 21, 2004, we see another string of (k)nots punctured by the timer on a stopwatch:

> It's not rhyming words at the end of a line. It's not form. It's not structure. It's not loneliness. It's not the sky. It's not love. It's not the color. It's not the feeling. It's not the meter. It's not the place. It's not the intention. It's not the desire. It's not the weather. It's not the hope. It's not the subject matter. It's not the death. It's not the birth. It's not the trees. It's not the words. It's not the things between the words. It's not the meter. It's not the meter . . . [timer beeps] It's the timing. (Bernstein 2018: 171)

In one of the most profound studies of the Baroque, Deleuze identifies the fold, in the form of pleats, curves, and twisting surfaces, as the quintessential aesthetics and operative function of the historical style. "The experience of the Baroque," writes Deleuze,

> entails that of the fold. . . . Included in things folded are draperies, tresses, tessellated fabrics, ornate costumes; dermal surfaces of the body that unfold in the embryo and create themselves at death; domestic architecture that bends upper and lower levels together while floating in the cosmos; novels that invaginate their narratives or develop infinite possibilities of serial form; harmonics that orchestrate vastly different rhythms and tempos; philosophies that resolve Cartesian distinctions of mind and body through physical means—without recourse to occasionalism and parallelism—grasped as foldings. (1993: xi–xii)

Benjamin, another aficionado of the historical style, writes that the baroque aesthetics is "to pile up fragments ceaselessly, without any strict idea of a goal, and in the unremitting expectation of a miracle, to take the repetition of stereotypes for a process of intensification" (1998: 178).

To add another wrinkle, or fold within a fold, to my grappling with Bernstein's poetry as a representation of the Deleuzian fold, here is what Bernstein has to say about Benjamin as a multipolar thinker: "Benjamin's form of reflective writing suggests a poetics of multiple layers or figures. A line of thought may seem to go off into one direction but then drops back to follow another trajectory, only this new direction is not a non sequitur but rather echoes or refracts both the antecedent motifs and—this is the uncanny part—the eventual ones. I mean this as a way of rethinking what is often called fragmentation or disjunction. Think of fragments not as discontinuous but as overlays, pleats, folds" (2016: 204).

"Voices I am following," Susan Howe said, "lead me to the margins" (1993: 4). An essay is really a footnote to its footnotes. How can it be otherwise?

9. Objectile, or the Other Charlie

"Schools are made to be broken" (Bernstein 2013: 10).

"One perception must immediately and directly lead to a further perception," so declared Charles Olson, who laid a cornerstone for the innovative poetic tradition at SUNY–Buffalo, where Bernstein would one day find his first institutional home. In two landmark mid-century essays, "Projective Verse" and "Human Universe," Olson drew a distinction between "language as the act of the instant and language as the act of thought about the instant." Calling for composition by field—that is, open form (as opposed to inherited, traditional forms)—Olson proposed projective verse as what follows the heartbeat and breath on a line, as opposed to the head and ear in a syllable. In the three cognate *P* words, namely, "projectile, percussive, and prospective," Olson saw the mandate for the kind of poetry he was advocating (see Olson 1997: 155–66, 239–49).

It is worth remembering that Olson had resigned from his governmental work partly because he was disgusted with the American Cold War machinery of propaganda and misinformation, a geopolitical gambit in which language was turned into bombastic dogmas, jingoistic phrases, and memorable lines ("Build the wall!"). In poetry, there is also the question of how words are used. "It is a matter, finally, of OBJECTS," Olson writes, "what they are, what they are inside a poem, how they got there, and, once there, how they are to be used." Revisiting the idea of "objectivism" as proposed by Williams and Pound in the earlier decades, Olson saw the virtue of the Objectivists, a school of poetry that would have a profound impact on

Bernstein (via a handful of mostly secular Jewish, politically radical writers, such as Louis Zukofsky, George Oppen, and Charles Reznikoff): "Objectivism is the getting rid of the lyrical interference of the individual as ego, of the 'subject' and his soul, that peculiar presumption by which western man has interposed himself between what he is as a creature of nature . . . and those other creatures of nature" (243, 247).

In Olson's rejection of psychological subjectivism, we find echoes of Bernstein's resistance to the "lyrical interference" of ego and his turn to the materiality of words. "I'm not that interested in myself," says Bernstein, "in recounting facts and observations about that" (1986: 394). Just as Olson's conception of word as object is kinetic not static, as he insists on language as "the act of the instant" rather than "the act of thought about the instant," Bernstein's quest in poetry, fully grounded in cultural materialism, is never a fetishism of materiality. If the key word in Olson's projective verse is "projectile," the functioning term in Bernstein's writing is objectile.

In his study of the fold, Deleuze suggests that we reconsider objects as objectiles: "The new status of the object no longer refers its condition to a spatial mold—in other words, to a relation of form-matter—but to a temporal modulation that implies as much the beginnings of a continuous variation of matter as a continuous development of form. . . . This new object we call objectile. . . . The object here is manneristic, not essentializing; it becomes an event" (1993: 19).

I now begin to see the pain my former Harvard colleague(s) must feel in reading Bernstein. Just as how he builds the book of *With Strings* as a vortex, his poems are often moving targets and shape-shifters, not striving for the climactic moment, but perpetuating the clinamenic movement. When the object of your focus keeps changing, what do you do? Even the best scholars forget to emphasize that Lucretius, whose *De Rerum Natura* (*Nature of Things*) introduced the idea of a swerving clinamen, further inspiring the Leibnizian fold and monad, Deleuzian objectile and rhizome, as well as today's quantum physics, wrote the piece in poetry. You may take away the idea, but you cannot take away the poem. And that is perhaps the most Epicurean about *De Rerum Natura*.

10. Echoes: A Test of Poetry

"This Charlie says: Jew's ear like motor car in lake: learn to adapt" (Bernstein 2016: 11).

Nothing tests poetry harder than translation. At the same time, nothing makes poetry more alive, or objectilistic, than translation. When a poem crosses linguistic boundaries, it loses its original mooring or cohesiveness. Words, syntaxes, and references fly off in all directions like quantum dots, errant clinamens. For a poet who is devoted to polyentendre and polyvocality, Bernstein is a particularly difficult poet to translate. He acknowledged that in a lecture delivered in China on September 30, 2011, to an audience who either had to read him in translation or found his poems in English rather daunting:

> What interested me here was that no matter how formally difficult a poem is in terms of syntax or structure, and many of my poems are difficult in that way, the overriding difficulty is cultural, especially in terms of vernacular, cultural reference, and social context. Nonstandard, vernacular, slang, or accented language in a poem, which is a fundamental formal device of much twentieth-century American poetry, loses its meaning when translated for the lexical or word-for-word meaning. In the case of my work, I often distort my cultural references, making it almost impossible to look up what the "original" reference is: a daunting problem for the translation. (Bernstein 2016: 8)

Here he refers to an interesting exchange he once had with a Chinese scholar, Zhang Ziqing, who was trying to translate his work. Puzzled by Bernstein's poems, Zhang asked him a series of questions, many of which sounded like simple requests for clarification of meaning but actually raised fundamental questions about our understanding of poetry. If close reading, still the basic tool for literary hermeneutics, intends to contain polysemy, these questions bust the door wide open rather than, as Benjamin claims in his famous essay on translation, shut the door on language. Derived from Zhang's probing questions, Bernstein's "A Test of Poetry" is a Dada readymade, putting poetry to a cardiac stress test, in the way Marcel Duchamp's "Fountain" interrogated the status of art:

> You write, *the walls are our floors.*
> How can the *walls* be floors if the floors
> refer to the part of the room which forms
> its enclosing surface and upon which one
> walks? In *and the floors, like balls,*
> *repel all falls*—does *balls* refer to
> nonsense or to any ball like a basket ball

or to guys? Or to a social assembly for
dancing? *Falls* means to descend
from a higher to a lower
or to drop down wounded or dead?
But what is *the so-called overall*
mesh?
(1999: 53)

Here the questioner should not be faulted for his persistent queries into the lexical meaning of words. His genuine puzzlement is not only a testament to the aesthetics of indeterminacy, or art of adjacency, that lies at the heart of Bernstein's work but also to the futility of trying to fix meaning in poetry. "Accuracy is the bogeyman of translation," Bernstein states. "For what can be accurately paraphrased is not the 'poetic' content of the work" (2011: 199). In the lines in question, "The walls / are our only floors and the floors, like balls, repel / all falls," from a poem titled "Fear of Flipping," the poet is more invested in the ring of echoes of *wall*, *ball*, *fall*, *all*, and even the half-rhyming *repel*, than the lexical meaning of these words. The ricochet of sounds and syllables, creating the titular fear of flipping, like a flip or slip of tongue, looks to walls to keep it inside or floors to hold it up.

"Disputes about translation are always a pretext for disputes about poetry," writes Bernstein. "Translation theory is poetics by another name. If I am interested in a certain kind of translation, it is because I am interested in a certain kind of poetry" (2011: 201). We know what kind of poetry Bernstein is interested in—echopoetics, regarding a poem as an echo chamber of meaning. "Echopoetics is the nonlinear resonance of one motif bouncing off another within an aesthetics of constellation. Even more, it's the sensation of allusion in the absence of allusion" (x). Echoes, then, are not merely acoustic but allusive. The Chinese translator was not wrong trying to chase down the literal meanings of words, "Does *balls* refer to / nonsense or to any ball like a basket ball / or to guys / Or to a social assembly for / dancing?" But the exact meaning of the word *ball*, like a ball, keeps on bouncing and falls into the constellation of *all*, *fall*, *wall*, and so on. In that echo chamber, the allusion of *ball* is, as Bernstein puts it, "a blank, a shadow of an absent source" (x). It's the same kind of swerving poetics one would find, for instance, in Gertrude Stein's series of "Chicken" poems in *Tender Buttons*: "Chicken is a peculiar third . . . Alas a dirty word, alas a dirty third alas a dirty third, alas a dirty bird" (1990: 54). What it requires of a reader or a translator is, as Bernstein insists, not to seek equivalence or adjudication but to provide responses, especially those "that are hard to support rationally," like hunches, homophonic translation, close listening, or a conversation that doesn't have to stop (2016: 190).

+ Coda: A Conversation

"Even when it's over it's not over" (Bernstein 2013: 91).

Here's a recent poem titled "Jellyfish with Jew's Ear" by Bernstein, dedicated to someone named Yunte Huang:

> Sometimes a fascist is just
> fascist but we don't talk
> that way around here. It'll
> be a slow boat to China
> before the moonbeams
> hit the stargaze, deep
> under the seventh seal,
> eight if we count you.
>
> *for Yunte Huang*

A reader, passing as yet another Charlie in this constellation of Charlies, responded to the poem via a missive to the author:

> Dear Professor Bernstein:
>
> I have some questions about your poem entitled "Jellyfish with Jew's Ear."
>
> When you write "Sometimes a fascist is just fascist," you mean at some other times they are not? Isn't your sentence a case of tautology? Or do you mean to say something like Gertrude Stein's "Rose is a rose is a rose"?
>
> In the lines "but we don't talk that way around here," why don't you talk that way? What way is that? Who do you refer to by "we"? Jews? Or all people who are not fascists? And where is "around here"? You mean New York City, where I know you live, or just your block, as your mother used to say?
>
> What's a "slow boat to China"? I often hear Americans say or even sing "slow boat to China." Why are Americans so crazy about taking a slow boat to China? Don't they like speed? Or is boat only a metaphor here, like the word "metaphor" itself?
>
> According to my dictionary, a stargaze is inviting your friends out to nature, to watch stars at night, and possibly have

other kinds of fun as well, you know what I mean (wink, wink). Is that why moonbeams like hitting them? Does "moonbeams" mean literally the beam-like light from the moon?

"The seventh seal" seems to be a reference from the Bible, or do you mean the cult movie of that title? In the Bible, the Lamb opens a seal of the book. Is the Lamb, i.e. Jesus, also the Jew in your title? Does your poem ultimately describe a confrontation between fascists and Jews?

In the phrase "if we count you," since your poem is "for Yunte Huang," is he the "you" in this line? Can any reader be this "you," even a fascist?

I love your title, not just because there's no slippage of meaning, but because I know the dish so well. It reminds me of a line from *Flower Drum Song* by the great Rodgers and Hammerstein, "The girl who serves you all your food / Is another tasty dish." Yum yum! Now I begin to see the point of taking it slow going to China.

Sincerely yours,
Charlie Chan

References

Bacon, Francis. 1934. *The Advancement of Learning*. Edited by G. W. Kitchin. New York: E. P. Dutton.

Benjamin, Walter. 1968. *Illuminations*. Translated by Harry Zohn. New York: Schocken Books.

———. 1996. *Selected Writings, Volume 1: 1913–1926*. Edited by Marcus Bullock and Michael W. Jennings. Cambridge, MA: Harvard University Press.

———. 1998. *Origin of German Tragic Drama*. Translated by John Osborne. New York: Verso.

Bernstein, Charles. 1986. *Content's Dream: Essays 1975–1984* (Los Angeles: Sun & Moon Press.

———. 1987. *The Sophist*. Los Angeles: Sun & Moon Press.

———. 1992. *A Poetics*. Cambridge, MA: Harvard University Press.

———. 1999. *My Way: Speeches and Poems*. Chicago: University of Chicago Press.

———. 2001. *With Strings: Poems*. Chicago: University of Chicago Press.

———. 2011. *Attack of the Difficult Poems*. Chicago: University of Chicago Press.

———. 2013. *Recalculating*. Chicago: University of Chicago Press.

———. 2016. *Pitch of Poetry*. Chicago: University of Chicago Press.

———. 2018. *Near/Miss*. Chicago: University of Chicago Press.
Cherkovski, Neeli. 2020. Review of Charles Bernstein's *Near/Miss*, in *Brooklyn Rail*. Accessed December 12, 2020. https://brooklynrail.org/2020/11/books/Charles-Bernsteins-NearMiss.
Deleuze, Gilles. 1993. *The Fold: Leibniz and the Baroque*. Translated by Tom Conley. Minneapolis: University of Minnesota Press.
Geertz, Clifford. 1973. *The Interpretation of Cultures*. New York: Basic Books.
Howe, Susan. 1993. *The Birth-mark: Unsettling the Wilderness in American Literary History*. Hanover, NH: Wesleyan University Press.
Hui, Andrew. 2019. *A Theory of the Aphorism: From Confucius to Twitter*. Princeton, NJ: Princeton University Press.
Jameson, Fredric. 1991. *Postmodernism; or, The Cultural Logic of Late Capitalism*. Durham, NC: Duke University Press.
Mackey, Nathaniel. 1993. *Discrepant Engagement: Dissonance, Cross-Culturality, and Experimental Writing*. Cambridge: Cambridge University Press.
McGann, Jerome. 1983. *The Romantic Ideology: A Critical Investigation*. Chicago: University of Chicago Press.
Nietzsche, Friedrich. 1986. *Human, All Too Human: A Book for Free Spirits*. Translated by R. J. Hollingdale. Cambridge: Cambridge University Press.
———. 1989. *On the Genealogy of Morals*. Translated by Walter Kaufmann and R. J. Hollingdale. New York: Vintage Books.
Olson, Charles. 1997. *Collected Prose*. Edited by Donald Allen and Benjamin Friedlander. Berkeley: University of California Press.
Perloff, Marjorie. 1999. *The Poetics of Indeterminacy: Rimbaud to Cage*. Evanston, IL: Northwestern University Press.
———. 2002. *21st-Century Modernism: The "New" Poetics*. Malden, MA: Blackwell.
———. n.d. "Funny Ha-ha or Funny Peculiar? Recalculating Charles Bernstein's Poetry" (unpublished manuscript).
Pound, Ezra. 1970. *The Cantos*. New York: New Directions.
Quartermain, Peter. 1992. *Disjunctive Poetics: From Gertrude Stein and Louis Zukofsky to Susan Howe*. Cambridge: Cambridge University Press
Stein, Gertrude. 1990. *Tender Buttons*. Los Angeles: Sun & Moon Press.

This Working Title Will Be Replaced: Charles Bernstein's Forever Forthcoming

Brian Kim Stefans

It's never comforting to open a new title by Charles Bernstein. This is, of course, by design. In one of his most celebrated essays, "The Artifice of Absorption" (1987), Bernstein writes that the "artifice" of the title is "a measure of a poem's / intractability to being read as the sum of its / devices & subject matters" (1992: 9). He later asks for a literary criticism "in which the inadequacy of our / explanatory paradigms is neither ignored / nor regretted but brought into fruitful play" (16). Even worse for the *reviewer*, he writes that, in his poems of the time, "antiabsorptive / techniques are used towards / absorptive ends," though in his "satirical" mode, "absorptive means are used / toward antiabsorptive ends. It remains / an open question" (30). To some degree, these ideas aren't far from a general goal of much "language" writing of the time, which was to make (to put it reductively) the *social* operations of language visible in the poem in which—given our time of naturally assuming a poem is a "lyric" and thereby an act of "personal expression" or, worse, confession—the *subjective* content, whatever it is

boundary 2 48:4 (2021) DOI 10.1215/01903659-9382314

in the poem that relates to the writer, is etiolated or entirely deleted. As for *reading* itself, Bernstein notes (writing of Ron Silliman's *Ketjak* and *Tjanting*), that the poem "does not preclude absorption / in the various subject matters of the text / but rather doubles one's attentional focus: *in / & beside*" (69, italics in original).

So then where *are* we? The reader is asked to apprehend the satirical *voicing* of the content of a poem to determine where it lies on the nexus of "absorptive" and "antiabsorptive"—how does one do *that*? The reader is asked to take whatever critical acumen—the frameworks, the buzzwords, the poetical/political convictions—one might have acquired in school or in one's own autodidactic reading and put it into "play" when trying to appreciate a poem? And when considering the "subject matter" of a text, we are asked to read "in" and "beside"—i.e., reading as *one's self* and yet *over one's own shoulder*? Can this self-divorced reading practice possibly lead to something like *pleasure*?

Readers—not to mention *auditors*—of Bernstein's poetry, since the time of "Artifice of Absorption," written during what I think of as the "heroic" period of "Language" writing, which was more closely aligned with something we might call a "formalist" or "constructivist" approach, are aware that his poetry and thinking have expanded since then. Notably, it has become impossible to ignore the "subject matter" of his poetry, which is to say, since Bernstein's early classics (to the degree "Language" writing has them) such as "Asylum" (1975, a "collage" of the writing of Erving Goffman) and "The Klupzy Girl" (1983), his most anthologized poem, the repeatedly over-typed poem "Veil" (1987), which Craig Dworkin avers "[does] not so much prevent reading as redirect and discipline usual reading habits," and favorites of my own, the books *Rough Trades* (1991) and *Dark City* (1994), Bernstein has allowed both more *emotional* content into his work—poems expressing love, loss, sadness, fear, anger, even nostalgia—while also making clear, if often in brief clusters, a sort of pointillism, that the poems are "about" something that is not, itself, the language.

It's one thing to cut and paste, mime, procedurally reorder, and otherwise borrow material from the "social"—whether that be political jargon, memorandums to fellow office employees, Basic English, naive letters to the managers of NYC subway stations, or academic treatises on interpersonal relations—and another to write (to quote countless pop songs) "from the heart." There is certainly a lot of *time* between the writing of "Artifice of Absorption" and *Topsy-Turvy*, his most recent collection (2021), but also a lot, or perhaps *loss*, of *space*, too—the world has contracted since networked media have become ubiquitous. While there is a plethora of differences between Bernstein's earlier poetry and what he's writing now, I'd like to concentrate on these subjective aspects, as they're one of the most salient features of *Topsy-Turvy*.

1. The Broken

To start, I'd like to focus on what can be called a "theme" (much as I hate this word) that runs through *Topsy-Turvy*, and that is of *brokenness*. Of course, much early "Language" theory implied, if not overtly stated, that language itself can only be viewed as "broken," if either because of a natural *indeterminacy* in language (derived from the writings of Saussure, Wittgenstein, Stein, and others), or because language as circulated through the media was inauthentic, "spectacular" (in the Situationist sense), deceptive, and/or generally compromised. But *Topsy-Turvy*, like much of Bernstein's recent work, moves beyond these concerns; the *brokenness* becomes visceral, fraught, even pathetic. Here are a few excerpts:

Three steps
ahead, knocked
to floor;
get up,
pushed two
steps behind,
knocked down
again; get
up.
("Zeno's Way," 5)

One time I'm in the hen coop
Next at a loading dock
Afraid I'll tumble down the stairs
Then that I may not
("Beeline," 10)

If you leave, do it later
Or don't: the history
Of dance crippled by
Riptides, and when that

Passes, this may.
("Screwball's Tragedy," 14 [entirety])

It was never my intention to do
Either—Just to keep bailing this open
Boat drifting out toward an infinite sea.
("Testament," 15)

as quick as you run as
quick as they'll catch you
upland on spoons or back-hand
on canastas.

I haven't slept in many
a year—and the fissures
reply, are you measuring
fears
("Girl with Pail for Hat," 65 [entirety])

Sliding
till you hit false bottom,
wrestling metaphor for
sleep.
("Loose Lips Lift All Slips," 99)

Death is the end of all sadness
Storm follows each moment of bliss
Here lies the road to true madness
Deeper than locks in abyss
Storm echoes surfeit of gladness
Loneliness lives by its wits
("The Wreck of Hope," 157 [entirety])

The "brokenness" of "Zeno's Way" can be linked to an abiding interest in Beckett (filtered through Buster Keaton) for whom all actions, even the most elegant, seem to find themselves among a catalog of disgraces. Altogether, this recurring motif—being "crippled" in dance, being "knocked to the floor," "bailing" a sinking boat, not being able to "run" without being caught, and so forth—strikes me as dramatizing a "description of a struggle" (my reference is to Kafka), a human *agon*, not merely an enactment of linguistic failure in "antiabsorptive" verse.

Some of this apparent self-dramatization might be a result of a loose "blues" form that Bernstein has adopted over the years. *Topsy-Turvy* starts with a lyric by Geeshie Wiley, who recorded in the 1930s and has been noted as possibly "the rural South's greatest female blues singer and musician."[1] One of Wiley's verses runs:

I went—to the depot—I
looked up—at the stars—
cried—some train don't come—
there'll be some walkin' done.

These notes of resignation, after an appeal to the "Lord" by the singer's father not to die in the "German war," subtly become part of the panoply of voices that Bernstein employs in this book. There will be "some walkin' done" after the train fails to arrive, but Bernstein hints that the intended destination—Mobile, Easthampton, wherever it is trains take you—is either unreachable or entirely illusory. The poem "Zeno's Way" continues:

Pushed back
one step.
Push ahead
three steps,
pushed back
one step,
pushed sideways
five steps.
Knocked out.
Wake up,
groggy, five
steps to
back in
place. Continue
on, as
before, as
after.
(8)

Bernstein's restatement of Zeno's paradox isn't paradoxical at all; to my mind, it resembles a seedy tale of drunkenness from an early Tom

1. Wikipedia, s.v. "Geeshie Wiley," accessed March 10, 2021. https://en.wikipedia.org/wiki/Geeshie_Wiley.

Waits tune. Yes, the final lines bring us to the famous ending of "Worstward Ho"—"Fail better."—but that begs the question: What are we *failing to do*? Given all the metatextual elements that Bernstein has been known for since "The Artifice of Absorption," how are we to understand this theme in the new work, especially as tied to the blues lyric that opens the book?

The word *broke* appears only in one of the poems of *Topsy-Turvy*, "Procuring Poetry," which Bernstein notes is "after" the Brazilian poet Carlos Drummond de Andrade's "Procura da poesia" (1945), but, strangely, also *after* "John Yau and Michael Palmer." The poem is prescriptive, a Rilkean "letter to a young poet," but given that Bernstein often *satirizes* such prescriptions in his poems—remember the "open question" above—it's hard to know what he intends here:

> No reworking
> your buried and melancholy childhood.
> No oscillating between mirror and
> disappearing memories.
> What disappeared wasn't poetry.
> What broke was no crystal.
> (128)

My sense is that "Procuring Poetry" is an homage to Andrade, which is to say, Bernstein eludes prescriptiveness itself while celebrating that of a great Modernist poet he admires. Andrade is just one of the many writers Bernstein alludes or reverts to, or directly quotes, in this collection; "Boat Ride on West Lake (Pastoral)" ends, for example, with the words of William Carlos Williams's "Pastoral": "No / one will / believe / this of / vast import / to the nation" (41). As much as it appears that Bernstein appears to agree with Andrade's prescriptions—the "crystal" that "broke" here seems to be that of the mirror itself, a symbol of lyrical narcissism—we are still being asked to read "in / & beside," through the broken mirror of the "self" itself.

As for the word *broken*, it appears twice, but not in poems. In his note to the poem "Shields Green," Bernstein quotes Frederick Douglass on Green, a man who had liberated himself from slavery, joined John Brown on his fateful raid, and was eventually executed in 1859: "Shields Green was not one to shrink from hardships or dangers. He was a man of few words, and his speech was *singularly broken*; but his courage and self-respect made him quite a dignified character" (88; italics mine). Douglass did, in fact, quote some of Shields's speech (speaking of John Brown): "I b'leve I'll go wid de ole man." Technically, however, this isn't "broken" speech at all, but rather dialect, AAVE, or just a very strong Southern accent. Bernstein's poem for Shields (his "nomination for an American hero worthy of commendation") is a concrete reflection on some of the most traumatic events of US history, a visceral illustration of the standard/nonstandard linguistic divide that Bernstein has written about often in his essays.

Broken is also linked to language in the note to the series of short translations, "Amberianum: Philosophical Fragments of Caudio Amberian," from the first-century "Jewish poet and sophist" who "[a]t his school in Rome . . . spoke in a broken or pidgin Latin that some of his students called 'barbaric.' The only records we have of his writing are the Latin transcriptions made by these notoriously unreliable and sometimes hostile students" (116). The poem itself comprises forty single-line Latin aphorisms with Bernstein's "translations" beneath each one; for example: "Vivis et vigeo. Argumentum injustitia deos. / The fact that you are alive and thriving is proof that the gods are not just." The kicker, perhaps unsurprisingly, is that Caudio Amberian never existed; Bernstein is both the author of the *Latin* and the "translation." Furthermore, it doesn't appear that there ever was a Jewish poet during Roman times (Juvenal, the satirist, is noted by scholars to have recorded Jewish life in Rome but wasn't a Jew himself). However, Caudio is more than a fiction in that he's been *inserted* into history; his Latin fragments, however they were written (I suspect there was some digital assistance here), are now part of the canon for Latin scholars to pore over.

In both the Shields poem and the aphorisms, *brokenness* is ascribed to some element of language and to that degree might not support my contention that the brokenness of *Topsy-Turvy* represents a great departure. However, the breaks aspire beyond the merely semantic, and merely the present day; instead, they point to events that gum up the works of the transparency of history itself. As for the fictional Caudio, the polyglot who "read Aramaic, Hebrew, and Greek," is it possible he was more a victim of anti-Semitism rather than simple mockery for his "broken or pidgin Latin"? Only Sid Caesar knows for sure.

2. The Transcendental

Bernstein has written wonderfully about "The Skaters," one of John Ashbery's most visionary and, in an indescribable way, *grave* but *light-hearted* poems. Bernstein's confession to not being able to relive the unadulterated joys of that poem in "If Sappho Were a UFO" strikes me as telling, which leads me to another "theme" that reappears in this book, and which doesn't so much appear in the "heroic" phase, which is that of the transcendental or even of "God." Bernstein dedicates a short poem, "If Sappho Were a UFO," to Ashbery, part of which runs:

> Nothing much else
> Glues me to this shredded fabric
> Of the marvelous, on sale all these years
> With no buyers and just three
> Authorized sellers.
> (4)

While Ashbery's relationship to "God" will forever remain obscure—the word frequently appears in his poetry, though he never released any sort of Eliotic profession of his faith—one can't help but think that Ashbery's "fabric / Of the marvelous," in Bernstein's phrase, points toward the transcendental, linked to his childlike belief in a benign universe where all acts and happenstances could be *justified*. One of Ashbery's later poems, "Anticipated Stranger," ends with a non sequitur: "God will find the pattern and break it." Perhaps the Ashberian non sequitur represents, in fact, a literal deus ex machina, an intrusion from *beyond* the mundane of worldly mechanics by a deity.

The word "God" itself appears twelve times in *Topsy-Turvy* (according to the magic of Adobe Acrobat's search function), though not in all cases quite meaningfully. Here's a selection:

> Her voice
> weeps
> sin-
> g-
> ing
> to
> God
> o-
> n a
> fre-
> quen-
> cy
> that tu-
> nes
> out he-

r
cries.
("Karen Carpenter," 8)

I'm game if you are
See you on other side
God says he's hiding
Hope to meet her 'fore I die
("Beeline," 10)

Dante loves God [...]
Danton loves God [...]
William Morris loves God [...]
("My Father Would Be a Yard Salesman," 59–64)

The only thing harder than being a poet is being married to one.

COMMENTARY: A reworking of Reb Gimlet's "The only thing harder than being a fool is being married to one," itself a reworking of Reb Negroni's "The only thing harder than being a Jew is being married to one," itself a reworking of Reb Gibson's "The only thing harder than being God is being married to God."
("Swan Songs," 108–11)

Here's real:
Lore our God
Annoyed echo
("She/Ma," 122 [entirety])

A flailing poet came to the Alter Cocker Rebbe for advice on how to improve his art. "Stop cursing God," Rebbe said defiantly. "I constantly praise God in my poems," insisted the poet.
("Whiskey on Rye," after Mark Twain, 147)

This is a pretty eclectic assemblage of God references. Some sound a bit satirical, as in the poem about Karen Carpenter, but even here we notice a poignancy about "God" in the mind of the singer (who suffered from extreme anorexia), not the scare quotes that one might associate with Bernstein's earlier collage poetics. "Beeline" develops on the loose blues meters that crop up in this book, though—again, poignantly?—God undergoes a gender switch here. The short poem "She/Ma" cannot, to my mind, be read with any hint of satire, and in fact seems to point to something like Buber's "I/Thou" relationship in the suggestion that the "real" is not merely material reality, and not a purely linguistic one either. One might argue that "lore" is a figure denoting collective speech acts (as expressed in the media, for example), communal myths, and so forth, and that the poet is suggesting we treat this as "God," but then what is it that is being *echoed* here? I'm not suggesting that Bernstein is positing a "God" but merely noting that this short poem and many of the fragments cited above cannot be read as parody or pastiche.

"My Father Would Be a Yard Salesman" (a play on the title of Robert Duncan's hermetic homage, "My Mother Would Be a Falconress") is an addition to the catalog of list poems Bernstein has written over the years. "God" appears three times in this one, perhaps most unusually in the reference to the French revolutionary George Jacques Danton, guillotined in 1794 for calling for an end to the Terror and wanting to moderate the excesses of "dechristianization" (he had converted to Christianity as a condition of his marriage to Louise Gély in 1793). But given the mix-and-match nature of "My Father"—Diogenes, St. Augustine, Michelangelo, and the English poet Ernest Dowson are all noted as being "morally repugnant," while "Jesus is the real thing" (as is Buddha), "Savonarola is too cerebral," "Luther leaves me wanting more," and Galileo and Moses Mendelssohn have a "Jewish cast of mind"—we're not quite sure which side of the "satirical" we are on. Notably, the Jesuit poet Gerard Manley Hopkins does *not* have a "Jewish cast of mind," the only figure so denoted in this list. Does this singularity signal to us that we must review this seemingly random association of famous historical and literary figures as somehow *accurate*? Is Marx really "adorable" and Hegel "shallow"?

The narrative poem "Jewish Heaven" is one of a few poems in this collection that clearly addresses religious belief, drawing what, to my mind, is a clear distinction between Christian (or more narrowly, evangelical) and Jewish belief systems. The protagonist is "Reb," a common honorific in Yiddish when referring to a rabbi, though here without a proper name ("Reb," of course, could also refer to a Confederate soldier, as in "Johnny Reb," but that does not seem to be the case here). At first, Reb "couldn't help smiling" when hearing the "dream of / evangelical heaven," which, in the words of the "born-again preach," contained "bucolic fields, placid / lakes, fruit-punched / valleys," and so forth (124). This same preach preached a "Jewish heaven" which was "noisy, / smelly, crammed / with bodies jammed / 'gainst another, / sardines in cans" (124). Reb confirms the preach's visions as he, too, "dreamed of two / heavens" (124). The Jewish one is, indeed, crowded, loud and smelly, "filled with all manner / of Jew, observant and / opposed" (125). But Reb, his "voice rising," continues:

> "And not just Jews.
> Sunnis and Shia,
> Hindus, Catholics,
> born-again and
> mainline, boisterous,
> gesticulating wildly
> in streets chock-full
> of Buddhists, blasphemers,
> unbelievers, even those
> never gave belief or
> unbelief a plug nickel
> of thought."
> (125)

This "Jewish heaven" (which resembles, notably, a Dantescan hell, at least as figured in Eliot's *The Waste Land*) is decidedly *pluralistic*, as busy as New York's Washington Square Park in the '50s and '60s where congeries of religious folks (many representing marginal, or purely invented, faiths), political extremists, and forthright "blasphemers" and "unbelievers" mingled without any hope of finding resolutions among themselves. To this degree, it's not "heaven"—a vision of the afterlife—at all. Reb continues:

> "In my dream, like yours,
> evangelical heaven is
> crazy Day-Glo green
> fields, pristine vistas that
> seem to go to infinity.
> Quiet as all get-out.
>
> "For six days and six
> nights I wandered through
> your heaven, walking in
> sublime meadows,
> climbing beauteous
> mountains, roaming
> rolling hills.

"I never felt such peace
in those six days and
those six nights. Nor
such solitude."
(125–26)

"Evangelical heaven" doesn't sound all that bad, provided you like Day-Glo green. There's "nature," for one, all laid out for man's pleasure, either on a purely therapeutic level or of the sort that inspires epic poems. Reb found "peace" there—who wouldn't want that?—not to mention a transcendentalist-tinged "solitude." But Reb's final reflection on the place, itself the final stanza of the poem, is the kicker:

"Nobody was there."
(126)

Freud famously argued in *Moses and Monotheism* that it wasn't until the advent of monotheistic religions that anything like religious discrimination appeared. While, on the surface, we can understand Bernstein's poem as a contest of monotheisms, Jewish versus Christian, in fact, we notice that the "Jewish heaven" is not monotheistic at all, or even *theistic*. In fact, it's crammed with the life that we know today, even if we experience it in terribly etiolated form through the media—clamorous, opaque, upsetting, *present tense*. More terrifying is the implication here that the search for "evangelical heaven" might very well lead to the active *deletion* of bodies for the sake of the governing "Day-Glo" dream—intimations of a new Holocaust, but "not just Jews."

In my knowledge, the most revealing writing that Bernstein has done on his sense of himself as a Jew is "An Autobiographical Interview" conducted through email with Loss Pequeño Glazier and first published in 1996. He notes that he became interested in a sort of nonidentity formation (described by Isaac Deutscher) of the "non-Jewish Jew," something of a "circus sideshow" to "'serious' Judaism." He also notes that, in his undergraduate work on Stein and Wittgenstein, he never mentioned Jewishness, but it was nonetheless "an obvious point of contact as well as a crucial, if implicit, reference point for me" (1999: 233). My favorite passage in the interview, however, is one most apposite to "Jewish Heaven" (and which resonates with my own upbringing as a half Korean, half European, quasi Christian, quasi Buddhist, quasi nothing, depending on the social context):

> My parents were assimilationists who nonetheless had a strong Jewish and later Zionist identification. As for many of their generation, this made for interesting contradictions. We were loosely kosher in the "beef fry" years, but in other years the bacon fried plentifully and tasted sweet. Or we were kosher on Friday night when my Aunt Pauline came to dinner but not the rest of the week. Of course, on Rosh Hashanah and Yom Kippur, when dozens of relatives descended on our apartment for gigantic and endless meals that I grew to dread for their tediousness, we were strictly kosher, with once-a-year Pesach plates and cakes made from matzoh meal. (Those who might "correctly" say you can't be a little bit kosher ignore the actual practice of Jewish ethnicity.) (231)

In this light, we can say that Bernstein's "Jewish heaven" is not a "heaven" but very much Jewish, at least of the New York variety in the '50s and '60s: foods swapped in an out for the sake of observance, dozens of relatives "descending" on a cramped apartment, verbal disagreements—he notes in this interview that his mother scolded him for being "the only Jew in New York who supported Jesse Jackson" and that he had "vituperative exchanges at dinner about Vietnam and about racism" with his father—and in the end, with *people*. Solitude is nice, but does anyone really want a heaven in which "nobody was there"?[2] Bernstein's views on the afterlife, in fact, are not far from Nietzsche's—it doesn't exist—though the poet's "afterlife" at least has bacon.

3. The Virtual

I've long been fascinated by the use of a particular word in one of Bernstein's other major essays, "Poetics of the Americas,"[3] which can be seen as his attempt at a rapprochement between the Eurocentric avant-garde techniques that the "Language" writers valorized in their "heroic" days and the plurality of Englishes that began to be used, or became more visible, in North American poetries immediately preceding the time of the

2. As Yogi Berra once said about a restaurant in New York, "Nobody goes there anymore. It's too crowded."
3. The essay first appeared in *Modernism/Modernity* in September 1996 (vol. 3, no. 3, pp. 1–23). I'm citing from a later "corrected" version that appears online at *Sybil/Sibilla*, https://sibila.com.br/wordpress/wp-content/uploads/2011/01/PoeticsOfAmericas-corrected.pdf.

essay's first publication in 1996. The word that intrigued me was *virtual* (I've added italics to all instances of the word below):

> [It] is hardly surprising that static conceptions of group identity represented by authentic spokespersons continue to ride roughshod over works and individuals whose identities are complex, multiple, mixed, confused, hyperactivated, miscegenated, synthetic, mutant, forming, or *virtual*.
>
> The point is to pursue the collective and dialogic nature of poetry without necessarily defining the nature of this collectivity—call it a *virtual* collectivity or . . . "this new yet unapproachable America": this unrepresentable yet ever presenting collectivity.
>
> The invention of an ideolectical English language poetry, as a poetry of the Americas, involves the replacement of the national and geographically centered category of English (or Spanish) poetry not with the equally essentialist category of American poetry but with a field of potentialities, a *virtual* America that we approach but never possess.
>
> [P]erhaps what we hear is a writing that moves beyond the present definitions and inscriptions of collective and individual identifications and toward a *virtual* or coming identity about which these confusions and comminglings, call them confabulations, hint; as if such writing leaves room for readers' multifoliate projections.

Virtual, of course, was a big buzzword in the time of the writing of this essay; it usually meant something like the digital re-creation or simulacrum of something we otherwise understood as "real," or material—a ghost, or phantom, suspended by the algorithms and wire frames of a programmer and animator. The second definition of *virtual* in the online *Merriam-Webster Dictionary* reflects this: "being on or simulated on a computer or computer network." However, it's the fourth definition from this same dictionary that seems most apposite to Bernstein's usage: "of, relating to, or being a *hypothetical* particle whose existence is inferred from *indirect* evidence" (italics added). In physics, the "virtual" is largely mathematical; like the Higgs boson at one time, it is an element that would fill in a gap in the Standard Model, a sort of "convenient truth" should the universe not be governed by dice rolls. But Bernstein's "virtual" is not *that*, either: like the "complex, multiple, mixed, confused," all the fun things Bernstein has celebrated in his poetry and essays, the "virtual" *exists*; it is not a hypothesis.

The virtual *is* an "ever presenting collectivity," even if it's not possible to provide it a *positive* identity or to "define" it; we *can* approach it, even if, like in Zeno's paradox, it can never be "possessed," as it is always in the process of *becoming* or *arriving* and, to this extent, *retreating*.

Years after first reading this essay, I was provided with some insight in the book *Without Criteria: Kant, Whitehead, Deleuze, and Aesthetics* by Steven Shaviro, an elegant, accessible, and illuminating consideration of the three philosophers in its title. He writes, "For Deleuze, the possible is an empty form defined only by the principle of noncontradiction" (2009: 33), which, in layman's terms, means that the "possible" is not yet "actual" because it has not come into existence, and yet there is nothing in our *reason* or in our science that would argue, a priori, against us positing that it *could be*. The event of the "possible" becoming "actual" would be quite trivial, to this degree—there is nothing truly *novel* in this event. "Possibility is a purely negative category; it lacks any proper being of its own," Shaviro writes, continuing: "Something that is merely possible has no claim to existence, and no intrinsic mode of being. Its only positive characteristics are those that it *borrows* from the real that it is *not*" (33; italics added).

As for the *virtual*, in Shaviro's words (quoting Deleuze):

> The virtual . . . is altogether *real* in its own right; it "possesses a full reality by itself." It is just that this reality is not *actual*. The virtual is like a field of energies that have not yet been expended, or a reservoir of potentialities that have not yet been tapped. That is to say, the virtual is not composed of atoms; it doesn't have body or extension. But the *potential for change* that it offers is *real* in its own way. . . . The virtual is a principle of emergence, or of creation. As such, it does not *prefigure* or *predetermine* the actualities that emerge from it. Rather, it is the impelling force, or the principle, that allows each actual entity to appear (to manifest itself) as something *new*, something without precedence or resemblance, *something that has never existed in the universe* in quite that way before. (34; italics added)

The virtual (here associated with the "potential") *exists*—it has a claim to the *real* that the merely "possible" doesn't. But the *virtual* is not *actual* to the degree that it, or rather its products, cannot be a subject of observation: we cannot turn rationalistic or scientific tools on the *virtual* because it hasn't yet acquired "body or extension." The *possible* is mundane, much as the possibility of an avalanche at 7:28 p.m. on the 16th of March, 2022, in Switzerland is mundane because, alas, it's conceivable or *thinkable* that such might happen. However, the *virtual* does not "prefigure or predetermine the actualities that emerge from it," which is to say, there is no *causal* relationship between the "virtual" and the actual—there are no states A, B, and C in the virtual that will, by *necessity*, produce results or states D, E, and F in the actual (let's call this the "world")—as there is between the "possible" and the actual.

The term *identity* plays a large role in how we think of contemporary social politics in terms of the individual—*identity politics*, duh—but in philosophical discourse, *identity* refers to an object's properties as it pertains to *itself*, and *only* to itself. Namely, if object *X* bears exactly the same properties as object *Y* (including those of time and space), are they the same object? What happens to nomenclature? Bernstein's emphases on, indeed celebrations of, the self-contradictions of singular "identities" in ethnographic, political, and religious terms represent, were one to tease out the logical implications, a unique intervention on our understanding of social "identity." One could certainly be "Asian American," and identify with a collectivity that names itself such, but one could not have *all* the same properties as another Asian American, or anyone or anything else, for that matter. It's hard enough to think of one apple as being the exact same as another—but Brian Kim Stefans and John Yau? But even if Brian Kim Stefans and John Yau and several others had the same identities—i.e., shared the exact same properties—what could we then say about them? What happens to "diversity" and "plurality"?

What happens to the innovative, maybe paradigm-shifting, artist who is only being written about through the frame of "identity politics"? According to Deleuze, and I'm extending this thinking to Bernstein, the actualities that emerge from the virtual are *always* novel—they are always new, though might appear "random" to science or indolent habits of thinking. The novel is always produced by the very *real* condition of the "virtual"—which is to say, *potentiality*. We can never know exactly what the properties of this "virtual" place are—Deleuze calls it elsewhere the "plane of immanence"—but we should be able to *think* it considering what we already know of the appearance of the novel—the eruption into actuality of the truly new—through history.

My sense is that much of the "discomfort" with reading a new book by Bernstein has increasingly less to do with his long commitment to troubling the "frames" of our reading as much as it is with his wanting to continue to illuminate this condition of the virtual. One could write that Bernstein is something like a "process philosopher" in the line of Whitehead, one of the three subjects of Shaviro's book, except that Bernstein doesn't only care about process just for itself but as it can be tied to something that is distinctly his own: a sort of "social justice" as a continuous *aspiration*, one whose ends simply don't exist *except* in the "virtual." He writes about this in terms of "American poetry" in "Poetics of the Americas" (it is "a field of potentialities, a virtual America that we approach but never possess"), but this concept can be generalized beyond Anglophone literature—Bernstein's ongoing critique of "Official Verse Culture"—to something like a metaphysically tinged social philosophy.

Tellingly, Bernstein has often recycled an old joke—or old *intervention*—by Tom Raworth in many of his poems. The Raworth poem titled "University Days," first published in 1971, runs in its entirety (including black bounding box):

this poem has been removed for further study

While it would be certainly unfair and inaccurate to write that this is one of Raworth's best poems, it's certainly been cited often: Nate Dorwood's 2003 volume on Raworth was titled *Removed for Further Study: The Poetry of Tom Raworth*, while the *Guardian*'s obituary for Raworth notes that "Raworth frequently relied on the university world to keep body and soul together, but remained instinctively detached from its more pedantic and hierarchical aspects," citing this poem as reflective of this ambivalent relation (Ward 2017). Bernstein, of course, has been an accomplished professor of literature at the University of Buffalo and the University of Pennsylvania. How often has he recycled this gesture? Let me count the ways:

> *This Poem Intentionally Left Blank*[4]
> —*With Strings* (2001)
>
> [THIS POEM REMOVED FOR INSPECTION AND VERIFICATION]
> —"A Poem Is Not a Weapon" (entirety), for/after Tom Raworth, *Girly Man* (2006)
>
> please wait
> —"Poem Loading . . ." (entirety), *Recalculating* (2013)

4. This is both the title and the poem. This page was intentionally left unpaginated.

13. There's no blank like the present.
—"Great Moments in Taches Blanches," a poem in numbered sections, *Recalculating*

POETRY WANTS TO BE FREE. (Or, if not, available for long-term loan.)
—"Manifest Aversions, Conceptual Conundrums, & Implausibly Deniable Links," *Recalculating*

No re-entry from this poem.
—"Loose Canons," final section, *Topsy-Turvy* (2021)

This Poem Is Not in Service
—Title of a poem from *Topsy-Turvy*

This page is closed for deinstallation.
—Words that appear on page 89 of *Topsy-Turvy*

Bernstein, with his love of Borscht Belt humor, is not only one to not let a good rehashable joke go to waste—take my wifi, please!—but with a "pataphysical" turn, returns again and again to the Raworth gesture cognizant of its increasingly failing returns, at least as a *joke*. Yes, it's a regular reminder of something like an instinctive, if not always maintained, detachment from the university's "more pedantic and hierarchical aspects." But in light of what we've read of Deleuze's philosophy of the "virtual," can we see these repeated evacuations of the *presence* of poetry, denials of the poem's *actualization*, as something like architectural signage pointing us in the direction of the parking lot, the restaurant, the main lobby, or anywhere but *here*? anything but *this*? Are these gestures more than comments on poetry, but a redirection of our attentions toward *potentiality*?

Where brokenness and the various references to "God" and religious belief in *Topsy-Turvy* meet is in a description of a form of transcendence that is entirely *immanent*, i.e., that does not point to anything outside the *real*, like to a God, or to some form of "intelligent design" or a telos. As Shaviro writes, "[D]eleuze most often describes the virtual as a transcendental field or structure, conditioning and generating the actual" (2009: 34). To my mind, this describes the "transcendental" aspect of Bernstein's poetry—not a deferral, not a pointing, but marking *potential* as an aspect of the real (if not actual). Bernstein is, to this degree, a philosophical poet, but not one who articulates philosophical systems so much as one who *enacts* philosophy itself. Any lack of obvious pleasures in his poetry—his jarring, gangly meters, his love for *le mot injuste*—should not be seen merely as a sort of intramural critique of the social operations of language, but rather, in addition, we should view Bernstein's calls to the virtual as signaling a preoccupation with *hope*. By this I mean: how do we drag these broken bones, how do we assimilate these failures at transcendence, how do we negotiate this commerce between the "I" and the "Thou," in a world that has closed off true *potential* in the confines of the *merely possible*? There *must be more*, there *is* more, in Bernstein's view, even as he's never so doctrinaire, or willing to compromise his sense of the virtual, of the ever *forthcoming* that already *is*, as to provide names or definitions for it.

References

Bernstein, Charles. 1992. *A Poetics*. Cambridge, MA: Harvard University Press.

———. 1999. *Close Listening*. Chicago: University of Chicago Press.

———. 2001. *With Strings: Poems*. Chicago: University of Chicago Press.

———. 2006. *Girly Man*. Chicago: University of Chicago Press.

———. 2013. *Recalculating*. Chicago: University of Chicago Press.

———. 2021. *Topsy-Turvy*. Chicago: University of Chicago Press.

Raworth, Tom. 1971. *Moving*. New York: Cape Golliard Press in Association with Grossman Publishers.

Shaviro, Steven. 2009. *Without Criteria: Kant, Whitehead, Deleuze, and Aesthetics*. Cambridge, MA: MIT Press.

Ward, Geoff. 2017. "Tom Raworth Obituary." *The Guardian*, April 16, 2017. https://www.theguardian.com/books/2017/apr/16/tom-raworth-obituary.

Contributors

Luigi Ballerini is a poet, essayist, and translator. Born in Milan in 1940, he divides his time between Italy and New York. He has taught Italian literature at NYU, UCLA, and Yale. He is the author of *A Feast of Weeds* and *Cephalonia*, and is the editor of the anthology *Those Who from Afar Look Like Flies*.

Runa Bandyopadhyay is a bilingual poet, essayist, critiqueer, and translator from Bengal, India. She is a scientist by profession but is addicted to inventive literature. She is the author of *Nocturnal Whistle*, in English, published in 2019, and twelve books of poetry, essays, and stories in Bengali. She coedited the anthologies *Hardcore Kaurab-2* with Barin Ghosal in 2013 and *Bridgeable Lines* with American poets in 2019.

Charles Bernstein is Donald T. Regan Professor of English, Emeritus, at the University of Pennsylvania. His most recent books are *Topsy-Turvy*, *Near/Miss*, *Pitch of Poetry*, *Recalculating*, and *Attack of the Difficult Poems*. In 2019, he was awarded the Bollingen Prize, the major US poetry prize, for lifetime achievement and for *Near/Miss*.

Dennis Büscher-Ulbrich is assistant professor of American cultural studies at the University of Kiel. His dissertation engages the poetry of Bruce Andrews through the work of Jacques Rancière. He coedited "Im/Possibility," a special issue of *Coils of the Serpent* (issue 8 [2021]), and "Marx and the United States," a special issue of *Amerikastudien / American Studies* (62, no. 4 [2017]). He is finishing a second book on riots, racialized superfluity, and the long crisis of capital.

Alí Calderón was born in 1982 in Mexico City. He is a professor at the Universidad Autónoma de Puebla, the director of the Mexico City International Poetry Festival, and the cofounder and editor of the electronic literary magazine *Círculo de Poesía*.

boundary 2 48:4 (2021) DOI 10.1215/01903659-9382328

Natalia Fedorova is a language artist, science/art and new media researcher, and curator. She teaches in the Department of Theory and Methodology for Teaching Arts and Humanities, St. Petersburg University.

Yi Feng is an associate professor at the Foreign Studies College, Northeastern University (Shenyang, China). Her primary research interest is American literature.

Jean-Marie Gleize is the author of over twenty books of poetry and literary criticism in France. His *Tarnac, un acte préparatoire* has been translated into English and published as *Tarnac, a Preparatory Act*. In addition to his scholarly work on modern and contemporary French, Arabic, and American poetry, he is the editor of the journal *Nioques*.

Susan Howe taught for many years at the State University of New York–Buffalo, where she held the Samuel P. Capen Chair of Poetry and the Humanities. She has received numerous honors and awards for her work, and in 2011 was awarded the Bollingen Prize in American Poetry from Yale University. Her most recent works include *Concordance* (2020) and *Debths* (2017).

Yunte Huang is professor of English at the University of California, Santa Barbara, a Guggenheim Fellow, and the author of *Charlie Chan* and *Inseparable*, both finalists for the National Book Critics Circle Award. He has published articles in the *New York Times*, *Wall Street Journal*, *Daily Beast*, and others, and has been featured on NPR, CBS, C-SPAN, and others.

Pierre Joris just published *Fox-trails, -tales & -trots* (poems & proses, Black Fountain Press). He completed his half-century Celan translation project with these two final volumes: *Memory Rose into Threshold Speech: The Collected Earlier Poetry of Paul Celan* (FSG) & *Microliths: Posthumous Prose of Paul Celan* (Contra Mundum Press). In 2020, he also published *A City Full of Voices: Essays on the Work of Robert Kelly* (CMP) & in 2019 *Arabia (not so) Deserta* (essays, Spuyten Duyvil) &, with Adonis, *Conversations in the Pyrenees* (CMP).

Abigail Lang is associate professor of American literature and translation at the Université de Paris (LARCA-UMR 8225) and a member of the Double Change collective, which promotes exchanges between US and French poetry. She is the author of *Leave to Remain* (2020, with Thalia Field) and *La Conversation transatlantique: Les échanges franco-américains en poésie depuis 1968* (2021).

Leevi Lehto (1951–2019) was an influential and prolific Finnish poet, translator (of, among others, Joyce's *Ulysses*, Ashbery, Bernstein), and publisher (ntamo 2007–17).

Marjorie Perloff is the author of many books on twentieth- and twenty-first-century poetry and poetics, most recently, *Unoriginal Genius: Writing by Other Means in the New Century* (2011). Her new book *Infrathin: An Experiment in Micropoetics*, is forthcoming in Fall 2021. Her memoir *Vienna Paradox* has been translated into many languages.

Ian Probstein is professor of English at Touro College. He has published numerous books and articles. His most recent book in English is *The River of Time: Time-Space, Language and History in Avant-Garde, Modernist, and Contemporary Poetry*. He has translated into Russian the complete annotated edition of T. S. Eliot's poetry and plays (St. Petersburg: Azbuka–antiqua, 2019) and Charles Bernstein's *Sign Under Test: Selected Poems and Essays* (Moscow: Russian Gulliver, 2020).

Ariel Resnikoff's most recent works include the poetry collection, *Unnatural Bird Migrator* (The Operating System, 2020), and with Jerome Rothenberg, the translingual epistolary collaboration, *A Paradise of Hearing* (The Swan, 2021). He received his PhD in comparative literature and literary theory from the University of Pennsylvania in 2019, and he is currently a Fulbright Postdoctoral U.S. Scholar at The Hebrew University of Jerusalem.

Brian Kim Stefans is professor of English at UCLA. His newest book is *Festivals of Patience: The Verse Poems of Rimbaud* (Kenning Editions, 2021). Recent books include *Word Toys: Poetry and Technics* (2017) and *"Viva Miscegenation": New Writing* (Make Now Books, 2013). His website, which includes his digital works, is www.arras.net.

Enrique Winter is one of Latin America's most prominent poets of his generation. His books *Skyscrapers*, *Suns*, and *Sign Tongue*—which was awarded both the Pablo de Rokha and the Goodmorning Menagerie prizes—are available in English. He is also a novelist and a translator of Dickinson, Chesterton, Larkin, Howe, and Bernstein. Winter leads the Creative Writing diploma at Pontifical Catholic University of Valparaíso (PUCV), Chile.